The Comprehensive Guide to
Medical Halachah

The Comprehensive Guide to MEDICAL HALACHAH

UPDATED AND EXPANDED EDITION OF
Medical Halachah for Everyone

by the author of
Lev Avraham and *Nishmat Avraham*

ABRAHAM S. ABRAHAM MD, FRCP

FELDHEIM PUBLISHERS
Jerusalem □ New York

First published 1990

Feldheim Publishers Ltd.
POB 6525/Jerusalem, Israel

Philipp Feldheim Inc.
200 Airport Executive Park
Spring Valley, NY 10977

Library of Congress Cataloging-in-Publication Data

Abraham, A. S.
　　[Lev Avraham.　English]
　　The comprehensive guide to medical halachah:
a comprehensive guide to Jewish medical law in sickness and
health = [Lev Avraham] / Abraham S. Abraham; [adapted
from the Hebrew by the author; translated by the author and
Naomi S. Cohen]. — Updated and expanded ed.
　　　　　　256 p.　23 cm.
　　Translation of: Lev Avraham.
　　"Updated and expanded edition of Medical halachah
for everyone"-t.p. verso.
　　Includes bibliographical references.
　　Includes index.
　　ISBN 0-87306-529-8 (hardcover)
1. Medical laws and legislation (Jewish law) 2. Medicine—
Religious aspects—Judaism. 3. Sick—Religious life.
4. Judaism—Customs and practices. I. Title.
　　[DNLM: 1. Ethics, Medical. 2. Judaism. 3. Legislation, Medical.
4. Religion and Medicine.　W 50 A159L]
LAW <GENERAL Abra 1990>
296.1'8—dc20
DNLM/DLC　　　　　　　90-3572
for Library of Congress　　CIP

10 9 8 7 6 5 4 3 2 1

Printed in Israel

בע"ה כז תשרי תש"ן.

כב' מכובדנו וידידנו הרב הדגול, פרופ' אברהם-סופר אברהם שליט"א אחדשה"ט
ושמעכ"ת,

שמחה שמחתי ורינה רניתי בראותי שב"ה נתקבל ספרו החשוב, הן בעולם התורני והן
בעולם הגדול, כספר שיש בו תועלת מרובה למחפש מרפא לנפשו, ובמיוחד בזמן שהוא
מחפש סייעתא דשמיא לגופו.

הספר חובר בטוב טעם ודעת וחכמה גדולה מצאתי בו. הוא הודפס בראשונה בלשון
הקודש, ואולם הביקוש לתרגמו לשפה האנגלית היה גדול, וזה עצמו מראה את
חשיבותו של ספרו ואת ברכתו במפעלו של מר.

רבות עברתי על הספר בלשון הקודש, וגם בזמן שתורגם הספר לשפה האנגלית ידידי
הנאמן שליט"א תמיד התייעץ אתי בדברי הלכה, כל דבר גדול או קטן, ובעניי עד כמה
שידי מגעת, בעזרת חונן הדעת, ביררנו וליבננו יחד את דבר ה' זו הלכה. גם עיינתי רבות
בהערות בשולי הדף, אשר הם כמפתח לגוף הספר, ומצויים בו מקורות למעינותיו,
ומצאתי בהם שידע מר להבחין מה להביא ומה שהשתיקה יפה להם.

ברכותי אל מעכ"ת שה' הטוב יהיה בעזרו לתת מרפא לחולי אחב"י ויחד עם זה להפיץ
אור תורתו שרבים נהנים מהם, עוד ועוד, לחבר ספרים עד אין קץ, ויזכה להגדיל תורה
ולהאדירה.

ידידו הנאמן המצפה להרמת קרן התורה וישראל
ונזכה לביאת גואל צדק בקרוב,

בברה"ת ובאה"ר
יהושע י. נויבירט.

Foreword by Chief Rabbi
Lord Immanuel Jakobovits
Chief Rabbi of Great Britain and the Commonwealth

This new and extensively revised edition of Professor Abraham's popular work will be widely greeted as helping to meet the growing demand for the presentation of practical rules founded in authentic Jewish sources on the moral and religious perplexities raised by the advance of medicine.

The work is thoroughly researched, intelligently written and attractively produced. It is a valuable addition to a new genre of halachic writings.

Not all rulings recorded in this work are unanimous; some of them may indeed represent what are still very moot points, still under intense discussion among leading rabbinical authorities. The halachic process has always been dynamic, and some conclusions may take a considerable period of enquiry and debate before they evolve as a new layer in the corpus of Jewish law.

Professor Abraham enjoys the rare distinction of combining rabbinical and medical expertise with the facility to express their interplay. Such a work is bound to enhance the relevance of Torah teachings to our times as well as the Jewish contribution to the solution of some of the most challenging moral problems besetting our civilization.

Preface

Almighty God, Lord of the Universe, Healer of all flesh, I thank You for the lovingkindness You have daily bestowed upon me, for the privileges of being able to study the Torah and live in the Land of Israel, and for the privilege of practicing medicine, treating and helping mankind. May it be Your will that I merit to walk in Your ways and fulfill Your *mitzvot*. Keep me from mistakes and guard me from errors in judgment; protect me from pride and bestow upon me the gift of healing. May it be Your will that I be worthy of sanctifying Your Name at all times, for that is the purpose of all Creation.

Ten years ago, with God's help, *Medical Halachah for Everyone* was first published; five years later, by His grace, a second edition was published. In addition, the three volumes of *Nishmat Avraham* which cover the medical aspects of the decisions codified in all four sections of the *Shulchan Aruch* have been published.

The present book is a completely rewritten and updated version of *Medical Halachah for Everyone*, with decisions on many problems not discussed in the original. As in the original, I have attempted, wherever possible, to express a definitive opinion. Some problems, however, are referred to in the Hebrew footnotes, as are the sources on which the decisions are based. Nevertheless, the reader should consult with his rabbi on each and every problem, since minor changes in details can result in different rulings. The book should be used for studying and understanding the way our Sages dealt with every problem—from the mundane to the exotic—and not as a handbook of halachic decisions.

As in the original edition, the additional subjects addressed in this volume have all been thoroughly discussed with and agreed to by my teacher, Rabbi Yehoshua Neuwirth, שליט״א, to whom I will forever be grateful.

Although this edition has been extensively rewritten, I must still express my thanks to Mrs. Naomi Cohen (née Hill), who originally translated part of *Lev Avraham* into English. The late Dr. Philip Birnbaum translated the short prayer (see Chapter 7, paragraph 3) and permitted me to use his translation of the *Havinenu* prayer (Chapter 7, paragraph 2). Needless to say, however, the responsibility for the final product is entirely mine.

To one who insists on remaining anonymous I express my thanks for his advice and deep friendship in all stages of the preparation of this book.

It remains a pleasure to know and work with my publisher, Mr. Yaakov Feldheim. The skillful and talented members of his editorial and design departments contributed significantly to the quality and appearance of this volume.

None of my books could have been written without the constant support, advice and encouragement of my wife, Sylvia. To paraphrase what the great Sage Rabbi Akiva said of his wife (כתובות סג ע״ג): "What is mine is hers." May all the blessings of the Torah be her reward.

Abraham S. Abraham, MD, FRCP

Jerusalem

CONTENTS

sores; washing hands; tearing paper wrapping; swabbing; driving to and from duty

1 / DEFINITION OF A SICK PERSON

Halachah recognizes four categories of sick patients with corresponding practical implications regarding the Sabbath, Yom Kippur, Pesach, forbidden foods, etc. These four types are defined in this chapter, with particular reference to the Sabbath.[1]

1. The seriously or dangerously ill (חולה שיש בו סכנה):[2] that is, the patient suffering from a potentially fatal condition.

a. A person who himself senses that he is seriously ill,[3] or whom a physician[4] or anyone with some knowledge of medicine[5] considers to be so.

b. One who, though not in immediate danger, may deteriorate into such a state unless given treatment in time;[6] for example, an insulin-dependent diabetic patient who has run out of insulin.

c. Patients with certain conditions held by the Talmud to be states of danger, even if contrary to current medical opinion;[7] for example, a woman within seven days of childbirth.[8]

Once such a potentially fatal condition has been diagnosed, one of two practical applications ensues:

(1) עיין המעין תמוז תשמ"ח עמ' 74.

(2) וראה יומא פה ע"א תוס' ד"ה ולפקח : שלא יוכל לבוא בשום ענין לידי מיתת ישראל.

(3) או"ח סי' שכח סע' ה.

(4) שם סע' י.

(5) מ"ב שם ס"ק כז ו־כח.

(6) מ"ב שם ס"ק יז, סי' שכא סע' יח ומ"ב ס"ק עה, שמירת שבת כהלכתה פל"ב סע' ח.

(7) סי' שכח מ"ב ס"ק ח, פמ"ג שם במ"ז ס"ק ב, מנחת שבת סי' צב ס"ק לב, זכרו תורת משה סי' צב בהגהותיו של הגר"יי שטייף ס"ק ריח., שדי חמד מערכת טי"ת כלל ה, שו"ת מהרי"ם שיק יו"ד סי' רמד, חזו"א נשים סי' כז ס"ק ג.

(8) סי' של סע' ד.

19

—If actual or possible danger to life is imminent,[9] everything necessary to save the patient's life must be done as speedily as possible, exactly as one would were it not the Sabbath.[10] In such a situation, one who delays treatment in order to seek a halachic decision is considered to have "shed blood," since the delay may result in a loss of life.[11]

—If, however, it is *certain* that there is no imminent danger to life in taking the time to consult competent halachic authority, this should be done in order to be properly guided as to when and how to set aside the Sabbath regulations.

DANGER TO A LIMB BUT NOT TO LIFE

In almost all situations in which there is danger to a limb the patient is held to be seriously ill and must be treated as such. For details, see *Nishmat Avraham.*[12]

2. The non-seriously or non-dangerously ill (חולה שאין בו סכנה): that is, the patient who has a generalized (systemic) illness but whose life is not in danger.

a. A person confined to bed or whose whole body is affected by illness or by pain,[13] even if he is not dangerously ill, for example, a person suffering from influenza or severe migraine.

b. One affected as in the previous group who, even though not confined to bed, is in a state in which most others in a similar condition would take to bed.[14]

c. A person not yet suffering from but prone to develop such an illness—for example, severe migraine, acute asthma, angina pectoris—unless given preventive treatment.[15]

(9) סי' שכח מ"ב ס"ק יז.

(10) שם סע' ב ו-ה.

(11) שם סע' ב ו-יג ומ"ב ס"ק ו.

(12) או"ח סי' שכח ס"ק מו (עמי קצה).

(13) או"ח שכח סע' יז.

(14) שם בהגה.

(15) מפי הגרש"ז אויערבאך שליט"א. ועיין גם חי' הר"ן לשבת קמ ע"א סוד"ה אי, אגלי טל מלאכת טוחן סע' טז.

d. A child until age two to three years (depending on its stage of development)[16] who is suffering even from only a mild illness.[17]

e. A woman from the eighth till the thirtieth day after childbirth.[18]

f. A person with an eye infection, however mild.[19]

For this category of patient a non-Jew may be instructed to carry out whatever is necessary for treatment, even if it involves setting aside Torah prohibitions that are applicable to a Jew.[20] A Jew may perform whatever is necessary for the care of these patients, provided that the prohibitions involved are Rabbinic and not from the Torah, and that the treatment is performed in a manner differing from the way it is ordinarily given.[21] Under such circumstances there is no need to seek the help of a non-Jew.[22]

3. The patient with a minor illness, aches or pains (חולה במקצת או מצטער הרבה):[23] for example, someone with nasal catarrh, an irritating cough or headache, ailments which do not affect the whole body and are not severe enough for the person to be confined to bed. Such a patient may not be treated by a Jew if desecration of the Sabbath is involved, even if the prohibition be by Rabbinic ordinance only; nor may the patient take medicaments. However, the patient may be treated by a non-Jew if only a prohibition by Rabbinic ordinance is involved.[24]

(16) שמירת שבת כהלכתה פל״ז סע׳ ב, חזו״א סי׳ נט ס״ק ג.

(17) סי׳ שכח סע׳ יז בהגה.

(18) סי׳ של סע׳ ד, שמירת שבת כהלכתה פל״ו סע׳ טו.

(19) שמירת שבת כהלכתה פל״יד סע׳ ח.

(20) סי׳ שכח סע׳ יז מ״ב ס״ק מז.

(21) מ״ב שם ס״ק נז.

(22) מ״ב שם ס״ק נד. וראה גם מ״ב ס״ק קב.

(23) תפארת ישראל בכללכת שבת דין אמירה לנכרי סע׳ ז(א).

(24) סי׳ שז סע׳ ה וסימן שכח במ״ב ס״ק נב.

4.   The patient with discomfort (מיחוש בעלמא): for example, one who is suffering from a mild cold or cough or a skin eruption, ailments which are not severe enough to affect the whole body.[25] No medication may be taken and treatment is not permitted[26] even by a non-Jew,[27] and even if it would involve a prohibition of Rabbinic origin only.[28]

(25) סי׳ שכח סעי״א א.

(26) שם

(27) מי״ב שם סי״ק ג ו־ק.

(28) מי״ב שם סי״ק ב.

2 / THE DUTY OF SEEKING AND COMPLYING WITH MEDICAL ADVICE

The preservation of life takes precedence over all the *mitzvot* of the Torah except those commandments concerning idolatry, murder and prohibited relations (such as incest and adultery).[1]

1.　One may not depend on the miraculous; it is one's duty to seek the services of a physician whenever necessary and to carry out the physician's instructions.[2]

2.　A seriously or possibly seriously ill person[3] (see Chapter 1, paragraph 1) who objects to the setting aside of Sabbath rules on his behalf should be told that such behavior represents false piety. A patient who persists may be compelled to submit to whatever is necessary,[4] provided this is based on expert medical advice.[5]

3.　A patient is forbidden to fast on Yom Kippur if according to expert medical opinion doing so may lead to serious results.[6]

---

(1) יו״ד סי׳ קנז סע׳ א

(2) ברכ״י סי׳ שלו ס״ק ב. וראה רמב״ם פי׳ המשניות פסחים פ״ד מ״ט ונדרים פ״ד מ״ד. שו״ת הרשב״א ח״א סי׳ תיג. שו״ת חת״ס או״ח סי׳ קעו. שו״ת בנין ציון סי׳ קיא. אמנם יש חולקים — עיין אבן עזרא על שמות כא:יט, רמב״ן על ויקרא כו:יא, כרתי ופלתי יו״ד סי׳ קפח ס״ק ה ושו״ת אבני נזר חו״מ סי׳ קצג. אולם הרמב״ן בעצמו כתב בתורת האדם פרק ענין הסכנה, "ואם החולה רוצה להחמיר, עליו נאמר ואך את דמכם לנפשותיכם אדרוש, ואל תהי צדיק הרבה". ועיין גם חזו״א קובץ אגרות ח״א אגרת קלו. חכמת אדם כלל קנא סע׳ כה. שו״ת ציץ אליעזר ח״ה רמת רחל סי׳ כ. שו״ת יחוה דעת ח״א סי׳ סא.

(3) פמ״ג או״ח סי׳ שכח בא״א ס״ק א.

(4) רמב״ם הל׳ שבת פ״ב ה״ג. רמב״ן מלחמת ד׳ סנה׳ עד, שו״ת רדב״ז סי׳ תתפה (ח״ג סי׳ תמד). משנה ברורה או״ח סי׳ שכח ס״ק ו.

(5) מ״ב שם ס״ק ה. שמירת שבת כהלכתה פל״ב סע׳ ה.

(6) או״ח סי׳ תריח מ״ב ס״ק ה. מטה אפרים שם סע׳ טו. שו״ת דברי מלכיאל ח״ה סי׳ לה. שו״ת יחוה דעת ח״א סי׳ סא. וראה גם ר״ן יומא פא ע״א ד״ה חוץ. שו״ת הרדב״ז סי׳ תתפה

4. A seriously ill patient (see Chapter 1, paragraph 1) who is required to partake of an otherwise forbidden food in order that his or her life be saved is duty-bound to do so.[7] One who refuses is, indeed, held guilty of "shedding blood" (endangering life), in this case the patient's own.[8]

5. A patient who has been warned by the physician not to partake on the *Seder* night of matzah or *maror* or wine because they may endanger life but insists on doing so not only has not performed a *mitzvah* but is actually guilty of a serious offense.[9] Even if such consumption may lead only to an illness that requires confinement to bed (חולה שאין בו סכנה; see Chapter 1, paragraph 2), the patient is exempt from such Pesach duties.[10]

(ח״ג סי׳ תמד). שו״ת מהר״יי אסאד או״ח סי׳ קס. שו״ת מהר״ים שיק או״ח סי׳ רס. שו״ת מנחת יצחק ח״ד סי׳ קב אות ב. שו״ת ציץ אליעזר ח״ח סי׳ טו פ״ג ח״יי וסי׳ כה פי״ד.

(7) שי״ך יו״ד סי׳ רלח ס״ק ה.

(8) ר״ן יומא פב ע״א ד״ה חוץ, שו״ת יביע אומר ח״ד חו״מ סי׳ ו אות ד.

(9) שו״ת מהר״יי אסאד סי׳ קס. שו״ת מהר״ים שיק או״ח סי׳ רס. שו״ת מנחת יצחק ח״ד סי׳ קב אות ב. שו״ת ציץ אליעזר חי״ב סי׳ מג.

(10) מ״ב סי׳ תעב ס״ק לב. חזון עובדיה עמ׳ קעג. מקראי קודש, פסח ח״ב עמ׳ קטז. שדי חמד. אסיפת דינים מערכת המציצה ו. מערכת חמץ ומצה סי׳ יד סע׳ יד.

3 / BEHAVIOR HARMFUL TO HEALTH

One must avoid anything that may be injurious to one's well-being and do everything that maintains and strengthens good health.[1]

1. Since smoking has been proven, beyond any shadow of a doubt, to be injurious to health and dangerous to life,[2] one should do one's utmost to avoid it.[3] According to some authorities, smoking is (in light of present medical knowledge) an offense prohibited by the Torah.[4] If, as a consequence of smoking, a person becomes ill and is thereby prevented from studying Torah or performing *mitzvot*, he is not considered as one who is exempt because of extraneous circumstances which prevent him from doing so. On the contrary, he is judged as one who willfully desists from Torah study or from performing *mitzvot*.[5]

One may not smoke in public places since cigarette smoke has been proven to be injurious also to those in the vicinity of the smoker who inhale it.[6]

2. The intake of narcotic drugs in any form, unless on specific medical instructions, is a grave offense.[7]

(1) רמב״ם הל׳ דעות פ״ד ה״א.

(2) אסיא, חוברת לז כסלו תשמ״ד, עמ׳ 5, 17, 21.

(3) ואי אפשר לאסור את העישון ע״פ דין תורה ולפי הפסוק: ונשמרתם מאד לנפשותיכם, כי אינו מזיק רק כעבור כמה שנים. וגם מכיון שנמצא בשימוש רחב ודשו בו רבים על זה נאמר שומר פתאים ד׳ (עיין שבת קכט ע״ב) — שו״ת אגרות משה יו״ד ח״ב סי׳ מט. וכן חו״מ ח״ב סי׳ עו. הגרש״ז אויערבאך שליט״א, לב אברהם ח״ב עמי יז. שו״ת יחוה דעת ח״ה סי׳ לט.

(4) שו״ת ציץ אליעזר חט״ו סי׳ לט. הגר״א נבנצל שליט״א, אסיא שם עמי 83

(5) החפץ חיים בליקוטי אמרים פי״ג. וראה גם באר הגולה בסוף חושן משפט.

(6) שו״ת אג״מ חו״מ ח״ב סי׳ יח. שו״ת ציץ אליעזר חט״ו סי׳ לט.

(7) שו״ת אג״מ יו״ד ח״ג סי׳ לה. וכן שמעתי מפי הגרש״ז אויערבאך שליט״א. וראה רמב״ם הל׳ רוצח פי״א ה״ה. שו״ת נודע ביהודה תניינא יו״ד סי׳ י, הובא בפ״ת יו״ד סי׳ כח ס״ק י.

25

3.   Obesity is well-known as a harbinger of many diseases. To quote Maimonides: "It is one's duty to avoid whatever is injurious to the body; therefore food should not be taken to repletion.[8] One should not be a glutton, but eat food conducive to health; and of such food he should not eat to excess; he should not be eager to fill his stomach, like those who gorge themselves with food and drink till the body swells.[9] Overeating is like a deadly poison to any constitution and is the principal cause of all diseases. Most maladies that afflict mankind result from bad food, or are due to the patient filling the stomach with an excess of foods even though these be (in themselves) wholesome."[10]

4.   It is well-known that physical exercise is healthy for the body, and in particular for the heart. Thus Maimonides said: "Another great principle of hygiene is as follows: As long as a person takes active exercise, works hard...he will be free from disease and will increase in vigor.[11] But if one leads a sedentary life and does not take exercise...he will throughout his life be subject to aches and pains and his strength will fail him."[12]

(8) הל׳ דעות פ״ד ה״א ו־ב.

(9) שם פ״ה ה״א.

(10) שם פ״ד הט״ו.

(11) שם ה׳׳יד.

(12) שם הט״ו.

4 / THE TORAH AND MEDICAL OPINION

1. Whenever medical opinion conflicts with the opinion of the Talmudic Sages, the latter is overridingly decisive[1] (see the next paragraph).

2. However, when medical opinion has implications which may enable a patient to avoid or be released from danger, or possible danger, it overrides all the rules of the Torah, except idolatry, murder and prohibited relations (such as adultery or incest).[2]

3. Chemical tests for blood are ordinarily not valid for deciding whether a woman is a *niddah* or not.[3] However, in cases of doubt, they may be used as auxiliary measures in order to reach a decision by competent halachic authority.[4]

4. Blood grouping or even HLA typing of white cells[5] is not, in itself, a halachically acceptable method for establishing parentage.[6] They may be used to provide *corroborative* evidence

---

(1) ראה רמב״ם הל׳ שחיטה פ״י ה״יב ו־י״ג. שו״ת הרשב״א ח״א סי׳ צח. שו״ת הריב״ש סי׳ תמז. שו״ת חת״ס יו״ד סי׳ קנח ו־קעה. שו״ת מהר״ם שיק יו״ד סי׳ קנב, רמד ו־רמח. שדי חמד מערכת טי״ת כלל ה. פמ״ג סי׳ שכח מ״ז ס״ק ב. מ״ב שם ס״ק ח. חזו״א נשים סי׳ כז ס״ק ג. מנחת שבת סי׳ צב ס״ק לב. דעת כהן סי׳ קמו ו־קמב. תפארת ישראל שבת פי״ט מ״ב. וראה נשמת אברהם אהע״ז סי׳ קעב ס״ק ה (עמי קע).

(2) שו״ת רשב״ץ ח״ג סי׳ רעא. שו״ת חת״ס יו״ד סי׳ קנג ואהע״ז סי׳ טז וח״ב סי׳ פב. שו״ת מהר״ם שיק יו״ד סי׳ קנה. או״ח סי׳ שכח סע׳ י ומ״ב ס״ק כה ו־כו. אולם ראה או״ח סי׳ תריח סע׳ א בבה״ל ד״ה חולה. שו״ת חת״ס יו״ד סי׳ קנח. שו״ת מהר״ם שיק יו״ד סי׳ רמב. שו״ת מהרש״ם ח״א סי׳ יג, כד, כה, קיד וח״ב סי׳ עב. יו״ד סי׳ קפז בפי״ת ס״ק ל. הרפואה והיהדות עמי 88 ו־284.

(3) שו״ת ציץ אליעזר חי״ג סי׳ פא ס״ק ג. הגרש״ז אויערבאך שליט״א, נשמת אברהם יו״ד סי׳ קצ ס״ק א (עמי פט).

(4) הגרי״י נויבירט שליט״א והגרש״ז אויערבאך שליט״א, נשמת אברהם שם.

(5) אסיא, חוברת לד תשרי תשמ״ג עמי 6.

(6) שו״ת ציץ אליעזר חי״ג סי׳ קד.

in establishing or denying parentage.[7] However, if tissue or white-cell typing should prove to be accurate and become widely accepted as having high specificity and sensitivity, it may be depended on to reach a decision.[8]

5. HLA typing of white blood cells may be utilized, in certain cases, to deny parentage,[9] such as when two babies have been interchanged.[10]

GENETIC ENGINEERING

6. The prohibition of *kilayim* (hybridization) applies only to whole animals or plants and not to parts of a DNA molecule.[11]

7. The use of procedures based on genetic engineering for the early detection or the treatment of hitherto incurable, genetically determined diseases must be encouraged.

8. The use of chorionic villous sampling in conjunction with the recently developed polymerase chain reaction, based on genetic engineering, makes possible the very early diagnosis of many infectious diseases. Moreover, with this technique, certain serious conditions, among them Tay-Sach's disease, Down's Syndrome, cystic fibrosis, hemophilia and thalassemia, can be detected very early in fetal development. It would appear that in the near future this will be possible even before the fetus is forty days old. If the technique proves to be reliable, the fact that such a defect will be detected during the first forty days following conception may have a most important bearing on halachic decisions concerning abortion.

(7) הגרש"ז אויערבאך שליט"א, נשמת אברהם אהע"ז סי' ד ס"ק א (עמי ל) וס"ק ו (עמי לז).

(8) הגרש"ז אויערבאך שליט"א, נשמת אברהם שם ס"ק ו (עמי לז).

(9) אסיא חוברת לד תשרי תשמ"ג עמי 6 וחוברת לה שבט תשמ"ג עמי 60. הגרש"ז אויערבאך שליט"א, נשמת אברהם אהע"ז סי' ד ס"ק ו (עמי לז).

(10) אסיא חוברת לד תשרי תשמ"ג עמי 17.

(11) כתב לי הגרש"ז אויערבאך שליט"א.

5 / LAWS CONCERNING FOOD

Problems may arise during ill health with regard to food and the various benedictions for the partaking of food. These problems are discussed in this chapter.

1. If a seriously ill patient (see Chapter 1, paragraph 1) needs to partake of otherwise forbidden foods in order that his or her life be saved, it is the patient's duty to do so, since the preservation of life takes precedence over almost all other *mitzvot*[1] (see the introduction to Chapter 2). Refusal is considered to be equivalent to "shedding blood" (endangering life), in this case the patient's own.[2]

2. On the Sabbath one may ask a non-Jew to cook for a non-seriously ill patient (see Chapter 1, paragraph 2) if necessary.[3] However, one must be careful in no way to help the non-Jew to cook, not even by putting the raw food into the utensil before it is placed on the stove,[4] or covering the utensil,[5] or stirring during cooking.[6] A healthy person may not partake of this food on the Sabbath.[7]

3. It is permitted, even for patients who are non-seriously ill (see Chapter 1, paragraph 2), to swallow *medicaments* derived from forbidden materials if these materials have pre-

(1) יו"ד סי' רלח בש"ך ס"ק ה.

(2) ר"ן יומא פב ע"א ד"ה חוץ. שו"ת יביע אומר ח"ד חו"מ סי' ו אות ד.

(3) או"ח סי' שכח סע' ט. שם סע' יז ברמ"א.

(4) מ"ב שם ס"ק נח.

(5) סי' רנד סע' ד ומי"ב ס"ק כג.

(6) סי' שיח סע' יח ומי"ב ס"ק קיד.

(7) שם סע' ס ברמ"א ומ"ב ס"ק יג. ולגבי אכילת אותו אוכל, אפילו לחולה עצמו במוצאי שבת, ראה נשמת אברהם או"ח סי' שיח ס"ק א (עמ' קנו). ולגבי הגעלת הכלים בהם בישל הגוי, ראה נשמת אברהם או"ח סי' שכח ס"ק נח (עמ' קצט).

viously been rendered unfit for consumption as human food.[8]

4. The same ruling applies even to materials forbidden by the Torah if they have undergone such chemical change as to render them unfit to be taken as *food*.[9] This is true even if in the original, forbidden state the material was of a category forbidden by the Torah for *use in any way*.[10] Exceptions to this ruling include meat cooked with dairy products[11] and actual *chametz* during Pesach[12] (unless the patient requires such a product as a life-saving measure).

5. A patient, even one suffering only from a minor illness (see Chapter 1, paragraph 3), a woman within thirty days of childbirth, a pregnant woman suffering discomfort because of her pregnancy or a nursing mother with insufficient milk,[13] who has eaten meat and who customarily waits six hours before partaking of dairy products, need, if necessary, wait only one hour after the meat. The appropriate benediction should be made after eating the meat,[14] and the mouth should be rinsed.[15]

6. Ordinarily meat has to be salted for one hour as part of the process of kashering.[16] However, for patients on low-salt diets the salting time may be reduced to the absolute

(8) שו"ת שבות יעקב ח"ב סי' ע. וראה רמ"א יו"ד סי' פז סע' י. וכן כתב הש"ך שם ס"ק לג. וראה גם פ"ת יו"ד סי' קנה ס"ק ו.

(9) שו"ת אחיעזר ח"ג סי' לא וחיו"ד סי' יא ס"ק ה.

(10) יו"ד סי' קנה סע' א בהגה. שו"ת רדב"ז ח"ג סי' תקמח.

(11) הגר"א יו"ד סי' קנה ס"ק כב.

(12) או"ח סי' תמה סע' ב.

(13) שו"ת יחוה דעת ח"ג סי' נח.

(14) ערוה"ש יו"ד סי' פט סע' ז. שו"ת חת"ס יו"ד סי' עג. כף החיים יו"ד סי' פט ס"ק כא. בן איש חי שנה ב פ' שלח לך סע' יא. חכ"א כלל מ סע' יג.

(15) דרכי תשובה יו"ד סי' פט ס"ק טו. בנוגע להתרת נדרים — ראה יו"ד סי' ריד סע' א ובש"ך ס"ק ב מחד גיסא, ואו"ח סי' תקפא במג"א ס"ק יב ודגול מרבבה יו"ד סי' ריד מאידך גיסא. וראה שעה"צ סי' תקפא ס"ק לג ושו"ת יביע אומר ח"ב סי' ל אות ז.

(16) יו"ד סי' סט סע' ו בהגה.

minimum of eighteen minutes[17] (but preferably to no less than twenty-three minutes[18]). For those on a salt-*free* diet, meat should be grilled directly over the fire after being washed but without prior salting (as is ordinarily done for liver), and then may either be eaten as such or cooked according to taste.[19] With regard to the use of other salts, such as potassium or ammonium chloride, see *Nishmat Avraham*.[20] (Such salts should be used only under medical supervision.)

7. The appropriate benedictions should be pronounced before and after partaking of any food or liquid (except water) for medicinal purposes, provided it is palatable.[21] This applies even if the patient eats or drinks it *because* of the illness and not because of appetite or thirst.[22] (Water is an exception, and a benediction is pronounced only if it is taken for thirst or palatability.[23]) However, the benedictions are not to be recited for what is actually unpalatable, even if it is beneficial[24] (see also Chapter 6).

8. A patient who is permitted (for a specific medical reason) to partake of foods which are ordinarily forbidden should, nevertheless, if an Ashkenazi, recite the appropriate benedictions before and after eating.[25] This is true whether the food itself is a forbidden one or whether it is a permitted food that may not be eaten on account of the time factor (such as on Yom

(17) או״ח סי׳ תנט סע״ב. ש״ך יו״ד שם ס״ק כה. שו״ת ציץ אליעזר חי״ג סי׳ לה ס״ק ב.

(18) או״ח סי׳ תנט במ״ב סי״ק טו. חזו״א או״ח סי׳ קכג ס״ק א. וראה בנשמת אברהם יו״ד סי׳ סט סק״ב (עמ׳ טז).

(19) יו״ד סי׳ סט סע׳ כא. וראה שם סי׳ עג סע׳ ה בהגה.

(20) יו״ד סי׳ סט ס״ק א (עמ׳ טז).

(21) או״ח סי׳ רד סע׳ ח. וראה שם שעה״צ ס״ק לז שאף אם טעמו אינו טוב, כיון שעכ״פ אינו רע, גם מברך.

(22) מ״ב שם ס״ק מג.

(23) מ״ב שם ס״ק מ.

(24) מ״ב שם.

(25) או״ח סי׳ רד סע׳ ט.

Kippur).[26] The seriously ill person (see Chapter 1, paragraph 1) who needs the food is doing no wrong in consuming it; on the contrary, the patient is performing the *mitzvah* of preserving (one's own) life.[27]

In the case of a Sephardi, either the patient should first eat or drink something permissible which requires the same benediction or, if that is not possible, the words of the benediction should be borne in mind without actually being uttered.[28]

However, if a patient has to consume a non-kosher food which is actually repulsive, no benediction should be pronounced.[29]

9. Three adults who have together partaken of a meal which included bread form a *zimmun* (quorum) for the purpose of the *Birkat Ha-mazon*.[30] A patient who, for medical reasons, has had to consume an otherwise forbidden food should not be included in the *zimmun*.[31] Similarly, three seriously ill patients (see Chapter 1, paragraph 1), lying in the same hospital room, who need to eat on Yom Kippur should not form a *zimmun*[32] (see Chapter 13, paragraph 17).

10. A patient who is fed via a stomach tube, whether inserted via the nose, the mouth or directly through the abdominal wall, should not recite the benedictions before or after food.[33]

---

(26) מ״ב סי׳ רד ס״ק מו

(27) מ״ב שם ס״ק מז.

(28) ב״ח סי׳ רד. החיד״א סי׳ קצו בשיורי ברכה. כף החיים סי׳ קצו ס״ק ח.

(29) מ״ב שם ס״ק מח.

(30) או״ח סי׳ קצב סע׳ א.

(31) פמ״ג סי׳ קצו מ״ז סוס״ק א. כף החיים שם ס״ק ט.

(32) כף החיים שם. שמירת שבת כהלכתה פל״ט סע׳ לא. וראה שם הערה קה בשם הגרש״ז אויערבאך שליט״א.

(33) מנחת חינוך מצוה שיג ס״ק ב. שו״ת מהרי״ם שיק סי׳ רן. שו״ת דברי מלכיאל ח״ה סו״ס רמא. שערי תשובה סי׳ קצז סוס״ק ח. שו״ת חלקת יעקב ח״ג סי׳ סח. שו״ת מחזה אברהם או״ח סי׳ קכט. אך ראה שערים מצויינים בהלכה סי׳ נ ס״ק ח. וראה נשמת אברהם

11.   A patient who has eaten less than an olive's bulk (30 cc.) of bread,[34] even if he is thereby satiated and unable to eat more, should not recite the benediction after meals.[35]

12.   If a patient is not likely to eat as much as an egg's bulk (50 cc.) of bread,[36] the benediction for the ritual washing of the hands should not be recited.[37]

13.   One who has a bandage or a band-aid on a finger, which should not be removed, should ritually wash the uncovered part of the hand and pronounce the benediction before eating bread.[38] On the Sabbath, care should be taken not to pour water on the bandage.[39] If all the fingers are completely bandaged to the tips, only the other hand should be washed and the benediction should be pronounced in the usual way.[40]

14.   In the case of a patient who is fed bread by an attendant, it is the patient (not the attendant) whose hands should be washed, even though the patient himself does not handle the bread.[41]

15.   A healthy person may not eat or drink before the

אוי"ח סי' רי ס"ק א (עמ' צג). ומה טוב, אם אפשר אם ישמע ברכת המזון מאחר שגם חייב בברכת המזון שיוציא אותו ידי חובתו — שו"ת מחזה אברהם שם. שו"ת ציץ אליעזר חי"ג סי' לה.

(34) סי' תפו ומ"ב ס"ק א. שיעורי תורה סי' ג סע' יג. שיעורין דאורייתא בשיעורי המצות ס"ק כג.

(35) שו"ת ציץ אליעזר חי"א סי' יג.

(36) אוי"ח סי' רצא סע' א ומ"ב ס"ק ב. שיעורין דאורייתא בשיעורי המצות ס"ק כא.

(37) אוי"ח סי' קנח סע' ב.

(38) שו"ת זבחי צדק ח"ב אוי"ח סי' יג. שו"ת רב פעלים חי"א אוי"ח סי' ח. שו"ת יחוה דעת ח"ב סי' יט.

(39) כן כתב לי הגרש"ז אויערבאך שליט"א.

(40) אוי"ח סי' קסב סע' י ומ"ב שם ס"ק סח. ואם אינו יכול ליטול ידיו כלל מחמת חולי, יכרוך ידיו במפה — מ"ב ס"ק סט.

(41) אוי"ח סי' קסג סע' ב. וראה נשמת אברהם שם ס"ק ב (עמ' פא).

morning prayers[42] (except for water, tea or coffee[43]); however, it is permissible for an ill person to do so.[44] If possible, the benedictions over the Torah should first be pronounced and the first paragraph of the *Shema* recited.[45] It is preferable to recite the prayers in private before eating, rather than eat first in order then to join a congregational prayer. However, after praying in private one should, if possible, join the congregation to hear *Kaddish, Barechu* and other prayers that require a *minyan*[46] (see Chapter 10, paragraph 159).

16. It is permitted for patients to eat from utensils that have not been immersed in a *mikveh*.[47]

17. A physician who in the middle of a meal is called out to see a seriously ill patient (see Chapter 1, paragraph 1) may continue with the meal on returning without pronouncing any further benedictions, despite the interruption, provided that he had in mind to continue the meal on his return[48] and had already eaten at least an olive's bulk of bread (30 cc.).[49] However, the hands should be washed again.[50]

18. If on the Sabbath a physician is called out for a seriously ill patient (see Chapter 1, paragraph 1) between the recital of *Kiddush* and the partaking of food, and the matter is

(42) או"ח סי' פט סע' ג ומ"ב ס"ק כא.

(43) שם ומ"ב ס"ק כב. שו"ת יביע אומר ח"ד סי' יא ו-יב. שמעתי מפי הגרש"ז אויערבאך שליטא"א.

(44) או"ח שם.

(45) מ"ב שם ס"ק כב וביה"ל ד"ה ולא.

(46) ביה"ל שם ד"ה וכן.

(47) שמעתי מפי הגרש"ז אויערבאך שליטא"א. וראה נשמת אברהם יו"ד סי' קכ ס"ק א (עמי לא).

(48) או"ח סי' קעח סע' ב בהגה. בן איש חי שנה א פ' בהעלותך סע' ב. כף החיים סי' קעח ס"ק יד.

(49) שמעתי מפי הגרש"ז אוירבאך שליטא"א.

(50) או"ח סי' קסד סע' ב וסי' קע סע' א ובמ"ב ס"ק ט. ולגבי ברכת על נטילת ידים ראה מ"ב סי' קסד ס"ק יג.

not urgent, he should eat an olive's bulk (30 cc.) of cake or drink at least 86 cc.[51] of wine in addition to the wine he drank for *Kiddush*; or, if even this is not possible, a total of at least 86 cc. of wine should be consumed. On returning, he may continue with his Sabbath meal without repeating *Kiddush*. In an emergency, when there is no time to eat or drink, *Kiddush* must be repeated on returning.[52]

For rules concerning interruptions in the middle of the *Seder* service, see Chapter 15, paragraph 16.

Regarding the separation of tithes or *challah* on the Sabbath and the Festivals, see Chapter 10, paragraph 32.

---

(51) דהיינו שיעור רביעית לפי הגר״ח נאה שיעורי תורה עמ׳ קעז. ולדעת החזו״א 150 ccs —
שיעורין דאורייתא בשיעורי המצוות ס״ק יח.

(52) או״ח סי׳ רעג סע׳ ה וסי׳ רעא במ״ב ס״ק עח.

6 / MEDICINES

A person should not think that healing lies in any given medicine or treatment *per se*, for the Almighty alone has the power
to heal. Rather, trust should be placed in the Almighty, that the
medicine or treatment about to be taken will be the means for a
cure.[1]

1.   Before receiving any treatment, be it medical or
surgical, or taking any medication (whether palatable or not), a
person should say,[2]

יְהִי רָצוֹן מִלְפָנֶיךָ ד' אֱלֹקַי, שֶׁיְהֵא עֵסֶק זֶה לִי לִרְפוּאָה כִּי
רוֹפֵא חִנָּם אָתָּה.

"May it be Your wish, O Lord my God, that what I am doing
shall cure me, for You are the Healer Who takes no reward."

After the treatment or medicine, he should say,[3]

בָּרוּךְ רוֹפֵא חוֹלִים

"Blessed be He Who heals the sick."

2.   A person who swallows an unpalatable medicine should
not recite a benediction for it[4] or for the water he may drink in
order to facilitate swallowing.[5] If another liquid is drunk to help
swallow the medicine or to conceal its bitter taste, the *Shehakol*
benediction should be recited over that liquid.[6]

(1) או"ח סי' רל סע' ד במ"ב ס"ק ו.

(2) או"ח שם ומג"א ס"ק ו. מ"ב ס"ק ו ושעה"יצ ס"ק ח.

(3) או"ח שם. וראה ט"ז ס"ק ג, פמ"ג א"א ס"ק ו ושעה"יצ ס"ק ט.

(4) או"ח סי' רד במ"ב ס"ק מג.

(5) שם סע' ז ומ"ב ס"ק מב.

(6) מ"ב שם.

3.   If the medicine itself is not unpalatable,[7] or if it is unpalatable but is mixed or coated with sugar or a similar material to conceal its unpalatability, one should not recite any benediction.[8]

(7) מ״ב שם ס״ק מג.

(8) אמרו לי הגרש״ז אויערבאך שליט״א והגרי״י נויבירט שליט״א. עיין נשמת אברהם
או״ח סי׳ רד ס״ק ד (עמי צא).

7 / DUTIES OF PRAYER

Prayers are recited three times daily on weekdays. This may not be possible during ill health. The problems are discussed in this chapter.

1. A person who is unable to stand during the *Shemoneh Esreh* prayer, even while leaning for support,[1] may recite it in a sitting position. If unable to sit, he may recite it while reclining,[2] if possible with the head and shoulders raised on pillows.[3] If this too is not possible, the patient should lie on his side,[4] at least slightly.[5] If even this is not possible, he may pray while lying flat.[6]

If the patient is unable to speak, he should pray in thought, as suggested in Scripture: "Commune with your heart upon your bed" (*Psalms* 4:5).[7] Even if one recovers during the very period of time relevant to that particular prayer, there is no need subsequently to recite it.[8]

2. A patient who finds it difficult to recite the standard *Shemoneh Esreh* may recite the shortened version, known as *Havinenu*[9] (if possible in the standing position[10]), as follows: He should recite the first three benedictions of the *Shemoneh Esreh*,

(1) או"ח סי' צד במ"ב ס"ק כח.

(2) או"ח שם סע' ו ומ"ב ס"ק כ.

(3) ראה נשמת אברהם או"ח סי' סג ס"ק א בשם הגרש"ז אויערבאך שליט"א.

(4) או"ח סי' צד סע' ו וסי' סג סע' א ומ"ב שם ס"ק ב ו-ד.

(5) נשמת אברהם סי' סג ס"ק א בשם הגרש"ז אויערבאך שליט"א.

(6) ראה ערוה"ש סע' ה.

(7) או"ח סי' צד סע' ו בהגה.

(8) מ"ב שם ס"ק כא ו-כז. וראה נשמת אברהם סי' צד ס"ק ג ו-ד (עמ' סב).

(9) או"ח סי' ק סע' א בביה"ל ד"ה או.

(10) או"ח שם.

38

then *Havinenu* (see below), and conclude with the three benedictions of the *Shemoneh Esreh* from *Retzeh* onward.[11] The text of *Havinenu* is as follows:

הֲבִינֵנוּ ד' אֱלֹקֵינוּ לָדַעַת דְּרָכֶיךָ, וּמוֹל אֶת לְבָבֵנוּ לְיִרְאָתֶךָ, וְתִסְלַח לָנוּ לִהְיוֹת גְּאוּלִים, וְהַרְחִיקֵנוּ מִמַּכְאוֹבֵינוּ, וְדַשְּׁנֵנוּ בִּנְאוֹת אַרְצֶךָ, וּנְפוּצוֹתֵינוּ מֵאַרְבַּע (כַּנְפוֹת הָאָרֶץ) תְּקַבֵּץ, וְהַתּוֹעִים בְּדַעְתְּךָ יִשָּׁפֵטוּ, וְעַל הָרְשָׁעִים תָּנִיף יָדֶךָ, וְיִשְׂמְחוּ צַדִּיקִים בְּבִנְיַן עִירֶךָ וּבְתִקּוּן הֵיכָלֶךָ וּבִצְמִיחַת קֶרֶן לְדָוִד עַבְדֶּךָ וַעֲרִיכַת נֵר לְבֶן יִשַׁי מְשִׁיחֶךָ, טֶרֶם נִקְרָא אַתָּה תַעֲנֶה, בָּרוּךְ אַתָּה ד' שׁוֹמֵעַ תְּפִלָּה.

"Grant us, Lord our God, wisdom to learn Thy ways; subject our hearts to Thy worship; forgive us so that we may be redeemed; keep us from suffering; satisfy us with the products of Thy earth; gather our dispersed people from the four corners of the earth; judge those who stray from Thy faith; punish the wicked; and may the righteous rejoice over the rebuilding of Thy city, the reconstruction of Thy Temple, the flourishing of the dynasty of Thy servant David and the continuance of the offspring of Thy anointed, the son of Jesse. Answer us before we call. Blessed art Thou, O Lord, who hearest prayer."[12]

Again, there is no need subsequently to repeat the whole *Shemoneh Esreh* even if the patient recovers during the time period appropriate for that prayer.[13]

3. If the patient finds it difficult to recite even the *Havinenu* prayer together with its preceding and concluding benedictions, the recital of the following short paragraph is adequate:[14]

(11) ברכות כט ע"א. טור או"ח סי' קי.

(12) הסידור השלם, ד"ר פ. בירנבאום.

(13) או"ח שם סעי' א.

(14) גשר החיים פ"א סי' ג ס"ק ה. טור או"ח סי' קי.

רִבּוֹן הָעוֹלָמִים, צָרְכֵי עַמְּךָ מְרוּבִּים וְדַעְתָּם קְצָרָה, יְהִי רָצוֹן
מִלְפָנֶיךָ ד' אֱלֹקַי, שֶׁתִּתֵּן לְכָל אֶחָד וְאֶחָד כְּדֵי פַרְנָסָתוֹ וּלְכָל
גְּוִיָּה דֵי מַחְסוֹרָהּ (רְפָאֵנוּ וְנֵרָפֵא) וְהַטּוֹב בְּעֵינֶיךָ עֲשֵׂה, בָּרוּךְ
אַתָּה ד' שׁוֹמֵעַ תְּפִלָּה.

"Lord of the worlds, the needs of Thy people Israel are
many and their knowledge is limited. May it be Thy will, Lord
my God, to grant a sufficient livelihood to each and every one,
and to each and every creature according to its needs, (heal us
that we be healed,) and do as seems good in Thy sight. Blessed
art Thou, O Lord, Who hearest prayer."[15]

However, unlike the ruling given in paragraphs 1 and
2 above, in this circumstance if the patient recovers sufficiently
during the relevant time the whole standard *Shemoneh Esreh*
should be recited in the usual way.[16]

4.   A patient who cannot concentrate in order to pray
should, if possible, recite the *Shema*, or at least the first verse.[17]

5.   A patient who, because of his medical condition,
has contemplated the words of the *Shema* without pronouncing
them has thereby complied with the duty of reciting the *Shema*.[18]
However, if he recovers sufficiently during the relevant time, he
should recite the *Shema* in the normal way.[19]

6.   At the end of the *Shemoneh Esreh* one has to take
three steps backward.[20] A person who is confined to a wheelchair
should, if possible, move the wheelchair backward (or have
someone else move it) for the required distance at the end of the
Shemoneh Esreh.[21]

(15) תורגם ע"י ד"ר פ. בירנבאום.

(16) או"ח סי' קי סע' ג ומ"ב ס"ק טו.

(17) או"ח סי' צד במ"ב ס"ק כא.

(18) או"ח סי' סב סע' ד.

(19) מ"ב שם ס"ק ז. ואפילו לדעת השו"ע. וראה גם ביה"ל ד"ה יצא.

(20) או"ח סי' קכג סע' א. וראה יומא נג ע"ב שאם לא עשה כן ראוי לו שלא התפלל.

(21) ראה או"ח סי' צד סע' ה ברמ"א. שמעתי מהגרש"ז אויערבאך שליט"א.

7. A person who is concerned about a close relative who is ill may include the latter by name either in the *Refa'enu* or in the *Shome'a tefillah* benediction of the *Shemoneh Esreh*.[22] The patient should be mentioned by name even if the patient is a parent of the supplicant[23] (see also Chapter 20, paragraph 9).

8. A physician who is called to see a seriously ill patient (see Chapter 1, paragraph 1) must go to attend to the patient even if he is in the middle of the *Shemoneh Esreh* or even if he has been called up to the reading of the Torah, and even if the time for that particular prayer will have passed by the time he has finished attending to the patient.[24]

9. A physician or other attendant who cannot leave his patients and who has no replacement must continue to tend to his patients, even if by doing so he will miss the opportunity to pray. When off duty he does not need to "make up" for the lost prayer.[25] However, this is so only if he started to attend to his patients before the period of time to which that particular prayer was related and he was so occupied for the whole period of time. If he came on duty only after the beginning of the period of time related to that particular prayer, he should "make up" for the lost prayer during the next service.[26]

Thus, for instance, if he had started to treat the patient or patients before the time when one may pray *Minchah*, and was involved until it was too late to pray *Minchah*, he does not need to repeat the *Shemoneh Esreh* of *Ma'ariv*. However, if he started to tend to patients after the beginning of the time that it was possible to pray *Minchah*, and as a result of his duties missed the opportunity to pray *Minchah*, he has to recite the *Shemoneh Esreh* of *Ma'ariv* twice—the first time for *Ma'ariv* and the second,

(22) אוי״ח סי׳ קטז מי״ב סי״ק ג.

(23) כף החיים סי׳ קיט סי״ק ו.

(24) שו״ת ציץ אליעזר ח״ט סי׳ יז פי״ז וח״י סי׳ יג.

(25) אוי״ח סי׳ צג סע׳ א ומי״ב סי״ק ח. סי׳ קו במי״ב סי״ק ג.

(26) אוי״ח סי׳ קח סע׳ ח.

to compensate for the lost *Minchah*.[27]

10. If a man is to undergo an operation scheduled for the early morning and he knows that he will not be able to lay *tefillin* or recite *Shacharit* that day after the operation, he should try to start praying after dawn, so that he reaches the benediction *Yotzer or* at first light,[28] and then put on the *tallit* and *tefillin*, recite the appropriate benedictions[29] and continue with the rest of *Shacharit*.[30] If the operation is scheduled to start even earlier, so that this is not possible, he may put on the *tallit* and *tefillin* immediately after dawn, without reciting the benedictions.[31] If time does not allow even for this, the *mitzvot* of *tallit* and *tefillin* may be performed before dawn (the benedictions are not recited);[32] *Shacharit* may be recited only after dawn.[33]

(27) אורח חיים סי' קח סע' א.

(28) וראה ביה"ל סי' פט סע' א ד"ה ואם, על זמן עמוד השחר וכן מג"א ס"ק ג. וע"ע א"ר והגר"א שם ושו"ת מלמד להועיל סי' ל.

(29) בכדי שיראה את חברו ברחוק ד' אמות. עיין או"ח סי' ל סע' א ופמ"ג סי' נח א"א ס"ק ב. כף החיים ס"ק יח. שו"ת אגרות משה או"ח חי"ד סי' ז.

(30) ועיין רמב"ם הל' תפילין פ"ד הי"א שאף עובר על לאו אם מניחם בלילה. אולם ע"ע באו"ח סי' ל סע' ב ומג"א ס"ק א.

(31) מהא דמ"ב סי' ל ס"ק יג וסימן נח ס"ק יג וביה"ל סע' א ד"ה זמן. כף החיים סי' נח ס"ק יז. ועיין תפארת ישראל ברכות סוף פ"א. ברכי יוסף סי' נח ס"ק ד. שערי תשובה על סי' תרסד. שו"ת אגרות משה או"ח חי"ד סי' ו. שו"ת יחוה דעת ח"ב סי' ח.

(32) שמעתי ממו"ר הגרי"י נויבירט שליט"א. וראה ערוך השולחן סי' ל סע' ה.

(33) וראה נשמת אברהם או"ח סי' נח ס"ק א (עמ' כד).

8 / *TEFILLIN* (PHYLACTERIES)

**It is the duty of every adult male Jew to lay *tefillin* on his arm
and head every day except the Sabbath and the Festivals.
Problems arise as a result of ill health or of injury to an arm
or the head.**

1.   The *tefillin* of the arm should be placed over the
lower half of the biceps muscle of the left arm, or of the right
arm in the case of a left-handed person (i.e., on the weaker of
the two arms).[1] A person who is injured so that he cannot lay
tefillin on that part of the arm should lay *tefillin* over the upper
half of the muscle,[2] but should not recite the benediction for
tefillin of the arm.[3]

2.   One who has lost the left *forearm* from the elbow
downward should put on the *tefillin* of the arm without reciting
the benediction.[4] When he puts on the *tefillin* of the head, if he is
a Sephardi he should recite only the one benediction, *Al mitzvat
tefillin*; if he is an Ashkenazi he should recite both *Lehaniach
tefillin* and *Al mitzvat tefillin*.[5]

3.   If *part* of the forearm remains, the benediction should
be recited as usual.[6]

4.   It is commendable for a person who has lost the
left arm or whose left arm has been amputated above the biceps
muscle, to have *tefillin* laid on the right arm; but the benediction

(1) או״ח סי׳ כז סע׳ א בהגה.

(2) ערוה״יש שם סע׳ ד. מ״ב ס״ק ד. בן איש חי שנה א פ׳ חיי שרה ס״ק ו.

(3) שו״ת יביע אומר ח״א או״ח סי׳ ג אות כ ו־כא.

(4) או״ח סי׳ כז סע׳ א בהגה.

(5) או״ח סי׳ כו סע׳ ב. סי׳ כז בביה״ל ד״ה בלא.

(6) סי׳ כז במ״ב ס״ק ה.

43

is not recited.[7] He should, of course, have *tefillin* put on the head.[8] With regard to the benediction, see paragraph 2 above.

5. A person *born* without a left arm has *tefillin* laid on his right arm,[9] and, of course, *tefillin* are put on the head. With regard to the benediction, see paragraph 2 above.

6. If the middle finger of a person's left hand has been amputated, he lays *tefillin* as usual but winds the strap around the index finger instead.[10]

7. A person whose left arm is in a plaster cast should, nevertheless, lay *tefillin* on the left arm.[11] If the box of the *tefillin* itself is in contact with the skin, though the *straps* are wrapped around the cast, he should recite the benediction for the *tefillin* of the arm.[12] However, if the box itself rests on the cast, he should recite only the benediction for the *tefillin* of the head as stated in paragraph 2 above. The *tefillin* of the arm should, as usual, be covered by a garment.[13]

8. One should lay *tefillin* on a paralyzed left arm just as one would if it were functioning normally[14] (see paragraph 13 below).

9. A patient who because of an intravenous infusion into the left arm is unable to wind the *tefillin* seven times round the forearm in the usual way should lay *tefillin* on the left arm as usual, except that after strapping the box over his biceps muscle

(7) שו״ת שבות יעקב ח״א סי׳ ג. שו״ת שאגת אריה סי׳ כז מ״ב ס״ק ו ושעה״צ ס״ק ז. כף החיים ס״ק ו. אך ראה שו״ת רמ״א סי׳ קכב, ב״ח, א״ר, הגר״א ס״ק ו ושו״ת פנים מאירות ח״ג סי׳ יא.

(8) כף החיים שם. שו״ת שאגת אריה שם.

(9) שו״ת שבות יעקב שם.

(10) שו״ת חלקת יעקב ח״ג סי׳ קג.

(11) שו״ת חלקת יעקב ח״ב סי׳ מג. שו״ת מנחת יצחק ח״ב סי׳ מו.

(12) מהא דמג״א סי׳ כז ס״ק ו ו־ח. מ״ב ס״ק טז ר־יח.

(13) מ״ב שם.

(14) שו״ת אגרות משה או״ח ח״א סי׳ ח.

he should draw the strap straight down to the left middle finger, without first winding it around the forearm. The benediction is pronounced as usual,[15] even if the *tefillin* can be strapped only over the biceps and not at all to the forearm or finger.[16]

10. One who has no right arm should have the *tefillin* laid upon the left arm by an attendant.[17]

11. If a person's right *hand* has been amputated, leaving the forearm intact, he lays *tefillin* on the right arm, which is now considered the weaker arm[18] (see paragraph 1 above). If the arm was amputated above the biceps muscle, he lays *tefillin* on the left arm.[19]

12. A person whose right arm is paralyzed should be helped to lay *tefillin* on the left arm[20] if, according to expert medical opinion, the arm will probably recover its function. If it is likely to remain paralyzed, the *tefillin* should be laid on the right arm.[21]

13. If a patient, in addition to suffering paralysis of the right arm, has lost all sensation in it, he is considered as having no right arm and should, therefore, have *tefillin* laid on the left arm.[22] Similarly, if paralysis and loss of sensation has affected his left arm, he should have *tefillin* laid on the right.

(15) מהא דסי' כז סע' ח.

(16) שמעתי ממו"ר הגריי"י נויבירט שליטי"א.

(17) או"ח סי' כז במ"ב סוסי"ק ו.

(18) מ"ב שם ס"ק כב וביה"ל ד"ה ואיטר יד.

(19) מ"ב שם ס"ק ו. וכן שמעתי מהגרא"י וולדינברג וממו"ר הגריי"י נויברט שליטי"א. וראה נשמת אברהם או"ח סי' כז ס"ק ב(ז) (עמי ח).

(20) מ"ב שם ס"ק כב. ובמקום שאין איש אחר שיקשור לו את התפילין, יכולה אשה לקשור לו (שו"ת מהרי"ם שיק או"ח סי' טו. שו"ת מהרי"י אסאד או"ח סי' יט. שו"ת יד הלוי ח"ב סי' א). וראה גם לענין ברכה. וראה מ"ב סי' יד סע' א בביה"ל ד"ה להצריך ובסימן תרמט ס"ק יד. וראה נשמת אברהם או"ח סי' כז עמי ט.

(21) כן כתב לי הגרש"ז אויערבאך שליטי"א.

(22) כן כתב לי הגרש"ז אויערבאך שליטי"א.

14. A person both of whose arms are paralyzed should have *tefillin* laid for him on the left arm, reciting the benediction as usual.[23]

15. One whose head is bandaged should, nevertheless, lay *tefillin* on his head. When the box of the *tefillin* and the knot both lie in contact with the body, if he is an Ashkenazi he recites the benediction *Al mitzvat tefillin* in the usual way, even if the straps lie on the bandage. However, if the box or the knot also lies on the bandage, he does not recite this benediction.[24] A Sephardi does not recite a benediction for the *tefillin* of the head in any case (see paragraph 2 above).

16. In the rare event of a man having his heart on the right side of the chest (dextrocardia), he should nevertheless lay *tefillin* on the left arm, since the essential criterion is that they be worn on the weaker of the two arms.[25]

17. A person suffering from severe diarrhea may not put on *tefillin*.[26] However, if the diarrhea is such that he is sure of being able to recite the *Shema* without having to defecate or pass flatus, he should lay *tefillin* immediately after the *Ahavah* prayer, pronounce the benediction for *tefillin* and recite the *Shema*.[27] In the case of an illness other than diarrhea, he should lay *tefillin*, unless his suffering is such as to preclude concentration on the *mitzvah*.[28]

18. If a man is to undergo an operation scheduled for the early morning and he knows that he will not be able to lay *tefillin* or recite *Shacharit* that day after the operation, he should try to start praying after dawn, so that he reaches the benedic-

(23) לקט הקמח החדש סי' כז ס"ק יב.

(24) מ"ב ס"ק טז.

(25) יסודי ישורון ח"א עמ' פג.

(26) או"ח סי' לח סע' א ומג"א ס"ק א.

(27) או"ח שם סע' ב.

(28) או"ח שם סע' א בהגה. וראה מ"ב ס"ק ה.

tion *Yotzer or* at first light,[29] and then put on the *tallit* and *tefillin*, recite the appropriate benedictions[30] and continue with the rest of *Shacharit*.[31] If the operation is scheduled to start even earlier, so that this is not possible, he may put on the *tallit* and *tefillin* immediately after dawn, without reciting the benedictions.[32] If time does not allow even for this, the *mitzvot* of *tallit* and *tefillin* may be performed before dawn (the benedictions are not recited);[33] *Shacharit* may be recited only after dawn.[34]

(29) וראה ביה"ל סי' פט סע' א ד"ה ואם, על זמן עמוד השחר וכן מג"א ס"ק ג. וע"ע א"ר והגר"א שם ושו"ת מלמד להועיל סי' ל.

(30) בכדי שיראה את חברו ברחוק ד' אמות. עיין או"ח סי' ל סע' א ופמ"ג סי' נח א"א ס"ק ב. כף החיים ס"ק יח. שו"ת אגרות משה או"ח ח"ד סי' ז.

(31) ועיין רמב"ם הל' תפילין פ"ד הי"א שאף היי"א עובר על לאו אם מניחם בלילה. אולם ע"ע באו"ח סי' ל סע' ב ומג"א ס"ק א.

(32) מהא דמ"ב סי' ל ס"ק יג וסימן נח ס"ק יג וביה"ל סע' א ד"ה זמן. כף החיים סי' נח ס"ק יז. ועיין תפארת ישראל ברכות סוף פ"א. ברכי יוסף סי' נח ס"ק ד. שערי תשובה על סי' תרסד. שו"ת אגרות משה או"ח ח"ד סי' ו. שו"ת יחוה דעת ח"ב סי' ח.

(33) שמעתי ממו"ר הגרי"י נויבירט שליט"א. וראה ערוך השולחן סי' ל סע' ה.

(34) וראה נשמת אברהם או"ח סי' נח ס"ק א (עמ' כד).

9 / RELIGIOUS DUTIES IN AN UNCLEAN ENVIRONMENT

This chapter discusses the carrying out of such duties as reciting prayers and the *Shema*, pronouncing the various benedictions and studying Torah in an unclean location or situation.

1. According to the Torah (*Deuteronomy* 23:15), a person may not engage in sacred matters, such as prayer or the study of Torah, in the presence of excrement;[1] and the Rabbis have extended this prohibition to apply to urine.[2] If the excreta are in front of the person, prayers may not be recited unless they are out of sight. If they are behind or to one side, so that he would have to turn his head to see them, he should move at least two meters away from the malodorous area.[3] In the case of urine, he may pour at least 90 cc. of water on it and then, if there is no odor,[4] he may proceed to pray, etc.[5]

2. These rules concerning excreta apply also to containers such as urine bottles or bedpans made of wood or unglazed pottery, even if they are empty.[6]

3. If the bedpan is made of metal, glass, glazed pottery or plastic and is clean and free of unpleasant odor, no distancing is required.[7]

---

(1) אור״ח סי׳ עט מ״ב ס״ק ב וביה״ל ד״ה צואה.

(2) אורח סי׳ עז מ״ב ס״ק ב.

(3) אורח סי׳ פז מ״ב ס״ק ג. וראה אור״ח סי׳ עט סע׳ א ומ״ב ס״ק ה וחיי אדם כלל ג סע׳ יד.

(4) אורח סי׳ עז מ״ב ס״ק ב.

(5) אורח שם סע׳ א.

(6) אורח סי׳ פז סע׳ א ומ״ב ס״ק ג.

(7) אורח שם סע׳ א ומ״ב ס״ק ו. שמירת שבת כהלכתה פכ״ב הערה קיג.

48

4. All the above rules apply by night as well as by day, and even if the patient has no sense of smell or is blind.[8]

5. If the excreta or containers are covered, prayers, etc. may be recited even in proximity to them as long as there is no odor,[9] even if the excreta are visible through a transparent cover.[10]

6. A bed that stands 24 cm. or more above the ground is not considered a covering for a bedpan under it, and the bedpan should therefore be removed or covered, even if there is no odor.[11]

7. A person who recited the *Shema* or *Shemoneh Esreh* and subsequently discovered a bedpan, etc., within two meters should repeat the prayer if the circumstances are such that finding such an object could have been anticipated.[12]

8. A person who is in an unclean location may neither recite nor meditate on the *Shema*, etc.[13]

9. A person is permitted to perform his religious duties if there is an adequate partition between himself and the excreta, provided that there is no odor. The partition must be at least[14] 80 cm. high[15] and 32 cm. wide,[16] such as may be provided,

(8) או״ח סי׳ עט סע׳ א. חיי אדם כלל ג סע׳ יב ו־יג.

(9) או״ח סי׳ פז סע׳ ג.

(10) משום דבכיסוי תלה רחמנא. סי׳ עו סע׳ א.

(11) כיון שרגליהן של מיטות שלנו גבוהות ג׳ טפחים ולא נקרא לבוד, ואם כן אין הכלי נקרא מכוסה. או״ח סי׳ פז מ״ב ס״ק ט. כף החיים שם ס״ק יב. וראה גם שו״ת ציץ אליעזר ח״ח סי׳ א.

(12) או״ח סי׳ פז מ״ב ס״ק ג.

(13) או״ח סי׳ סב סע׳ ד בהגה. סי׳ עו סע׳ ח ביה״ל ד״ה צריך. וראה שם מ״ב ס״ק ט.

(14) לשיטת הגר״ח נאה ספר שיעורי תורה סי׳ ג סע׳ יח. אולם לשיטת החזו״א הטפח הוא 9.6 סמ׳ — ספר שיעורין דאורייתא.

(15) או״ח סי׳ שטו מ״ב ס״ק י.

(16) או״ח סי׳ פז סע׳ ג ביה״ל ד״ה מותר.

for instance, by a curtain affixed to a frame, top and bottom.[17]

10. A critically ill patient may recite the deathbed confession even in an unclean location, but without uttering the Names of the Almighty.[18]

11. A patient who has urinary incontinence is permitted to perform his religious duties, provided he does not sense the actual passage of urine and as long as his outer garments are clean.[19]

12. A person who has a catheter in the bladder, through which urine passes into a bag, is permitted to perform his religious duties.[20]

13. A person who has urine drawn through a catheter should recite the *Asher yatzar* benediction. If the urine drains continuously, he should recite the benediction only if the drip has ceased.[21]

14. A patient who passes feces through an artificial opening (colostomy or ileostomy) may engage in religious duties if the external opening is clean and covered.[22]

15. A person suffering from diarrhea should recite the *Asher yatzar* benediction after each bowel movement.[23] If the diarrhea is continuous, he should not pronounce the benediction until the movements have ceased.[24]

16. A person who passes flatus may not recite the

(17) אורח סי' רמ סע' ו ביה"ל ד"ה עד. סי' שטו במ"ב ס"ק ו ו-ט ושעה"צ ס"ק ו ו-יא.

(18) אורח סי' תרו שעה"צ ס"ק כב — מו"ר הגרי"י נויבירט שליטא. והוסיף הגרש"ז אויערבאך שליטא שטוב שלא יכוין למצות וידוי כמו בשופר.

(19) שו"ת רמ"א סי' צח. מור וקציעה סי' פ. שו"ת ציץ אליעזר ח"ח סי' א.

(20) שו"ת ציץ אליעזר שם. וראה נשמת אברהם אור"ח סי' עו ס"ק ט (עמ' מ).

(21) שו"ת הר צבי אור"ח ח"א סי' ו. שו"ת ציץ אליעזר ח"ח סי' א. וראה נשמת אברהם שם.

(22) שו"ת ציץ אליעזר ח"ט סי' ו. שו"ת מנחת יצחק ח"ו סי' יא ו-יב.

(23) אורח סי' ז מ"ב ס"ק ב. ברכי יוסף שם ס"ק ב. כף החיים שם ס"ק ב.

(24) אורח סי' צב סע' א.

Shema or study Torah until the odor has disappeared.[25] If he has no sense of smell, he may recite the *Shema,* etc.[26]

17. A person who is confined in a non-Jewish hospital in which the wards have non-Jewish religious objects should try to pray outside the ward or, at least, in a secluded corner,[27] even if by doing so he does not face toward Jerusalem.[28] If he is bedridden and this is not possible, he should pray with his eyes closed[29] and without bowing during the *Shemoneh Esreh.*[30]

(25) או״ח סי׳ עט סע׳ ט ומ״ב ס״ק לא ו־לב.

(26) מהא דמג״א שם ס״ק ט.

(27) או״ח סי׳ צד סע׳ ט בהגה. שו״ת תרומת הדשן סי׳ ו.

(28) שם מ״ב ס״ק ל.

(29) שערים מצויינים בהלכה סי׳ יח ס״ק ז.

(30) שמעתי מפי מו״ר הגרי״י נויבירט שליט״א.

10 / THE SABBATH

Since there are occasions when a patient's requirements con-
flict with observance of the Sabbath, it is essential to know
which takes precedence. This chapter outlines how the Sabbath is to be observed under various circumstances. Most of
the following paragraphs apply to the Festivals as well. Exceptions include paragraphs 18-31; but competent halachic authority
must be consulted in each case. See also Chapters 1 and 11.

GENERAL RULES: THE SERIOUSLY ILL PATIENT[*]

1. Thus wrote Maimonides: "When the laws of the
Sabbath are set aside for a seriously ill person, this should not be
given over to non-Jews, minors, servants or women, lest they
should come to regard Sabbath observance as a trivial matter,
but this is to be preferably done by adult Jews and Sages.[1]
Furthermore, it is forbidden to delay setting aside the Sabbath
regulations for the sake of a person who is seriously ill, for
Scripture says (*Leviticus* 18:5): 'Which if a man do he shall *live* by
them,' that is to say, he should not die as a result of observing
them. Hence, we learn that the ordinances of the Torah are
meant to bring to the world not vengeance, but mercy, lovingkindness and peace. It is with regard to heretics, who assert that
such behavior is a violation of the Sabbath and therefore prohibited, that Scripture says (*Ezekiel* 20:25): 'Wherefore I also
gave them statutes that were not good, and ordinances whereby
they should not live.' "[2]

*see Chapter 1, paragraph 1

(1) ראה שמירת שבת כהלכתה פל״ב סעי׳ ו.

(2) רמב״ם הל׳ שבת פי״ב ה״ג. וראה דעת מחמירה — או״ח סי׳ שכח סעי׳ יב בהגה ומ״ב
סי״ק יד.

2. One is required to set aside the laws of the Sabbath, including those involving acts that are forbidden by the Torah, in case of danger[3] or possible danger to human life.[4] In doing this one should be as alert and as speedy as possible.[5] One who delays setting aside the Sabbath laws in order to first consult competent halachic authority is considered as having "shed blood," because such delay may indeed result in a deterioration of the patient's condition.[6] However, when there is no risk of danger to life in taking the time to consult a competent halachic authority, that should be done.[7]

3. If a seriously ill person (see Chapter 1, paragraph 1) objects to the setting aside of Sabbath laws on his behalf, he should be told gently that such objection is false piety. If he persists, he may be compelled to accede to whatever measures are necessary,[8] provided that they are based on expert medical advice.[9]

4. One should set aside the Sabbath laws for a seriously ill patient (see Chapter 1, paragraph 1) even if only to prolong life[10] or reduce pain (which may itself hasten death) for a short while.[11]

5. These rules apply equally to a fetus in any stage of gestation.[12]

(3) או״ח סי׳ שכח סע׳ ב.

(4) שם סע׳ ה ומ״ב ס״ק יז. וראה שמירת שבת כהלכתה פ״מ סע׳ א ופל״ב הערה ב.

(5) או״ח שם סע׳ ב.

(6) או״ח סי׳ שכח במ״ב ס״ק ו.

(7) ערוך השולחן או״ח סי׳ שכח סע׳ ב.

(8) או״ח סי׳ שכח במ״ב ס״ק ו. שמירת שבת כהלכתה פל״ב סע׳ ה.

(9) מ״ב שם ס״ק ה. שמירת שבת כהלכתה שם הערה טו.

(10) או״ח סי׳ שכט סע׳ ד. וראה גם בביה״ל שם ד״ה אלא. ברכ״י שם ס״ק ד. שו״ת שבות יעקב ח״א סי׳ יג.

(11) כן כתב לי הגרש״ז אויערבאך שליט״א.

(12) קרבן נתנאל על הרא״ש, יומא פ״ח ס״ק י. טור או״ח סי׳ תריז. דעת תורה סי׳ תריז ס״ק א. ביה״ל סי׳ של סע׳ ז ד״ה או ספק. שו״ת ציץ אליעזר חי״א סי׳ מג. שמירת שבת

6. The Sabbath laws should be set aside to treat a patient who has attempted suicide.[13]

7. If it is clear that for a particular seriously ill patient (see Chapter 1, paragraph 1) treatment may be postponed until after the Sabbath without any risk of harm to the patient, one may not set aside any of the Torah prohibitions.[14]

8. A Torah prohibition may be set aside on the Sabbath in order to treat a seriously ill patient (see Chapter 1, paragraph 1) more efectively even if it is possible to render treatment, but less effectively, without setting aside the prohibition. Thus, even if there is a hospital that can be reached on foot, it is permitted to transport a patient to a better-equipped hospital or to one that the patient prefers (but not if the preference is on account of financial considerations). It is permitted to telephone the patient's family physician, or a specialist, who may have to travel by car, even if a local physician might be reached who would not need to travel. A heater may be activated for such a patient if it is more satisfactory than extra blankets.[15]

9. The request to immediately set aside a Torah prohibition for a seriously ill patient (see Chapter 1, paragraph 1) must be accepted if it comes from the patient himself,[16] from an accredited physician,[17] or, if a physician is not immediately avail-

כהלכתה פל״ב הערה יג. אולם ראה שעה״צ סי׳ תריז ס״ק א, וראה מה שכתב הגרש״ז אויערבאך שליט״א בנשמת אברהם או״ח סי׳ שכח הערה 47. וראה חזו״א יו״ד סי׳ קנה ושו״ת מנחת יצחק ח״ד סי׳ קכג לגבי תינוק שנולד בחודש השמיני להריון.

(13) שו״ת חלקת יעקב ח״א סי׳ עב. שו״ת אג״מ או״ח ח״א סי׳ קכז. שו״ת ציץ אליעזר ח״ח סי׳ טו פ״ד וח״ט סי׳ יז פ״ב אות ו.

(14) או״ח סי׳ שכח סע׳ ד. מ״ב ס״ק טז וביה״ל ד״ה שממתין. שמירת שבת כהלכתה פל״ב סע׳ כג.

(15) שמירת שבת כהלכתה פל״ב סע׳ לח ,מה ו-פג.

(16) או״ח סי׳ שכח סע׳ ה מ״ב ס״ק כה.

(17) או״ח סי׳ שכח סע׳ י ומ״ב ס״ק כה ו-כו. שמירת שבת כהלכתה פל״ב סע׳ כא.

able, from anyone who has some knowledge of medicine.[18]

10. Whenever possible one should try to minimize the setting aside of Sabbath laws, provided that this is in no way detrimental to the patient. Similarly, one may not set aside a Torah prohibition if equally effective treatment can be given by setting aside a prohibition of Rabbinic origin only. A procedure that may be done just as effectively in a manner different from the usual may not be carried out in the usual manner.[19]

11. Just as one must minimize, when possible, the setting aside of Sabbath laws, so must one reduce to a minimum the amount of ordinarily prohibited work that is done, rendering only that which is necessary for the patient's welfare. Thus, even when it is imperative to write, the writing must be kept to the essential minimum (for the patient).[20] When there is time to do so, a right-handed person should write with the left hand and a left-handed person with the right.[21]

12. If in the physician's opinion a patient's condition is likely to deteriorate to the point of danger or possible danger to life, the patient is already regarded as being seriously ill, and all regulations concerning such patients apply.[22]

13. A patient who is in danger of losing a limb will, under most circumstances, be considered as seriously ill and must be treated accordingly.[23]

(18) אוי"ח סי' שכח סע' י מ"ב ס"ק כז.

(19) שמירת שבת כהלכתה פל"ב סע' כח.

(20) שמירת שבת כהלכתה שם סע' מט.

(21) מ"ב סי' שם ס"ק כב אות ז.

(22) אוי"ח סי' שכח מ"ב ס"ק יז. סי' רעח ביה"ל סוד"ה בשביל. סי' תריח סע' א מ"ב ס"ק ב וביה"ל ד"ה חולה.

(23) אוי"ח סי' שכח מ"ב ס"ק מט. פמ"ג מ"ז ס"ק ז. ערוך השולחן שם ס"ק יח. וראה גם תוס' סוכה כו ע"א ד"ה אפילו ומאירי ע"ז כח ע"א ד"ה עין. שו"ת ציץ אליעזר ח"ח סי' טו פ"י ס"ק ט.

GENERAL RULES: THE NON-SERIOUSLY ILL PATIENT*

14. On the Sabbath one may instruct a non-Jew to care for a non-seriously ill patient (see Chapter 1, paragraph 2), even if the care involves setting aside a Torah prohibition.[24] A Jew may not set aside a Torah prohibition for such a patient. However, a Jew may perform an act which is Rabbinically prohibited; if possible, this should be done in an indirect manner.[25] The patient himself is permitted to take medications as necessary.[26]

15. A patient who is in danger of losing the functional capacity of a limb (without danger to life) is considered to be in this category.[27] Thus, if the patient has a peripheral nerve palsy or has recovered from an operation or trauma, and requires continued physiotherapy in order to restore full function to a limb, he may be treated, if necessary, on the Sabbath.

MINOR ILLNESS, ACHES AND PAINS**

16. A person who feels very uncomfortable because of a localized ailment (see Chapter 1, paragraph 3) may not be treated on the Sabbath by a Jew, even if this involves a Rabbinic prohibition only, nor may he take any medicines. He may, however, be treated by a non-Jew if this involves a Rabbinic prohibition only.[28]

17. A person who has only minor discomfort (see Chap-

* see Chapter 1, paragraph 2
** see Chapter 1, paragraphs 3 and 4

(24) או״ח סי׳ שכח מ״ב ס״ק מז.

(25) מ״ב שם סוס״יק קב.

(26) או״ח סי׳ שכח סע׳ לז בהגה. מ״ב שם ס״ק קכא. ביה״ל שם ד״ה כן. שמירת שבת כהלכתה פל״ג סע׳ ד.

(27) קצות השולחן סי׳ קלח בבדי השולחן סוס״יק יח.

(28) דהיינו שבות דשבות באמירה לנכרי — או״ח סי׳ שז סע׳ ה. סי׳ שכח מ״ב ס״ק נב. וראה שמירת שבת כהלכתה פל״יד סע׳ ג ופלי״ח סע׳ יד-טז.

ter 1, paragraph 4) may take no medication, nor receive treatment even from a non-Jew, even if it involves a Rabbinic prohibition only.[29]

FOOD AND ITS PREPARATION

18. Anything that a seriously ill patient (see Chapter 1, paragraph 1) thinks would be of *direct* help to recovery should be performed on the Sabbath, even if it involves setting aside a Torah prohibition, as long as the physician does not consider it actually harmful. Refusal to provide such treatment might be so distressing to the patient as to aggravate his condition.[30]

Therefore, one may cook on the Sabbath for a seriously ill patient who asks for hot food and claims that food kept hot overnight might be harmful (see paragraph 22 below). Similarly, one may heat water for such a patient who asks for a hot drink or bath.[31]

19. It is preferable, if possible, to prepare on Friday what the patient might need on the Sabbath, in order to minimize desecration of the Sabbath.[32]

20. It is permitted to draw water from a water heater on the Sabbath for a seriously ill patient (see Chapter 1, paragraph 1), though cold water thereby enters the tank and is heated.[33] Once the water has been drawn, the faucet should not be closed, unless it is possible that more hot water may be needed on the Sabbath for such a patient.[34]

(29) או״ח סי׳ שכח סע׳ א. מ״ב ס״ק ב, ג, ו־ק.

(30) או״ח סי׳ שכח סע׳ י ביה״ל ד״ה ורופא. שמירת שבת כהלכתה פל״ב סע׳ כו.

(31) ביה״ל שם.

(32) או״ח סי׳ של מ״ב ס״ק א.

(33) שמירת שבת כהלכתה פל״ב סע׳ פב.

(34) וכתב לי הגרש״ז אויערבאך שליט״א: גם אם יש ספק מותר. ויש לדון שאם המים הנכנסים הם מעט מאד, אפשר שהם מתחממים תיכף גם אם הברז נשאר פתוח, וגם מכיון שבסגירת הברז הוא רק ״מצמצם״ ולא מבשל ממש, אפשר דמותר לסגור מיד גם בספק רחוק, עכ״ל.

21. Whenever possible, one should try to minimize the setting aside of Sabbath laws for a seriously ill patient (see Chapter 1, paragraph 1), provided that this is in no way detrimental to the patient. Thus, if food must be cooked on the Sabbath, one should prepare only the amount required by the patient, and no more should be added to the utensil even before heating. However, if the food is needed without delay, no time should be spent measuring exact quantities.[35]

22. One may cook on the Sabbath for a seriously ill patient (see Chapter 1, paragraph 1) who demands freshly cooked hot food and who claims that the food cooked before the Sabbath may be harmful. This is true only if the request is reasonable and one is convinced that the patient sincerely senses a need for freshly cooked food.[36]

23. It is preferable to cook or heat food by electricity, if available, rather than by gas. Lighting a gas burner involves two prohibitions—lighting the match and then the gas—whereas switching on the electricity involves only one. If possible, the electricity should be turned on in an unusual manner.[37]

24. It is immaterial whether a person lights the larger or the smaller of two gas burners. However, one must not light a small flame with the intention of subsequently increasing it, since this is tantamount to lighting twice. Rather, one should first open the gas tap as much as is needed and then light the burner.[38] If, however, it subsequently becomes necessary, one may increase or decrease the flame. It is forbidden to turn off or turn down the flame once the food has been taken off the burner.[39]

(35) או״ח סי׳ שכח סע׳ טז ומ״ב ס״ק מד.

(36) שמירת שבת כהלכתה פל״ב סע׳ עג. וראה שם שמדובר על חולה שהשבת יקרה לו וירא לחלל בחנם.

(37) שמירת שבת כהלכתה שם סע׳ עו.

(38) שם הערה קיד ו־קצח.

(39) שם סע׳ עז וראה הערה קצט.

25. If a gas stove is used, it should be lit with a match and not with an ignitor.[40]

26. No one other than a seriously ill patient (see Chapter 1, paragraph 1) may partake on the Sabbath of food that was cooked on the Sabbath.[41] The food may, however, be tasted to check its palatability.[42]

27. Food so prepared is considered *muktzeh* for anyone other than such a patient and may, therefore, be handled only for his needs.[43]

28. Such food, if left over, may be consumed by others immediately after the termination of the Sabbath[44] (compare with paragraph 30 below).

29. If a seriously ill patient (see Chapter 1, paragraph 1) is in a non-Jewish hospital, every effort should be made to ensure that kosher food be available. If kosher food must be brought in, it must be prepared and brought in for the Sabbath before the commencement of the Sabbath. If this was not done and no kosher food is available on the Sabbath, a non-Jew should be asked to bring in the food. If this is not possible, a Jew may bring in the food from the outside on the Sabbath even if there is no *eruv*,[45] because eating non-kosher food might psychologically affect the patient adversely and lead to an aggravation of his condition. If the patient will not be affected by the fact that the food is not kosher—for instance, in the case of a

(40) שם הערה קצה.

(41) או״ח סי׳ שיח סע׳ ב מ״ב ס״ק יב.

(42) שם מ״ב ס״ק יא.

(43) או״ח סי׳ שכח מ״ב ס״ק נח. וראה פרטי דינים שמירת שבת כהלכתה פל״ב סע׳ עט.

(44) ואין צריך לחכות זמן ״בכדי שיעשו״ — או״ח סי׳ שיח מ״ב ס״ק יא. גם אין מקום לשאלה בנוגע לכשרות הכלים שבהם בישל בשביל החולה — שמירת שבת כהלכתה פל״ב סע׳ עח.

(45) ויעשה זאת בשינוי, אם אפשר.

young child[46] or a patient who is mentally confused[47]—one should give non-kosher food rather than set aside Sabbath laws.[48]

30. One may request a non-Jew to cook or warm food on the Sabbath for a non-seriously ill patient (see Chapter 1, paragraph 2) if it is required for the patient's health.[49] A Jew may take no part in this cooking; he may not place the food into the utensil before it is put on the stove,[50] nor cover the utensil while it is cooking,[51] nor stir the food on the stove.[52] A healthy person may not partake of this food on the Sabbath.[53] Regarding the consumption of such food after the Sabbath, see *Nishmat Avraham*[54] (compare with paragraph 28 above).

31. One may ask a non-Jew to draw hot water from a water heater, even for a non-seriously ill patient[55] (see Chapter 1, paragraph 2).

UNTITHED PRODUCE

32. A patient whose only available food on the Sabbath is definitely, or even probably, untithed produce of the Land of Israel, should separate the required tithes on the Sabbath rather than eat untithed produce. Similarly, he should separate *challah* from bread and cakes.[56] Outside the Land of

(46) או״ח סי׳ שכח מ״ב ס״ק לט.

(47) קיצור שולחן ערוך סי׳ צב סע׳ ח.

(48) שמירת שבת כהלכתה פ״מ סי׳ יז. וראה או״ח סי׳ שכח סע׳ יד ומ״ב ס״ק לט לגבי שחיטה בשבת.

(49) או״ח סי׳ שכח סע׳ יט מ״ב ס״ק סג.

(50) מ״ב שם ס״ק נח.

(51) או״ח סי׳ רנד סע׳ ד מ״ב ס״ק כג.

(52) או״ח סי׳ שיח מ״ב ס״ק קיד.

(53) שם סע׳ א בהגה מ״ב ס״ק יג.

(54) ראה נשמת אברהם או״ח סי׳ שיח ס״ק א (עמ׳ קנו) לגבי אכילת האוכל אחרי צאת השבת ושם בסי׳ שכח ס״ק נח (עמ׳ קצט) לגבי הגעלת כלים. וראה גם ספר לוית חן על על הל׳ שבת מאת הגר״ע יוסף שליט״א, אות מב.

(55) או״ח סי׳ רנג מ״ב ס״ק ק.

(56) שמירת שבת כהלכתה פ״מ סע׳ יח.

Israel, he should not separate *challah* on the Sabbath, but should leave part of the bread uneaten until after the Sabbath and then separate from it a portion for *challah*.[57]

TURNING ON AND TURNING OFF LIGHTS

33. A light should be switched on before the Sabbath in a room adjoining that of a patient, thereby anticipating his needs, and reducing the need to set aside the Sabbath laws. Similar considerations apply to a woman during the ninth month of pregnancy.[58]

34. If it becomes necessary to have light for a patient, if feasible, he should be moved to a room which is already lighted. If this is not feasible, but a portable source of light with a long enough cord is available in another room, it should be moved into the patient's room. Only if this is not possible or not sufficient, or in an urgent situation, may a light be turned on for a seriously ill patient (see Chapter 1, paragraph 1) on the Sabbath.[59]

35. A light may be switched on (see paragraph 34) for the needs of a seriously ill patient (see Chapter 1, paragraph 1) on the Sabbath in order to be able to treat him better, or because the patient is afraid to lie in the dark,[60] or in order that he may feel confident that he is being attended to properly.[61] Thus one may turn on a light for a blind patient who is seriously ill, even if his attendants do not need the light. His mind is thereby set at ease, knowing that his needs will be satisfied without delay.[62]

36. Whenever possible, switching on a light should be done in an unusual manner, as long as this does not result in

<hr>

(57) שם הערה נו.

(58) או"ח סי' של מ"ב ס"ק א. בן איש חי שנה ב פ' תצוה סעי' יד.

(59) וראה שמירת שבת כהלכתה פל"ב סעי' סה.

(60) או"ח סי' רעח ביה"ל ד"ה לכבות.

(61) שמירת שבת כהלכתה פל"ב סעי' סג.

(62) או"ח סי' של סעי' א ומ"ב ס"ק ג ו-ד.

undue delay.[63] Thus one should switch on a light with the elbow rather than with the hand.[64]

37. One may turn off a light in order to enable a seriously ill patient (see Chapter 1, paragraph 1) to sleep[65] if the patient cannot be moved to a darkened room,[66] if the light cannot be dimmed sufficiently by covering it,[67] or if it cannot be moved outside the room. One may also reset a timer ("Sabbath clock") connected to a light so that it will turn off the light earlier than originally set.[68]

38. One should, whenever possible, reduce the setting aside of Sabbath rules to the essential minimum. Therefore, if there are two electric switches in the room of a seriously ill person, one of which is connected to one light bulb, whereas the other is connected to two, the former should be turned on, if the light of the one bulb will suffice. Similarly, if a person has to connect the electric current through a main switch, such as a time clock, which is also connected to lights that are not needed for the patient, he should, if there is time, first turn off the switches of the lights that are not needed and only then turn on the main switch. All this is to be done, if feasible, in an unusual manner (see paragraph 36 above).[69]

39. If there are two lights of different sizes, the smaller one should be turned on if it suffices, because a smaller wire is thus heated.[70] A neon light is preferable if available.[71]

(63) או״ח סי׳ שכח סעי׳ יב בהגה ומ״ב ס״ק לה.

(64) שמירת שבת כהלכתה פל״ב סעי׳ סד.

(65) או״ח סי׳ רעח סעי׳ א.

(66) ביה״ל שם ד״ה מותר.

(67) מ״ב שם ס״ק א.

(68) שמירת שבת כהלכתה פל״ב סעי׳ ע.

(69) שם סעי׳ סו.

(70) שם סעי׳ סז.

(71) שם הערה קע.

40. The light bulb in a refrigerator should be removed or inactivated before the Sabbath. If this has not been done, the refrigerator door may be opened in order to obtain food or medicines for a seriously ill patient (see Chapter 1, paragraph 1); however, it should not be closed if the light is thereby switched off. If food or drugs in such a refrigerator may be needed for a seriously ill patient (see Chapter 1, paragraph 1) later that same Sabbath, and they cannot be stored elsewhere—for example, with a neighbor whose refrigerator light has been inactivated—or, if stored elsewhere might not be available when needed, and if they would spoil if kept in an open refrigerator, and cannot be replaced if they do spoil, then the refrigerator door should be closed. Before the door is closed the light bulb should be removed, in order to prevent it from being relit when the door is next opened.[72]

41. A diabetic patient who measures his blood glucose several times each day in order to inject the appropriate dose of insulin may use a glucometer on the Sabbath. If possible, the glucometer should be switched on before the Sabbath; if this is not possible, it should be switched on, when feasible, in an indirect manner.[73]

42. Unless the patient is seriously ill (see Chapter 1, paragraph 1) and needs immediate care, a nurse should not be called on the Sabbath by pressing a switch that turns on an electric light. The nurse may, however, be called by a mechanical bell, even for a non-seriously ill patient[74] (see Chapter 1, paragraph 2).

43. A non-seriously ill patient (see Chapter 1, paragraph 2) confined to bed who urgently needs to relieve himself and who can call a nurse only by activating a light should, if possible, ask a non-Jew to do this. Otherwise, the button should

(72) שם סעי׳ עא.

(73) מפי מו״ר הגרי״י נויבירט שליט״א.

(74) שמירת שבת כהלכתה פי״מ סעי׳ יט.

be pressed in an indirect fashion.[75]

44. A non-Jew may be asked to turn on a light in order to find out what is needed for a non-seriously ill patient (see Chapter 1, paragraph 2), and he may also be requested to switch it off so that the patient may sleep. A Jew is forbidden to turn a light on or off in these circumstances.[76]

45. A Jew other than the patient is permitted to make use of a light turned on by a non-Jew on behalf of a non-seriously ill patient[77] (see Chapter 1, paragraph 2).

46. A patient should not make use of a light which a Jew has turned on in *desecration* of the Sabbath. On the other hand, a light that has been turned on by a Jew *on behalf of a seriously ill patient* (see Chapter 1, paragraph 1) may be enjoyed by a healthy Jew.[78]

THE USE OF A TELEPHONE

47. If on the Sabbath one needs to call a physician or an ambulance for a seriously ill patient (see Chapter 1, paragraph1), or for a patient who is only possibly so, and the physician cannot be reached in time without setting aside Sabbath laws, even Torah prohibitions should be set aside as necessary. Thus one may telephone the physician at home or via a beeper number.[79] The patient should not be left alone in order to seek other methods of communication if a telephone is available.[80]

48. When possible, a nearby physician should be called, so as not to require him to travel in order to see the patient. However, if a particular physician has greater knowledge or

(75) שם.

(76) או״ח סי׳ שכח סע׳ יז ומ״ב ס״ק מז.

(77) או״ח סי׳ רעו סע׳ א.

(78) שם ביה״ל ד״ה אין בו. שמירת שבת כהלכתה פל״ב סע׳ סט.

(79) שמירת שבת כהלכתה שם סע׳ לו.

(80) שם סע׳ לז.

experience, or if he is the patient's personal physician, or if the patient himself requests a particular physician because he feels that he would be best treated by him, such a physician should be called, even if that involves setting aside Sabbath laws. This ruling does not apply where the choice is dependent upon monetary considerations.[81]

49. One may enter a telephone booth to call a physician or an ambulance for a seriously ill patient (see Chapter 1, paragraph 1) on the Sabbath even though when one enters the booth a light goes on automatically. The same applies to transporting such a patient into an elevator in which the light is activated as the door opens.[82] The appropriate button for the floor may be pressed, even if this activates a light. When possible, this should be done in an unusual fashion (see paragraph 36 above).

50. After telephoning on behalf of a seriously ill patient (see Chapter 1, paragraph 1), one may leave the telephone booth even though a light is thereby turned off automatically, if one's immediate presence is required by the patient. If, however, one is no longer needed by the patient, one should, if possible, block the doorway so as to prevent the automatic turning off of the light.[83]

51. If a telephone must be used on the Sabbath on behalf of a seriously ill patient (see Chapter 1, paragraph 1), the receiver should be lifted off the hook in an indirect or unusual manner, such as by using both hands.[84]

52. Unlike writing (see paragraph 56 below), there is no need to minimize the number of words spoken over the telephone on the Sabbath on behalf of a seriously ill patient (see

(81) שם סעי' לח.

(82) ראה שמירת שבת כהלכתה פ"מ סעי' מא.

(83) שם פלי"ב סעי' מג וראה שם פרטי דינים.

(84) שם סעי' מ.

Chapter 1, paragraph 1), and one may also add "Good morning" and "Thank you." However, conversation should be limited to that which is related to the patient's care.[85]

53. When the call is finished the receiver should be replaced, even if the phone is no longer needed, because if not replaced, the telephone of the physician or the ambulance station will remain disconnected and thereby unavailable for both outgoing and incoming calls.[86]

54. One may call a non-observant physician in preference to an observant one if the former has greater experience or expertise or if the patient has greater trust in him, even though the latter can be called without having to set aside the Sabbath laws and the former would *desecrate* the Sabbath unnecessarily (that is, by acts that are unconnected with the patient's care).[87]

55. A physician may answer the telephone on the Sabbath (see paragraph 51 above) since the call might be related to a seriously ill patient.[88]

See also Chapter 32, paragraph 15, regarding the use of an internal telephone.

WRITING

56. If one needs to write on the Sabbath on behalf of a seriously ill patient (see Chapter 1, paragraph 1), this must be limited to what is absolutely essential, because writing any unnecessary word, letter or even punctuation is a transgression of a Torah prohibition.[89] Unless the matter is urgent, a right-handed person should write with his left hand, and vice versa.[90]

(85) שם סעי מא.

(86) שם סעי מב. וראה שם הערה קיד.

(87) שם סעי מה.

(88) שם סעי מז.

(89) כי חצי שיעור אסור מן התורה. שם סעי מח.

(90) שם סעי מט.

57. A patient who needs ambulatory Holter monitoring (that is, a twenty-four-hour continuous electrocardiogram) should ordinarily not have this done over the Sabbath. If, however, the matter is fairly urgent, but may still be done on an ambulatory basis, the patient should be monitored from Friday to the Sabbath and not from the Sabbath to Sunday. The patient may not carry the attached Holter into the street unless there is an *eruv*. When the Holter is attached to the patient's body on Friday, the skin should be shaved clean so that no hair will be pulled out when the Holter is removed on the Sabbath. If the hair was not shaved, the adhesive should be removed carefully, if necessary using acetone or ether, which should be poured onto the area and not applied with cotton wool or gauze (see paragraph 61 below). The Holter with its attached leads should then be put away carefully until it is returned to the hospital, and it may not be switched off until after the Sabbath.[91]

MEDICATION

58. As mentioned above (paragraph 2), one may do all that is necessary for the welfare of a seriously ill patient[92] (see Chapter 1, paragraph 1). Most hospitalized patients are at least in the category of the non-seriously ill (see Chapter 1, paragraph 2), and may, therefore, take medication and be given sub-cutaneous or intra-muscular injections on the Sabbath, if necessary.[93]

59. A patient who has to take medication only on certain days every week should, if possible, arrange to have the Sabbath be one of the days on which he does *not* take medication.

91) שמעתי מהגרש"ז אויערבאך שליט"א.

92) או"ח סי' שכח סע' ב.

93) שמירת שבת כהלכתה פל"ב סע' נח. ובנוגע לזריקות תוך ורידית לחולה שאין בו סכנה, יש אוסרים (הגרש"ז אויערבאך שליט"א, מובא בשו"ת ציץ אליעזר ח"ט סי' יז פ"ב אות כ. שמירת שבת כהלכתה פל"ב סע' נח) ויש מתירים (שו"ת ציץ אליעזר ח"ח סי' טו פי"ד, ח"ט סי' יז פ"ב, חי"ד סי' כה פי"א).

60.   One may tear the paper wrapping off a medication or a syringe,[94] but, if possible, one should not tear through print.[95]

61.   One should not swab with alcohol- or iodine-soaked cotton wool or gauze, even if it is held with forceps and even if it was soaked before the Sabbath.[96] Instead, one should do either of the following:

a. If available, one should use nylon (non-absorbent) swabs rather than absorbent cotton wool or gauze.[97]

b. If these are not available, alcohol or iodine should be poured onto the part of the body concerned, which should then be wiped dry with absorbent cotton wool, gauze[98] or tissue.[99]

62.   A person who started taking a course of daily medication before the Sabbath should not interrupt it on the Sabbath if continuity is medically advisable.[100] A woman may continue to take on the Sabbath tablets to enable her to conceive,[101] to prevent conception (where halachically approved),[102] or to regularize her menstrual cycle.[103]

63.   A person suffering from hemorrhoids may take

(94) או״ח סי׳ שיד מ״ב ס״ק כה. חזו״א או״ח סי׳ סא ס״ק ב. כף החיים סי׳ שם ס״ק פה.

(95) או״ח סי׳ שם סע׳ יג מ״ב ס״ק מא. וראה מ״ב שם ס״ק יז, כף החיים סי׳ שז ס״ק קד ונשמת אדם כלל כט ס״ק ב.

(96) הגרש״ז אויערבאך שליט״א מובא בשו״ת ציץ אליעזר ח״ט סי׳ יז שמירת שבת כהלכתה פל״ב סע׳ יא.

(97) שמעתי ממו״ר הגרי״י נויבירט שליט״א. וראה שו״ת ציץ אליעזר ח״ח סי׳ טו פי״ד אות יא. ואין משום צובע בחיטוי מקום הזריקה ביוד וכדומה, לא לגבי הצמר גפן (מהא דשו״ע הרב סי׳ שב בקונטרס אחרון) ולא לגבי העור (או״ח סי׳ שג מ״ב ס״ק עט) — מובא בשמירת שבת כהלכתה פל״ב סע׳ נט.

(98) שמירת שבת כהלכתה שם.

(99) שו״ת הר צבי או״ח ח״א סי׳ קצ. שו״ת אגרות משה או״ח ח״ב סי׳ ע.

(100) מנחת שבת סי׳ צא ס״ק ט. שו״ת אגרות משה או״ח ח״ג סי׳ נג. שו״ת ציץ אליעזר ח״ח סי׳ טו פט״ו אות טו. שמירת שבת כהלכתה פל״ד סע׳ יז.

(101) שו״ת חלקת יעקב ח״ג סי׳ כג.

(102) שו״ת ציץ אליעזר ח״י״א סי׳ לז. וראה שמירת שבת כהלכתה פל״ד הערה פב.

(103) שמעתי ממו״ר הגרי״י נויבירט שליט״א.

laxatives on the Sabbath. A patient with angina pectoris may take such drugs as are necessary before or after sexual intercourse.[104] An asthmatic may inhale medication by means of a "spinhaler" or other such device, to prevent an acute attack.[105]

64. Even a patient who has completely recovered may continue to take medication to prevent a relapse.[106]

65. A healthy person may take preventive medicine as advised.[107] Thus a healthy person may take vitamins on the Sabbath as a preventive measure.[108] A seriously or non-seriously ill patient (see Chapter 1, paragraphs 1 and 2) may, of course, take vitamins as necessary. However, a person who has only a minor illness or discomfort (see Chapter 1, paragraphs 3 and 4) may not take vitamins on the Sabbath, even if he has been taking them regularly during the week.[109]

66. A pregnant woman may, if necessary, be immunized on the Sabbath against an infection to which she has been exposed if this is of serious import to her or to the unborn baby. She may travel on the Sabbath for such immunization if it is urgently needed.[110]

67. A person who is constipated may not take a laxative or insert a suppository,[111] nor may he be given an enema[112] on the Sabbath, unless the constipation is so severe as to affect his whole body[113] (see Chapter 1, paragraph 2).

(104) שו"ת מנחת יצחק ח"א סי' קח.

(105) שמעתי ממו"ר הגרי"י נויבירט שליט"א.

(106) שמירת שבת כהלכתה פל"ד סע' יז.

(107) נשמת אברהם או"ח סי' שכח ס"ק ג (עמ' קסד) בשם הגרש"ז אויערבאך שליט"א.

(108) שו"ת אגרות משה או"ח ח"ג סי' נד.

(109) שמירת שבת כהלכתה פל"ד סע' כ.

(110) שמירת שבת כהלכתה פל"ב סע' יג.

(111) או"ח סי' שכח מ"ב ס"ק קיח ו־קמא.

(112) שם מ"ב ס"ק קנ.

(113) קצות השולחן סי' קלח בבדה"ש ס"ק יד. שמירת שבת כהלכתה פל"ד סע' יא.

68. One may, of course, travel or set aside other Torah prohibitions on the Sabbath in order to obtain medication that is necessary for a seriously ill patient (see Chapter 1, paragraph 1). If such a patient asks for a particular drug, even if the physician does not consider it necessary, one may still set aside Sabbath laws in order to obtain it, lest the patient be disturbed and his condition thereby deteriorate. If there is no risk that the patient will become disturbed as a result of not having his request fulfilled on the Sabbath, and the nature of the illness is known, the Sabbath laws may not be set aside.[114] It is obvious that the Sabbath laws may not be set aside for this purpose if the physician considers the drug to be actually harmful to the patient.[115]

69. Patients such as diabetics requiring insulin or those suffering from angina pectoris, who have been instructed by their physician always to carry sugar or nitroglycerine tablets, respectively, in case of emergency, are permitted to carry them into the street on the Sabbath where there is no *eruv*, provided that:

a. It is not a public domain[116](competent halachic authority should be consulted).

b. The medication (or sugar) is carried in an unusual fashion, such as under the hat.

c. The purpose of the patient's going out is to attend a synagogue service or to study Torah.

d. The diabetic patient, if possible, continues to walk in the street without stopping till he reaches his destination. If such a person should need to take the sugar in the street, he should first enter a private courtyard or building and only then

---

114) או"ח סי' שכח סע' א ביה"ל ד"ה ורופא.

115) שם מ"ב ס"ק כה.

116) רשות הרבים גמורה ראה שמירת שבת כהלכתה פי"ז סע' ג.

take what is required.[117]

A person may not go out into the public domain while sucking a candy or tablet.[118]

70. A person with a mild ache or pain should take no medication on the Sabbath.[119] If the pain affects the whole body, medication is permitted, as in the case of any non-seriously ill patient[120] (see Chapter 1, paragraph 2).

POSTPONING TREATMENT

71. If a particular form of treatment is needed because of danger to life, but it is not of immediate urgency, it should be postponed until after the Sabbath if it involves a Torah prohibition. Otherwise, it may be performed on the Sabbath, but, if possible, it should be performed in a way different from the usual manner.[121]

72. Thus surgery should be deferred until after the Sabbath if there is no danger of this resulting in a deterioration of the patient's condition and possible risk to life.[122]

73. If a patient needs treatment in the morning and the evening, or treatment in two stages, the evening or second treatment should, if possible, be postponed until after the Sabbath.[123]

BLEEDING

74. It is forbidden to suck blood from a wound or

117) הגרש״ז אויערבאך שליט״א מובא בנשמת אברהם או״ח סי׳ שא ס״ק ב (עמ׳ קכה). שמירת שבת כהלכתה פי״מ סע׳ ז. וראה שו״ת ציץ אליעזר חי״ג סי׳ לד שאוסר במקום שאין עירוב.

118) שבת קב ע״א. ספר חסידים סי׳ רסה. או״ח סי׳ שנ סע׳ ג ומ״ב ס״ק יג. שמירת שבת כהלכתה פי״ח סע׳ ב.

119) או״ח סי׳ שכח סע׳ לז.

120) שמירת שבת כהלכתה פל״ד הערה ז.

121) שם פל״ב סע׳ סא.

122) שם פי״מ סע׳ לח.

123) שם פי״מ סע׳ מ.

from the gums on the Sabbath.[124] (Even on a weekday one may not lick blood that has exuded from an external wound.[125])

75. On the Sabbath one should wash away the blood from a bleeding wound and then cover the wound.[126] If the bleeding is severe, the wound should be bandaged without delay.[127]

76. A nosebleed should be controlled by external pressure, and only if that is insufficient should the nose be packed on the Sabbath.[128]

77. A person with hemorrhoids that bleed on defecation should cleanse the area with water rather than wiping with cloth or paper on the Sabbath. If that is not possible, toilet paper may be used.[129]

78. A splinter may be removed on the Sabbath even with a needle or forceps, but care should be taken as much as possible to avoid bleeding.[130]

79. One may use styptic surgical powder on a wound on the Sabbath in order to stop bleeding.[131]

BANDAGING A WOUND

80. One may clean a wound on the Sabbath with water or hydrogen peroxide.[132] Regarding the use of absorbent

(124) או"ח סי' שכח מ"ב ס"ק קמז.

(125) יו"ד סי' סו סע' י.

(126) או"ח סי' שכח סע' מח. וראה מג"א שם ס"ק נב.

(127) שם מ"ב ס"ק קמו. או"ח סי' שכ מ"ב ס"ק נט ושעה"צ ס"ק סה. חיי אדם כלל כד סע' ו. שו"ת ציץ אליעזר ח"ח סי' טו פי"ד ס"ק טו.

(128) או"ח סי' שכח סע' מח מ"ב סוס"ק קמו. שם סי' שכ מ"ב ס"ק נט. שמירת שבת כהלכתה פל"ה סע' טו.

(129) מנחת שבת סי' פ ס"ק קנא. שו"ע הרב סי' שב בקונטרס אחרון.

(130) שמירת שבת כהלכתה פל"ה סי' יז מהא דאו"ח סי' שכח מ"ב ס"ק פח ושעה"צ ס"ק סג. וראה שם סי' שח סע' יא ביה"ל ד"ה הקוץ.

(131) מהא דאו"ח סי' שכח סע' כט.

(132) שמירת שבת כהלכתה פל"ה סי' יא.

cotton wool, see paragraph 61 above.

81.   One may bandage a wound on the Sabbath to prevent infection. A clean, superficial wound with no risk of infection should not be dressed with ointment, but a dressing may be replaced by a clean dry one.[133]

82.   A bandage that is too long should not be cut to length on the Sabbath, but the whole bandage should be applied to the wound. A bandage should not be split lengthwise in order to knot the ends together, and one should be careful not to pull threads out of a bandage.[134]

83.   A bandage should be secured with a single knot and bow (as with shoelaces) on the Sabbath, with the intention of untying it within twenty-four hours,[135] or it should be held with a safety pin or special bandage clips. When necessary, a double knot may be used if the bandage is changed daily.[136]

84.   One should not use adhesive tape in order to fasten a bandage on the Sabbath, unless the tape is disposed of each time the bandage is opened.[137]

85.   On the Sabbath one may squeeze ointment from a tube directly onto a wound that is very painful. Ointment from a jar may be applied with a spatula. It may then be covered with gauze or a bandage. However, care should be taken not to *spread* the ointment onto the gauze or bandage or the wound itself. One may apply gauze on which ointment was spread before the Sabbath.[138]

(133) או"ח סי' שכח סע' יב. שמירת שבת כהלכתה פל"ה סע' כ.

(134) או"ח סי' שכח סע' יג. שמירת שבת כהלכתה פל"ה סע' כא.

(135) או"ח סי' שיז סע' ה ומ"ב ס"ק כט.

(136) שם שעה"צ ס"ק נב. שמירת שבת כהלכתה פל"ה סע' כב. וראה או"ח סי' שיז סע' ד ביה"ל ד"ה שאינם, דבמקום הצורך אפילו יותר מיום אחד לא מיקרי של קיימא, ומותר.

(137) שמירת שבת כהלכתה פל"ה סע' כה. וראה שם הערה ס"ק סג.

(138) שם סע' ח.

86.   One may use a band-aid on the Sabbath, but the protective paper covering the two adhesive tabs should, if possible, be removed before the Sabbath.[139]

87.   A butterfly dressing may be applied on the Sabbath in order to juxtapose the ends of a cut.[140]

88.   One may not rip adhesive tape off hairy skin on the Sabbath, because this inevitably uproots hair.[141] However, if removal of the tape is necessary, it is permitted.[142] When possible, the adhesive tape should be doused with a solvent, as long as the solvent was prepared for this purpose before the Sabbath.[143]

89.   A person may go out into the public domain on the Sabbath with an arm in a sling, even where there is no *eruv*.[144] This applies also to a bandage, provided that it was not applied purely for the purpose of preventing soiling of the patient's clothes,[145] and to a plaster cast. A sling should be prepared before the Sabbath; however, if this was not done, it may be tied on the Sabbath with a single knot and bow, with the intention of untying it within twenty-four hours.[146]

TAKING OF TEMPERATURE

90.   The temperature of a non-seriously ill patient (see Chapter 1, paragraph 2) may be taken on the Sabbath[147]

(139) ואם הוא מכין את הפלסתר לפני כניסת השבת ע"י הסרת הגזה והחזרתה למקומה מיד אחרי כן, יהיה מותר לו להסיר את הגזה שוב בשבת בעת הצורך — שמעתי מהגר"י אברמסקי ז"ל.

(140) שמירת שבת כהלכתה פלי"ה סעי' כד.

(141) שם סעי' כט.

(142) שם הערה ס"ק עג בשם הגרש"ז אויערבאך שליט"א. שו"ת יביע אומר ח"ה סי' ל.

(143) שם סעי' כט.

(144) שם פי"ח סעי' כ מהא דאו"ח סי' שא סעי' נא.

(145) שמירת שבת כהלכתה פי"ח סעי' יט מהא דאו"ח סי' שא סעי' כב וסעי' יג ומ"ב ס"ק מח.

(146) או"ח סי' שיז סעי' ה ומ"ב ס"ק כט.

(147) הגרש"ז אויערבאך שליט"א במאורי אש דף לג ע"ב. שו"ת חלקת יעקב ח"ג סי' כד. שו"ת אג"מ או"ח ח"א סי' קכח. שו"ת מנחת יצחק ח"ג סי' קמב. שו"ת ציץ אליעזר ח"ג סי' י. שמירת שבת כהלכתה פ"מ סעי' ב.

and, if the thermometer will be needed again on the Sabbath, the mercury may be shaken down.[148] The temperature should be recorded by attaching a paper clip to a previously prepared list of numbers, or by putting a previously prepared numbered slip of paper into the patient's chart. If there is a possibility that the reading of one patient will be interchanged with that of another, they should be written down by a non-Jew.[149] Temperature may also be taken, but not recorded, by a woman who is under investigation for sterility.[150]

91. A thermometer is not *muktzeh* on the Sabbath.[151]

92. One may immerse a thermometer in alcohol or another cleansing fluid and then dry it with cotton wool or a cloth before using it on the Sabbath; one may not cleanse it with wet cotton wool[152] (see paragraph 61 above).

93. A contact thermometer, which consists of a strip of special tape that registers temperature when placed on the skin, may be used on the Sabbath, provided that it registers temperature by a change only in the color of the tape, or by a change in the color or visibility of figures previously discernible on the tape.[153] However, a contact thermometer which is *blank* before use and on which figures can be seen only after it has been in contact with the skin, may not be used on the Sabbath.[154]

(148) שו״ת ציץ אליעזר חי״א סי׳ לח שמירת שבת כהלכתה פי״מ הערה ז. וכן שמעתי מפי הגרש״ז אויערבאך שליט״א.

(149) שמירת שת כהלכתה פי״מ סעי׳ ד.

(150) שו״ת ציץ אליעזר חי״א סי׳ לח ו־חי״ב סי׳ מד סי״ק ה. שמירת שבת כהלכתה שם סעי׳ ב.

(151) שם הערה ג.

(152) שמירת שבת כהלכתה שם סעי׳ ב. ועי״ע שו״ת ציץ אליעזר חי״ח סי׳ טו פיי״ד אות יא ו־חי״ט סי׳ יז פי״ב ס,ק לג.

(153) שמירת שבת כהלכתה שם בשם הגרש״ז אויערבאך שליט״א. שו״ת ציץ אליעזר חי״ד סי׳ לא.

(154) שמירת שבת כהלכתה שם. שו״ת מנחת יצחק חי״ז סי׳ כב. שו״ת מחזה אליהו סי׳ סה־סו. אך בשו״ת ציץ אליעזר חי״ד סי׳ ל־לא ושו״ת יחוה דעת חי״ד סי׳ כט מתירים.

RAISING BODY TEMPERATURE

94.   A hot-water bottle may be used on the Sabbath by any person who ordinarily uses it also on weekdays,[155] as well as by patients of all categories.[156]

95.   In cold weather an electric blanket may be used on the Sabbath by any person and, of course, by patients of all categories.[157] One may ask a non-Jew to switch it on or reset it. A Jew is allowed to move the blanket but may not reset the temperature. It is wise to cover the switch to avoid inadvertently changing the temperature setting.[158]

96.   When necessary, a non-Jew may be asked to switch on the central heating for a child or for a non-seriously ill patient[159] (see Chapter 1, paragraph 2).

LOWERING BODY TEMPERATURE

97.   It is permitted to use an ice bag or bottle for lowering temperature, and one may crack ice in order to fill the bag or bottle.[160]

98.   A non-Jew may be asked to turn on an electric fan or an air conditioner for a non-seriously ill patient[161] (see Chapter 1, paragraph 2). A Jew may not alter the speed of a fan or adjust an air conditioner but may change the direction of a fan or move it (as much as the length of the cord allows) for the benefit of the patient.[162]

(155) שמירת שבת כהלכתה פל״ד סעי׳ יא.

(156) או״ח סי׳ שכו מ״ב ס״ק יט. ויזהר שההבקבוק יהיה יבש לגמרי בשעה שממלא אותו או ישפוך לתוכו מכלי שני — שמירת שבת כהלכתה שם הערה סא.

(157) שו״ת חלקת יעקב ח״א סי׳ מ ו־ח״ג סי׳ קפא. שו״ת אג״מ או״ח ח״ג סי׳ נ.

(158) שו״ת אג״מ שם. נשמת אברהם סי׳ שכו ס״ק ג.

(159) או״ח סי׳ רעו סעי׳ ה ו־סי׳ של מ״ב ס״ק כא. שמירת שבת כהלכתה פל״ח סעי׳ ח, וראה שם שאם מצטערים מן הקור מותר גם בשביל בריאים.

(160) או״ח סי׳ שכ סעי׳ י. שמירת שבת כהלכתה פל״ג סעי׳ טו.

(161) שמירת שבת כהלכתה פל״ח סעי׳ ט. וראה שו״ת מנחת יצחק ח״ג סי׳ כב ו־כד שאם מצטער הרבה מחמת החום מותר גם עבור הבריא.

(162) שמירת שבת כהלכתה פי״ג סעי׳ לה.

EXERCISE AND PHYSIOTHERAPY

99. A healthy person may not be treated by physiotherapy[163] or massage[164] on the Sabbath, nor may he exercise.[165] They are permissible for a patient even if he is non-seriously ill[166] (see Chapter 1, paragraph 2).

100. One may perform simple movements in order to free stiff limbs or lessen pain.[167]

101. A patient with chronic lung disease who has been instructed by a physician to perform breathing exercises or to receive chest physiotherapy every day may do so on the Sabbath.[168]

102. One may not engage in occupational therapy on the Sabbath.[169]

USE OF APPLIANCES

103. A vaporizer may, of course, be used on the Sabbath for a seriously ill patient (see Chapter 1, paragraph 1), and water may be heated for that purpose. However, since various models are available, competent halachic authority should, when possible, be consulted in each case.[170]

104. A deaf person may use a hearing aid which was turned on before the Sabbath.[171] One may adjust the volume on the Sabbath if that does not result in a wire reaching red heat

(163) מהא דאו"ח סי' שכח סע' מב ומ"ב ס"ק קכט.

(164) מ"ב שם ס"ק קל. שו"ת שרידי אש ח"ב סי' ל. יסודי ישורון חי"ה עמ' שפח.

(165) כיון דמוכחא מילתא ואסור משום שחיקת סממנין — או"ח סי' שא מ"ב ס"ק ז.

(166) שו"ת מלמד להועיל או"ח סי' נג. יסודי ישורון ח"ד עמ' רצז. שמירת שבת כהלכתה פלי"ד סע' כג.

(167) שם סע' כב.

(168) שו"ת ציץ אליעזר חי"ב סי' מה.

(169) שו"ת מלמד להועיל או"ח סי' נג. שמירת שבת כהלכתה פי"ד סי' לח.

(170) שמירת שבת כהלכתה פל"ז סי' טו. וראה נשמת אברהם או"ח סי' רנב סע' א (עמ' קז).

(171) שו"ת יביע אומר ח"א סוסי' יט.

when the current is increased[172] or ceasing to glow when the current is reduced.[173] Expert technical advice should be sought before the Sabbath.

105. A hearing aid may not be worn outside the private domain on the Sabbath unless there is an *eruv*.[174]

106. Braces worn to straighten teeth may be worn on the Sabbath even in a public domain.[175]

107. A person who has a catheter with a bag attached permanently inserted in the bladder may go out into the public domain on the Sabbath even if there is no *eruv*.[176] The bag should be emptied before going out.[177]

108. Similarly, a patient who has an attached colostomy or ileostomy bag may go out into the public domain on the Sabbath even if there is no *eruv*. If possible, the bag should be emptied and cleaned before going out.[178]

HOSPITALS IN WHICH THE SABBATH LAWS ARE NOT OBSERVED AND NON-JEWISH HOSPITALS

109. Even a non-seriously ill patient (see Chapter 1, paragraph 2) may stay in a hospital where the Sabbath laws are not observed, but, when possible, he should try to obviate the transgression of Torah rules by the staff on his behalf.[179]

110. A patient who is taken to an emergency room on

(172) שמירת שבת כהלכתה פל״ד סע׳ כח.

(173) הגרש״ז אויערבאך שליט״א שם הערה קז.

(174) שו״ת הר צבי או״ח ח״א סי׳ קעג. שמירת שבת כהלכתה פל״ד סע׳ כח. וראה שו״ת מנחת יצחק ח״א סי׳ לז ו־ח״ב סי׳ יז וסי׳ קיב שכתב להתיר, אולם חזר בו בח״ב סי׳ קיג (אחרי שראה את ההר צבי).

(175) שמירת שבת כהלכתה פל״ד סי׳ כט.

(176) שו״ת ציץ אליעזר חי״ד סי׳ נח. וראה גם שו״ע הרב סי׳ שא סע׳ י וערוה״ש סי׳ שא סע׳ סו.

(177) שמעתי מהגרש״ז אויערבאך שליט״א. וע״ע שו״ת ציץ אליעזר שם.

(178) שמעתי מהגרש״ז אויערבאך שליט״א. ואם אחרי כן יוצאת צואה בזמן הליכתו ברה״ר לית לן בה כיון שאינו פסיק רישא וגם לא ניחא ליה.

(179) שמירת שבת כהלכתה פ״מ סע׳ טו.

or before the Sabbath and is discharged on the Sabbath or who is discharged from a ward on the Sabbath should not ask for a discharge letter.[180] It is preferable that the patient stay in the hospital till after the Sabbath. If he is in the category of a non-seriously ill patient (see Chapter 1, paragraph 2) and there is a possibility that he may require further treatment at home on the Sabbath, for which the details of his hospital stay may be important, a non-Jew may be asked to write the letter.[181]

111.   If the hospital authorities demand payment on the Sabbath for treatment, the patient should ask permission for payment to be deferred till after the Sabbath.[182] If treatment is refused unless payment is made immediately, something of value, such as a watch, should be given as security, to be redeemed after the Sabbath. If this is not acceptable, one may pay but may not take change owed to him until after the Sabbath.[183]

112.   If a seriously ill patient (see Chapter 1, paragraph 1) needs an operation on the Sabbath and the surgeon refuses to perform it unless the patient or a member of his family signs an authorization form, the person required to do so should sign, but in an unusual fashion, such as with the left hand[184]; only if he cannot possibly do otherwise may he sign in the ordinary way.[185] In any event, he should preferably sign his initials only, and with no flourishes.

See also Chapters 26, 27, 32 and 33.

(180) שם סעי׳ מד.

(181) שם.

(182) או״ח סי׳ שו מ״ב ס״ק כד. שו״ת ציץ אליעזר ח״ז סי׳ כח. יסודי ישורון ח״ד עמ׳ רעב. שערים מצויינים בהלכה סי׳ צ ס״ק ז.

(183) שמירת שבת כהלכתה שם סעי׳ יב.

(184) או״ח סי׳ שם מ״ב ס״ק כב או״ק ז.

(185) שמעתי ממו״ר הגרי״י נויבירט שליט״א.

DRIVING

113. One must, of course, drive on the Sabbath for the purpose of saving life.[186]

114. A car door may be opened even if, thereby, a light goes on inside the car. However, if the need for the car can be anticipated, the light should be disconnected before the Sabbath. While one is in the car with the door closed and the light off, it is preferable to disconnect the light so that it will not be relit when the door is opened (but only if the delay involved does not prejudice the prognosis of the seriously ill patient [see Chapter 1, paragraph 1]). If the disconnection was not or cannot be effected, the car door should not be closed when the journey is over, so that the light will not be extinguished. If it is possible to adjust the switch so that the light remains on, the door may be closed.[187]

115. Headlights may be turned on at night (when possible, in an unusual manner), but, here too, one may not extinguish or dim them at the end of the journey. Where local regulations forbid stationary cars to remain with their headlights on, the latter should be covered, if possible—for instance, with a blanket—so as to block the light. This may be done only if there is an *eruv* to permit carrying the blanket. The lights may not be extinguished even if this results in a monetary fine. However, if the car is likely to be needed again for a seriously ill patient (as in the case of an ambulance or the car of a busy doctor) and leaving the headlights on may cause difficulty in restarting the engine, they may be switched off (in an unusual manner).[188]

116. After the patient has left the car, it may not be driven any further, even to avoid its being left in a non-parking area. However, if the car is blocking the entrance to an emer-

(186) אוו״ח סי׳ שכח סע׳ ב.

(187) שמירת שבת כהלכתה פי״מ סע׳ נד.

(188) שם סע׳ נו.

gency room and may present difficulties to other seriously ill patients, it may be moved. If possible, it should be pushed rather than driven away from the entrance.[189]

117. A non-Jew may be asked to turn off the car engine at the end of the journey or, if not available, a minor should be asked to do so. If no minor is available, an adult Jew may turn off the ignition switch in an unusual manner.[190] However, if this results in lights automatically going on or off, the engine should be left running, unless overheating of the engine may endanger others.[191]

118. The driver may carry (in an unusual manner) all the documents necessary for driving, even where there is no *eruv*. After having brought the patient to a hospital, the driver should leave such documents in the car, unless there is an *eruv*.[192]

119. The ignition keys must be left in the car, since they are *muktzeh*.[193] However, if they are used also for opening the car doors or if other keys, such as house keys, are on the same ring or chain, they are not *muktzeh*[194] and may be carried if there is an *eruv*.[195]

See also Chapter 26, paragraphs 9 and 10.

CHILDBIRTH

120. A woman during childbirth is considered to be in the category of a seriously ill patient (see Chapter 1, paragraph 1), and the Sabbath laws are set aside for her as neces-

(189) שם סע' נז.

(190) שם סע' נט.

(191) שם סע' נט ו-ס.

(192) שם סע' סו.

(193) שם פ"כ סע' עז.

(194) שם פ"כ סע' פג.

(195) שם פ"מ סע' סו.

sary.[196] However, since childbirth is a natural, physiological phenomenon, the Sages have ruled that whenever possible the Sabbath prohibitions are to be set aside in an indirect or unusual manner[197] or by a non Jew.[198]

121. These rules apply to a woman who has given birth or who has had a miscarriage forty days or more after her last ritual immersion in the *mikveh*.[199]

122. A woman who has reached the ninth month of pregnancy should, before every Sabbath eve, prepare those things which she might require if she were to give birth on the Sabbath, thereby reducing the need for her to set aside the Sabbath laws.[200] She should write out two copies of her name and other pertinent information, one for the ambulance driver and one for the hospital administrative staff, so that any Jew among them will not need to write this information on the Sabbath. Should she forget to do so, she may still call for an ambulance and be taken to the hospital.[201] A light should be kept on at home throughout the Sabbath.[202]

123. Unless it can be easily arranged, a woman close to term is not obliged to stay near the hospital in order to avoid traveling on the Sabbath.[203]

124. When a woman feels repeated, regular labor pains[204] or if the membranes have ruptured and she will soon, though not

(196) אריח סיי של סעי א.

(197) שם ומייב סייק ה. וראה שם מייב סייק ה שאפילו למייד דגבי פקוח נפש לא בעיה שינוי, הכא שאני.

(198) קיצור שוייע סיי צג סקייב. מנחת שבת שם סקייג.

(199)אוייח סיי תריז סעי ד ביהייל דייה יולדת. כף החיים סיי של סייק ב.

(200) אריח סיי של מייב סייק א. בן איש חי שנה ב פי תצוה סעי יד.

(201) שמירת שבת כהלכתה פלייו סעי ו.

(202) כף החיים סימן של סייק א.

(203) שמירת שבת כהלכתה פלייו סעי ז בשם החזוייא ובשם הגרשייז אויערבאך שליטייא. וראה אמרי יושר קונטרס הפסקים סייק צח בשם החזוייא.

(204) שמירת שבת כהלכתה פלייו סעי ח.

necessarily immediately,[205] give birth, one may telephone for an
ambulance, and she may travel to her hospital of choice even if
there is another hospital nearer home[206] (but not if the choice is
based on financial considerations). Her husband or another
person may accompany her, to comfort her and set her mind at
ease.[207] She may take with her all that she may require on the
Sabbath, even where there is no *eruv*, provided that it is needed
for her health and is not available in the hospital.[208]

125. Although it is permitted to take such a woman to
the hospital on the Sabbath, anything not immediately necessary, such as turning on the light in her room, should not be
done until she is actually in labor, that is, when the cervix is fully
dilated,[209] or she is bleeding, or she is no longer able to walk.[210]

126. A woman who thought she was about to give
birth and was brought to the hospital, where it transpired that it
was a false alarm, and who was therefore discharged on the
Sabbath, may not return home in a car driven by a Jew. If there
is no place nearby where she can stay until after the Sabbath and
it would be difficult for her to remain within the hospital until
then, she may return home in a car driven by a non-Jew,[211]
provided that her home is within the Sabbath boundaries of the
city (*techum Shabbat*).[212]

127. A woman is considered to be in the category of a
seriously ill patient (see Chapter 1, paragraph 1) for a week after

(205) או"ח סי' של מ"ב ס"ק ט. וראה שעה"צ ס"ק ז.

(206) תפארת ישראל שבת פי"ח ס"ק לג. חזון יחזקאל תוספתא שבת פט"ז הי"ב. תוס'
שבת קל ע"א ד"ה רבי.

(207) מהא דאו"ח סי' של ומ"ב ס"ק ג וביה"ל ד"ה ומדליקין. שו"ת אג"מ או"ח ח"א סי'
קלב. שמירת שבת כהלכתה פל"ו סע' יא ופ"מ סע' ע.

(208) שמירת שבת כהלכתה פ"מ סע' ע. וראה שם פל"ו הערה יח.

(209) או"ח סי' של סע' ג ומ"ב ס"ק ט.

(210) שם וביה"ל ד"ה כיון. שמירת שבת כהלכתה שם סע' ט.

(211) כדין חולה שאין בו סכנה שעושין צרכיו ע"י נכרי — או"ח סי' שכח סע' יז.

(212) שמירת שבת כהלכתה פל"ו סע' י.

childbirth,[213] with some differences between her status during the first seventy-two hours after childbirth and the subsequent ninety-six hours (see paragraph 130 below):

a. During the first seventy-two hours,[214] one must set aside all Sabbath laws for her on the advice of a physician or a midwife or, in their absence, of any person who knows something of medicine, even if the mother herself does not agree.[215] The Sabbath laws are set aside to do whatever the mother requests for her health, even if the physician does not consider it necessary.[216] When possible, this should be done in an indirect or unusual manner,[217] or by a non-Jew[218] (see paragraph 120 above).

b. The following rules apply for the subsequent ninety-six hours:[219] If the physician or the midwife considers it necessary to do something that involves setting aside the Sabbath laws, it should be performed even against the mother's wishes. If a person other than the physician or the midwife requests it and the mother considers it unnecessary, her opinion prevails.[220] If the mother expresses no opinion, in the absence of a physician anyone present is held competent to pass judgment as to whether the Sabbath laws need to be set aside.[221] If the mother says that she needs it for her health, even if the physician considers it unnecessary, the Sabbath laws are set aside for her as she requests.[222] In all cases this should be done, when possible, in an indirect or unusual manner (see

(213) אוי"ח שם סעי' ד.

(214) שם ומ"ב ס"ק יא וביה"ל ד"ה כל. דהיינו מ"ב שם ס"ק י, שו"ת בנין ציון סימן כה.

(215) שם מ"ב ס"ק יב.

(216) מ"ב שם סוס"ק יד.

(217) שם סעי' א.

(218) קיצור שו"ע סי' צג ס"ק ב. מנחת שבת שם ס"ק ג. שמירת שבת כהלכתה פל"ו סעי' יג.

(219) אוי"ח סי' של סעי' ד ומ"ב ס"ק י.

(220) שם מ"ב ס"ק יד. וראה שם שעה"צ ס"ק יא. שו"ת אבני נזר אוי"ח סי' תנג.

(221) אוי"ח ומ"ב שם.

(222) מ"ב שם.

paragraph 120 above) or by a non-Jew.[223]

128. Although the periods of seventy-two and ninety-six hours referred to in paragraph 127 above are equal in length to three and four days, respectively, the rules set out there apply for just the number of hours in question, and change when that period comes to an end, regardless of the time of day at which this occurs. In particular, either period might end during the Sabbath, and the rules change accordingly, and this must be borne in mind when caring for the new mother.[224]

129. After the seventh day and until the thirtieth day after childbirth, as long as there are no complications,[225] the mother is considered as a non-seriously ill patient (see Chapter 1, paragraph 2), and, as for all such patients, only Rabbinically ordained prohibitions may be set aside.[226]

130. If there are complications, she is considered as a seriously ill patient (see Chapter 1, paragraph 1) and Torah prohibitions also are set aside when necessary.

THE NURSING MOTHER

131. When a mother cleans her nipples before nursing on the Sabbath, she should not use wet absorbent cotton for this purpose, even if it is held with forceps.[227] She should clean them as described in paragraph 61 above.

132. A mother may express some of her milk into the baby's mouth if it does not start sucking, so as to encourage it to take the breast.[228] She should not express her milk into a utensil.[229]

(223) ראה לעיל הערה 197 ו-198.
(224) שמירת שבת כהלכתה פל"ו סע' יג.
(225) מ"ב שם ס"ק טו ושעה"צ ס"ק יג.
(226) או"ח סי' שכח סע' יז. וראה שם מ"ס ב"ק נז.
(227) שמירת שבת כהלכתה שם סע' יז.
(228) או"ח סי' שכח סע' לה ומ"ב ס"ק קיב. וראה שם שעה"צ ס"ק פא.
(229) שם סע' לד.

133. A nursing mother suffering discomfort because of a surplus of milk may relieve her discomfort by expressing the surplus milk into the sink[230] or a diaper.[231]

134. Surplus milk may also be drawn with a suction pump, but no more than 17 cc. should be collected at one time before disposing of the milk.[232] Preferably, a small quantity of liquid soap or a similar substance should be placed in the pump receptacle before drawing the milk, so as to render it unfit for consumption; the pump is then used in the normal way.[233]

135. If the baby cannot suck at the mother's breast, or if the baby is in the hospital without the mother and the mother has to bring it her own fresh milk every day, she may draw her milk into a utensil even on the Sabbath.[234]

136. If a nursing mother has infected nipples which require treatment on the Sabbath, she may take any medication or other form of treatment as is needed.[235]

THE SABBATH CANDLES

137. A Jewish woman should kindle Sabbath and Festival candles even if she is in the hospital. Even if she has someone to light candles in her home, she may, if she wishes, light candles in the hospital and pronounce the benediction.[236] If she is able to get out of bed, she should light them by the table at which she will eat. If not, she should light them at her bedside, where she will eat, and the candles should not be

(230) או״ח סי׳ של סע׳ ח ומ״ב ס״ק לב.

(231) שמירת שבת כהלכתה פל״ו סע׳ כ מהא דסי׳ שב מ״ב ס״ק ס.

(232) שו״ת אבני נזר או״ח סי׳ מז. קצות השולחן סי׳ קלח בבדי השולחן ס״ק ל. ולגבי השיעור של 17 סמ״ק, ראה שמירת שבת כהלכתה הערה סא.

(233) שמעתי ממו״ר הגרי״י נויבירט שליט״א.

(234) שמירת שבת כהלכתה פל״ו סע׳ כא מהא דאו״ח סי׳ תריז סע׳ א ביה״ל ד״ה עוברות.וראה חזו״א או״ח סי׳ נט ס״ק ג ו־ד. שו״ת יביע אומר ח״ה סוסי׳ לב.

(235) שמירת שבת כהלכתה פל״ו סע׳ כב.

(236) שמירת שבת כהלכתה פמ״ה סע׳ ו.

moved to another room.[237]

If she is at home and cannot get out of bed, her husband should light the candles by the dining table,[238] or she may kindle them by her bed and then have them moved (by someone who has not yet ushered in the Sabbath) to the dining table where her family will eat.[239]

138. A bedpan should not be used in the presence of Sabbath candles, unless the patient is covered with a sheet.[240]

139. The Sabbath candles may be kindled well before sunset, to usher in the Sabbath early, but not earlier than one and a quarter hours before sunset[241] (an hour to be understood here as one-twelfth of the daylight time between dawn and dusk). (Regarding Festivals, see Chapter 11, paragraph 4.) During the summer when many communities usher in the Sabbath long before sunset, a non-Jew may be asked to do such work as may be necessary after the Sabbath has been ushered in, provided that it is still before sunset. Moreover, a Jew who has not yet ushered in the Sabbath also may do whatever work is necessary for the Jew who has already ushered in the Sabbath.[242] Therefore, both a non-Jew and a Jew (who has not yet ushered in the Sabbath) may be asked to tend to the needs even of a patient who has only a minor illness.

140. Ordinarily, if a woman forgets to light Sabbath candles she thereafter should light one more than it had been her custom to light until then.[243] However, if her failure to light candles was the result of illness, she is not required to add a candle thereafter.[244]

(237) שם פל״ו סע׳ טז ו־פמ״ה סע׳ ו.

(238) ראה או״ח סי׳ רסג סע׳ יד ומ״ב ס״ק יא.

(239) שם מ״ב ס״ק מח. שמירת שבת כהלכתה פמ״ג סע׳ לט.

(240) ראה כף החיים סי׳ רעה ס״ק מב. שמירת שבת כהלכתה פמ״ג סע׳ מא.

(241) שעות זמניות או״ח סי׳ רסג סע׳ ד.

(242) שמירת שבת כהלכתה פמ״ו סע׳ כב. וראה שם הערה קיח.

(243) או״ח שם סע׳ א בהגה.

(244) מ״ב שם ס״ק ז. שמירת שבת כהלכתה פמ״ג סע׳ ה.

141. If a woman realizes that the light of the Sabbath candles will not be enjoyed by herself or anyone else, she should not kindle them, since the benediction would then be pronounced unnecessarily.[245] Accordingly, a woman who has to enter the hospital just before the Sabbath should not light candles at home, unless her husband or some other member of the household remains to enjoy the candlelight after dark. Similarly, a woman who is taken into the operating theater before the Sabbath and is not likely to regain consciousness until after the candles have burnt out should not kindle them if there are other women in the ward who do so. If the other Jewish women do not light candles, she may light hers in order to act on their behalf.[246]

142. A physician or a nurse who is on duty Friday night should light candles for the Sabbath and pronounce the benediction, unless a member of his or her family does so at home[247] (see paragraph 137 above).

143. A nurse[248] or a physician may light candles in the hospital dining room[249] (see paragraphs 144 and 145 below). Staff members should be sure that there is light in all the rooms they might need at night.[250]

144. In a Jewish hospital in which arrangements are made for candles to be lit in the dining room, the staff is in-

(245) מ"ב שם ס"ק ל.

(246) שמעתי ממו"ר הגרי"י נויבירט שליט"א. וראה נשמת אברהם או"ח סי' רסג ס"ק ד (עמי קי) ושם עמי שמא אות ו.

(247) או"ח סי' רסג סעי' ב. בן איש חי שנה ב פי נח סעי' ה.

(248) מסתבר שאשה קודמת לאיש במצוה זו או"ח סי' רסג סעי' ג ומ"ב ס"ק יב. בן איש חי שם סעי' ה. שמירת שבת כהלכתה פמ"ג סעי' ו.

(249) או"ח שם סעי' ח. בן איש חי שם סעי' יא. קיצור שו"ע סי' עה סעי' ט. שמירת שבת כהלכתה פמ"ה סעי' ז.

(250) שמעתי ממו"ר הגרי"י נויבירט שליט"א מהא דאשל אברהם (בוטשאטש) על סי' רסג סעי' ה.

cluded and staff members do not individually light candles[251] (see paragraph 143 above).

145.   If for any reason the candles cannot be lit in the dining room, each staff member should light candles in a bed-room[252] or another room that will surely be used in the evening (after dark), and the benediction should be pronounced.[253] The candles should be of sufficient size so that they will not burn out before the room is used.[254]

146.   If candles are not available, an electric light should be switched on for this purpose, but the benediction should not be pronounced.[255] If the electric lights were already on, before the Sabbath they should be switched off and then turned on again for the specific purpose of the *mitzvah*.[256]

147.   The husband of a blind woman should light the Sabbath candles and pronounce the benediction.[257] A blind woman who lives alone lights them herself (guided if necessary) and pronounces the benediction.[258]

(251) או״ח שם סע׳ ז מ״ב ס״ק ג. קיצור שו״ע שם סוסע׳ ט.

(252) או״ח שם סע׳ ו ומ״ב ס״ק כט.

(253) מ״ב שם ס״ק לב וביה״ל ד״ה בחורים. ערוה״יש שם סע׳ ד.

(254) מ״ב שם ס״ק ל.

(255) משום ספק ברכות להקל כי קיימת מחלוקת הפוסקים לגבי הברכה. ראה שו״ת הר צבי או״ח ח״א סי׳ קמג, יסודי ישורון ח״ג עמ׳ קמח, שו״ת מחזה אברהם ח״א סי׳ מא, שו״ת מלמד להועיל ח״א סי׳ מז ושמירת שבת כהלכתה פמ״ג סע׳ ד. לעומתם, ראה שו״ת לבושי מרדכי מהד״ג סי׳ נט, שערים מצויינים בהלכה סי׳ עה ס״ק ז, משפטי עוזיאל או״ח סי׳ ז ושו״ת יביע אומר ח״ב סי׳ יז. וראה שמירת שבת כהלכתה שם הערה כב בשם הגרש״ז אוירבאך שליט״א שמבדיל בין חשמל הבאה מתחנת הכוח דהרי זה חשיב בשעת הדלקה כמדליק בלא שמן ובין מדליק עם נר המופעל ע״י מצבר אשר הזרם כבר צבור ונמצא בתוכו ששפיר מסתבר שיכולים גם לברך, עכ״ל. וראה נשמת אברהם או״ח סי׳ רסג ס״ק ג (עמ׳ קח).

(256) שמירת שבת כהלכתה פמ״ג סע׳ לב.

(257) או״ח סי׳ רסג מ״ב ס״ק יד. קיצור שו״ע סי׳ עה סע׳ יג.

(258) קיצור שו״ע שם. שמירת שבת כהלכתה פמ״ג סע׳ י ונשמת אברהם או״ח סי׳ רסג ס״ק ד (עמ׳ קז) ועמ׳ שמא אות ו.

KIDDUSH

148. Both women and men are required to recite or hear *Kiddush*[259] and to partake of at least three meals on the Sabbath.[260]

149. One may not eat, or drink even water, on the Sabbath eve before reciting or hearing *Kiddush*.[261] However, a person who needs to take tablets before eating may do so before *Kiddush*, with as much water as is necessary to swallow them. No other beverage may be drunk.[262]

150. The *Kiddush* cup should hold at least 86 cc. of wine or grape juice[263] and of this slightly more than half should be drunk[264] within four minutes.[265] If the one who recited *Kiddush* is unable to drink the wine, or the minimum quantity mentioned, one of the others present should do so.[266]

151. Wine or grape juice[267] for *Kiddush* should be made available in the hospital on the Sabbath,[268] and it is advisable that it be wine or grape juice that was previously heated to the boiling point.[269] If no wine or grape juice is available, *Kiddush*

(259) או״ח סי׳ רעא סע׳ ב. וראה מ״ב שם ס״ק ד.

(260) מהא דאו״ח סי׳ רצא סע׳ ו. יסודי ישורון ח״ה עמ׳ תמג. שו״ת דברי מלכיאל ח״ו סי׳ ד.

(261) או״ח סי׳ רעא סע׳ ד. וראה מ״ב שם ס״ק יא.

(262) שמירת שבת כהלכתה פנ״ב סע׳ ג.

(263) דהיינו רביעית יין שיעורי תורה סי׳ ג ס״ק ו. חזון עובדיה עמ׳ קכז. ויש אומרים 150 סמ״ק שיעורין דאורייתא בשיעורי המצוות ס״ק יח.

(264) או״ח סי׳ רעא סע׳ יג. וראה שם ביה״ל סוד״ה של רביעית, שאפילו לדעת המחמירים (הערה הקודמת) מספיק אם הוא שותה כמלוא לוגמיו שלו.

(265) מ״ב שם ס״ק עג. ערוך השולחן סי׳ רב סע׳ ח. שיעורין דאורייתא בשיעורי המצוות ס״ק כט. שיעורי תורה סי׳ ג ס״ק טז. שמירת שבת כהלכתה פמ״ח סע׳ י.

(266) או״ח שם סע׳ יד.

(267) או״ח סי׳ ערב סע׳ ב. יסודי ישורון ח״ג עמ׳ ריד. חזון עובדיה עמ׳ קכה.

(268) וראה יו״ד סי׳ קכג סע׳ א ו־סי׳ ב סע׳ ה. יסודי ישורון ח״ג עמ׳ קכו וח״יד עמ׳ קפז. שו״ת מנחת יצחק ח״ג סי׳ כו (ד). שו״ת אג״מ יו״ד ח״א סי׳ מו.

(269) יו״ד סי׳ קכג סע׳ ג.

should be recited over two whole loaves of bread.[270] If even these are not available, a slice of bread suffices.[271]

152. *Kiddush* should be recited where the meal is to be taken,[272] and should be immediately followed by the meal.[273] If, however, a physician or a nurse is occupied and unable to partake of the full meal after *Kiddush*, at least 45 grams[274] of bread or cake[275] should be eaten. If this is not available, an additional 86 cc. of wine or grape juice should be drunk (that is, a minimum total of 130 cc.).[276]

153. If for any reason *Kiddush* was not recited on Friday night, it should then be recited on the Sabbath morning, but *Va-yechullu* should be omitted.[277]

154. On the Sabbath morning also one may not eat before *Kiddush*.[278] Therefore, a man on night duty (who is obligated to recite *Shacharit* later) may eat only until half an hour before dawn.[279] Immediately after dawn, he should wash his hands three times,[280] recite *Shacharit*[281] and *Kiddush*, and then take light refreshment. A full meal should not be eaten until

(270) או״ח סי׳ ערב סע׳ ט. וראה שם סי׳ רעד מ״ב ס״ק א שגם הנשים חייבות בלחם משנה. וראה פרטי דינים בשמירת שבת כהלכתה פנ״ג סע׳ טו-יח.

(271) או״ח סי׳ רעד מ״ב ס״ק ב. שו״ת משיב דבר ח״א סי׳ כא.

(272) או״ח סי׳ רעג סע׳ א.

(273) שם סע׳ ג בהגה.

(274) מחצית השקל או״ח סי׳ רצא. וכן משמע דעת מרן בשו״ע שם סע׳ ה. השיעור של 45 גרם, דהיינו שיעור של ביצה או״ח סי׳ רצא סע׳ א מ״ב ס״ק ב. שיעורין דאורייתא בשיעורי המצוות ס״ק כא. ולכל הפחות יאכל חצי מזה או״ח סי׳ רעג מ״ב ס״ק כא.

(275) או״ח סי׳ רעג מ״ב ס״ק כה.

(276) או״ח שם סע׳ ה ומ״ב ס״ק כה ו-כז.

(277) או״ח סי׳ רעא סע׳ ח.

(278) או״ח סי׳ רפט סע׳ א.

(279) והאיסור הזה הוא רק לאנשים ולא לנשים הגרש״ז אויערבאך שליט״א.

(280) ולענין ברכה ראה או״ח סי׳ ד סע׳ יג ומ״ב ס״ק כט.

(281) ואם הוא טרוד בעבודתו, אפילו לפני הנץ החמה, מהא דאו״ח סי׳ נח סע׳ ג ומ״ב ס״ק יב ממו״ר הגרי״י נויבירט שליט״א.

after *Musaf* for the Sabbath has been recited.[282]

A woman should recite the morning benedictions before *Kiddush*,[283] and she may then eat a full meal.[284]

155. The morning *Kiddush* also should be recited at the dining table.[285]

156. On the Sabbath morning, *Kiddush* may be recited over wine or grape juice or any alcoholic drink of choice.[286]

157. If in the course of a meal a physician or a nurse is called out to treat a patient, the meal may be continued upon return without the need to pronounce the benedictions of *Birkat Ha-mazon* (on what has already been eaten) or repeat *Ha-motzi* (on what is about to be eaten).[287]

158. One may drink tea or coffee before prayers on the Sabbath morning (see Chapter 5, paragraph 15). If, however, this is insufficient for a patient and he needs to eat before praying, he should first recite *Kiddush*.[288] Since, if necessary, he is allowed to eat a full meal before prayers, he must first recite *Kiddush*, and may not drink even water before doing so.[289] If possible, he should recite also the benedictions for the Torah and the first paragraph of the *Shema*[290] (see Chapter 5, paragraph 15).

159. A person who feels weak but is not really ill should pray in private,[291] recite *Kiddush* and then eat, rather

(282) או"ח סי' רפו סע' ג. וראה שו"ת יביע אומר ח"ה סי' כב.

(283) או"ח סי' קו מג"א ס"ק ב. וראה שם מ"ב ס"ק ד. שו"ת יביע אומר ח"ו סי' יז.

(284) שמעתי ממו"ר הגרי"י נויבירט שליט"א. וראה שמירת שבת כהלכתה פנ"ב סע' יג.

(285) או"ח סי' רפט סע' א.

(286) שם סע' ב. וראה שמירת שבת כהלכתה פנ"ג סע' יט.

(287) בן איש חי שנה א פ' בהעלותך סע' ב. כף החיים סי' קעח ס"ק יד.

(288) או"ח סי' רפט סע' א ביה"ל ד"ה חובת.

(289) הגרש"ז אויערבאך שליט"א.

(290) או"ח סי' פט סע' ג מ"ב ס"ק כב. שמירת שבת כהלכתה פ"מ סע' מה.

(291) או"ח סי' רפו מ"ב ס"ק ט ושעה"צ ס"ק ט. וידלג על פסוקי דזמרא הגרש"ז אויערבאך שליט"א.

than eat first and then pray with a congregation. After the meal he should go to the synagogue to listen to *Kaddish, Barechu* and other prayers that are recited only in the presence of a *minyan*[292] (see Chapter 5, paragraph 15).

160. A patient who is unable to drink wine or eat bread is exempt from reciting *Kiddush* both in the evening and in the morning.[293] Such a patient should listen to *Kiddush* being recited by someone else.[294] If that is not possible, when saying the *Amidah* he should bear in mind that the benediction *Mekaddesh ha-Shabbat* includes the *mitzvah* of *Kiddush*. If by the morning the patient is able to drink wine or eat bread, he should recite the Friday evening *Kiddush*, omitting the *Va-yechullu* passage.[295]

HAVDALAH

161. On the termination of the Sabbath, one may perform no work before reciting the *Havdalah* benediction during the *Amidah* prayer[296] or reciting *Baruch ha-mavdil bein kodesh l'chol*.[297] One may partake of no food nor drink any liquid other than water without first reciting *Havdalah* over wine[298] or another halachically acceptable beverage.[299]

162. The benediction *Borei meorei ha-esh* should preferably be recited in the presence of light from a flame. If that is not available, light from a clear electric bulb may suffice, but not

(292) אוו״ח סי׳ פט ביה״ל ד״ה וכן.

(293) שמירת שבת כהלכתה פ״מ סע׳ מז מהא דאוו״ח סי׳ ערב שע״ת ס״ק ב. מנחת שבת סי׳ עז ס״ק כב ובהשמטות שם. שו״ת אג״מ אוו״ח ח״ב סי׳ כו.

(294) אוו״ח סי׳ רעב סע׳ ט ברמ״א.

(295) אוו״ח סי׳ רפט מ״ב סוס״ק י.

(296) אוו״ח סי׳ רצט סע׳ י.

(297) אוו״ח שם ומ״ב ס״ק לד.

(298) שם סע׳ א ומ״ב ס״ק לה.

(299) אוו״ח סי׳ רצו סע׳ ב ומ״ב ס״ק ח. וראה שמירת שבת כהלכתה פ״ס סע׳ ג־ח.

from a fluorescent lamp or an opaque (frosted) light bulb.[300] Competent halachic authority should be consulted.

163. A blind person should preferably hear *Havdalah* from someone else.[301] If no one else is available, the benediction *Borei meorei ha-esh* should not be pronounced.[302]

(300) שמירת שבת כהלכתה פס״א סעי לב. וראה שם עדויות על הבעל צפנת פענח, הגר״ח מבריסק והגרח״ע גרודזנסקי זצ״ל שהבדילו מפעם לפעם על מנורת חשמל. וכן, מעשה רב אצל הגר״י אברמסקי זצ״ל שהבדיל על אור של מנורת חשמל להוציא מלבן של אותם החושבים שאין בהדלקת חשמל משום איסור דאורייתא של הבערת אש עדותו של פרופ. דוב הימן שליט״א. וראה ספר מאורי אש של הגרש״ז אויערבאך שליט״א עמי צב ע״ב שדעתו נוטה להחמיר מפני שהאור אינו קבוע אלא מתחדש ונוצר כל הזמן ע״י תחנת הכוח. וקיימת מחלוקת הפוסקים, מהם מתירים (שו״ת מחזה אברהם או״ח סי׳ מא. שערים מצויינים בהלכה סי׳ צו ס״ק ו. יסודי ישורון ח״ה עמי תצד) ומהם אוסרים (או״ח סי׳ רצח סעי טו ביה״ל ד״ה או בתוך. בן איש חי שנה ב פי ויצא סעי יד. שו״ת יביע אומר ח״א סי׳ יז ו־ יח. שו״ת הר צבי או״ח ח״ב סי׳ קיד).

(301) כף החיים סי׳ רצח ס״ק נח. וראה נשמת אברהם או״ח סי׳ רצח ס״ק א (עמי קכג).

(302) או״ח סי׳ רצח סעי יג ומ״ב ס״ק לד. ולפי הגר״ע יוסף שליט״א גם שאר ההבדלה אינו אומר. וראה כף החיים סי׳ רצח ס״ק סח.

11 / THE *YAMIM TOVIM* (FESTIVALS)

The rules concerning observance of the Festivals are similar to those for the Sabbath, with certain differences which are discussed in this chapter.

1. What is forbidden for a non-seriously ill patient (see Chapter 1, paragraph 2) on the Sabbath is similarly prohibited on the Festivals.[1]

2. Different rules apply to the second days of the Festivals, which are observed only in the Diaspora. Any form of treatment which is prohibited by Rabbinic ordinance on the first day of the Festival is permitted on the second day[2] (see paragraph 3 below).

3. However, on Rosh Hashanah the rules of the first day are applicable also to the second day.[3]

4. The rules regarding the lighting of candles on the eve of the Festival are the same as those for the Sabbath eve[4] (see Chapter 10, paragraphs 137-147). But, unlike the rule for the Sabbath, if one did not light the candles before the Festival began, they may be kindled after nightfall, provided that the flame is transferred from an already existing one.[5] Care should

(1) מ"ב סי' תקלב ס"ק ה. וראה או"ח סי' תצה סע' א. קיצור שולחן ערוך סי' צח סע' לג.

(2) שמירת שבת כהלכתה פל"א סע' כח. או"ח סי' תצו סע' ב ומ"ב ס"ק ז. מנחת יו"ט סי' צה סע' קכא ו-קכב.

(3) או"ח סי' תצו סע' ב ומ"ב ס"ק ה ו-ו. שו"ת אבני נזר או"ח סי' שצד ו-שצה. שמירת שבת כהלכתה שם.

(4) או"ח סי' רסג סע' ה וסי' תקיד סע' יא ומ"ב ס"ק מח.

(5) שו"ת כתב סופר או"ח סי' סז. שו"ת רב פעלים ח"ב סי' נח. בן איש חי שנה ב פ' במדבר סע' טו. שדי חמד אסיפת דינים מערכת יו"ט אות לז. או"ח סי' תקב מ"ב ס"ק ד. שו"ת יחוה דעת ח"ג סי' לג. וראה שו"ת שואל ומשיב שתיתאה סי' סב.

be taken not to extinguish the match or the candle used to transfer the flame; rather one should allow it to burn itself out.[6]

5. A physician or a nurse who recites *Kiddush* on the Festival eve should pronounce the *Shehecheyanu* benediction with *Kiddush* and not when lighting the candles.[7]

6. On the eve of the seventh day of Pesach (and in the Diaspora also on the eve of the eighth day), the *Shehecheyanu* benediction is not recited.[8]

CHOL HA-MOED (THE INTERMEDIATE DAYS OF THE FESTIVAL)

7. On *chol ha-moed* a physician may give and a patient receive any necessary medical treatment, active or prophylactic,[9] just as on an ordinary weekday.[10] It is preferable not to arrange elective medical or dental appointments for *chol ha-moed* if this can be avoided.[11]

8. A physician may receive payment for services rendered on *chol ha-moed*.[12]

9. Although shaving is not ordinarily permitted on *chol ha-moed*,[13] a patient may shave if this is part of his treat-

---

(6) או"ח סי' תקיד סע' א.

(7) שו"ת שארית שמחה סי' ח. וראה גם שאילת יעב"ץ סי' קז. וראה או"ח סי' רסג מ"ב ס"ק כג וסי' תר מ"ב סוס"ק ד.

(8) או"ח סי' תצ סע' ז.

(9) חיי אדם כלל קי סע' יז ונשמת אדם ס"ק ב. שו"ת אגרות משה או"ח ח"ג סיק עח. שמירת שבת כהלכתה פס"יו סע' כ.

(10) או"ח סי' תקלב סע' ב ומ"ב ס"ק ה.

(11) כי ההיתר הוא משום דבר האבד ולא משום אוכל נפש שמעתי ממו"ר הגרי"י נויבירט שליט"א והסכים עמו הגרש"ז אויערבאך שליט"א. שמירת שבת כהלכתה פס"יו הערה פח. שו"ת אג"מ או"ח ח"ג סי' עח. הגר"מ פיינשטיין זצ"ל בספר זכרון שלמה על הל' חול המועד, פסקי הלכות אות טז.

(12) הגרש"ז אויערבאך שליט"א. וראה סי' תקמב סע' א בהגה ומ"ב ס"ק ד וביה"ל ד"ה ודבר.

(13) או"ח סי' תקלא סע' ב.

ment.[14] But a man who recovers from an illness during *chol ha-moed* should not shave during these days, even if he was unable to shave before the Festival because of illness.[15]

10. A hearing aid may be taken in for repair during *chol ha-moed* even if the wearer will not receive it back in time to use on *chol ha-moed*.[16] The same ruling applies to the repair of eyeglasses.[17]

11. A telephone may be repaired during *chol ha-moed* on behalf of an aged or sick person.[18]

12. A computer may be used on *chol ha-moed* for entering or printing out data or text for the benefit of a patient.[19]

13. During *chol ha-moed* one may engage only in research that was started before the Festival, and then only if postponement would result in financial loss. A manuscript may not be prepared during these days, even if only as a draft.[20]

(14) מג"א שם ס"ק יב. מ"ב ס"ק כא וביה"ל סע' ח ד"ה כל. וראה שמירת שבת כהלכתה פס"ו הערה קכג.

(15) או"ח שם סע' ג.

(16) ראה שמירת שבת כהלכתה פס"ו הערה פח בשם הגרש"ז אויערבאך שליט"א. וכעת כתב לי מו"ר הגרי"י נויבירט שליט"א ששמע מהגרש"ז אויערבאך שליט"א שמותר גם אם לא יקבל אותם בחזרה רק אחרי חול המועד.

(17) שם.

(18) שם.

(19) שם הערה ריא.

(20) שמעתי ממו"ר הגרי"י נויבירט שליט"א.

12 / ROSH HASHANAH (THE NEW YEAR)

1. A man may not eat on Rosh Hashanah during the day before hearing the *shofar*,[1] just as he may not eat before reciting the *Shema*, listening to the reading of the *Megillah* and performing the *mitzvah* of *lulav* at their respective times.[2] However, one may partake of light refreshment after reciting *Kiddush* if one feels a real need to do so.[3]

2. A woman who feels the need to eat before hearing the *shofar* should recite *Kiddush* before eating;[4] she should recite the morning benedictions before *Kiddush*.[5]

3. A man who blows the *shofar* on behalf of men who are unable to go to the synagogue should pronounce the benedictions *Lishmoa kol shofar* and *Shehecheyanu* even if he himself has already fulfilled the *mitzvah* of *shofar*.[6]

4. A man may blow the *shofar* on behalf of a woman. If she is a Sephardi, the benedictions should not be pronounced;[7] if an Ashkenazi, the benedictions should be pronounced by the woman. In the latter case, if several women are present, one of them should pronounce the benedictions.[8]

Regarding medical treatment on Rosh Hashanah, see Chapter 11, paragraphs 1-3.

---

(1) מג"א סי' תרצב ס"ק ז בשם תוספתא שבת פי"א ה"ד.

(2) מהא דאו"ח סי' תרצב מ"ב סוס"ק טו וסי' תרנב סע' ב. וראה נשמת אברהם סי' תקפה ס"ק א (עמ' רצא).

(3) או"ח סי' תרנב מ"ב ס"ק ז.

(4) קיצור שולחן ערוך סי' קכט סע' יט.

(5) או"ח סי' קו מג"א ס"ק ב. וראה שם מ"ב ס"ק ד. שו"ת יביע אומר ח"ו סי' יז.

(6) או"ח סי' תקפה סע' ב בהגה וסי' תקפט סע' ו בהגה.

(7) או"ח סי' תקפט סע' ו.

(8) שם בהגה.

13 / YOM KIPPUR
(THE DAY OF ATONEMENT)

This chapter discusses the various categories of ill persons with regard to their consumption of food on Yom Kippur. All the rules relating to the four categories of patients defined in Chapter 1 apply to Yom Kippur as they do to the Sabbath.

1. A person who is seriously ill (see Chapter 1, paragraph 1), or who might become so if he refrains from food, not only is permitted to eat on Yom Kippur but, indeed, is obligated to do so.[1] A person who is non-seriously ill (see Chapter 1, paragraph 2) may neither eat nor drink even the smallest quantity on Yom Kippur.[2]

2. A seriously ill patient (see Chapter 1, paragraph 1) who refuses to eat or drink on Yom Kippur is held responsible for endangering his or her own life,[3] as the Torah says (*Genesis* 9:5): "And surely your own blood of your souls will I require."

3. The opinion of the patient himself, or of the physician, or of any person with some medical knowledge, is sufficient to determine that the patient is obliged to eat.[4]

4. The opinion of the patient himself that he is in need of food overrides that of a physician who disagrees.[5] But, in such a case, the patient should be reminded that it is Yom Kippur, in case he has forgotten,[6] unless such information would cause him distress.[7]

(1) או״ח סי׳ תריח סע׳ א מ״ב ס״ק ב וביה״ל ד״ה חולה.

(2) שו״ת חת״ס ח״ן סי׳ כג. שו״ת שאגת אריה סי׳ עו.

(3) מ״ב שם ס״ק ה.

(4) מ״ב שם ס״ק א.

(5) מ״ב שם ס״ק ד.

(6) מ״ב שם ס״ק ה.

(7) שמירת שבת כהלכתה פל״ט הערה יג.

5. Should the patient ask for food when the physician is of the opinion that food would actually do the patient harm, the patient must abide by the expert opinion of the physician.[8]

6. It is clear that a patient who is seriously ill (see Chapter 1, paragraph 1) must, according to his own feelings or the opinion of his physician (see paragraph 3 above), consume all that is necessary for his well-being.[9] But, if small quantities will undoubtedly suffice to sustain the patient until after Yom Kippur without endangering him, the rules set out below apply. These rules are based on two measures: (a) the maximum quantity of solid and/or liquid that may be consumed in a period of time and (b) the minimum period of time during which they may be consumed.[10]

a. Measures of this type are always given in *Halachah* in terms of volume, rather than weight.[11] The maximum quantity of solid food that may be taken is about 30 cc.,[12] which for most foods is about 30 grams by weight (which in the case of solids is easier to measure). The maximum quantity of liquid that may be taken is the amount that fills one cheek,[13] which is usually about 45 cc.[14] It is advisable, but not obligatory, that these measurements be made before Yom Kippur.[15]

---

(8) ערוך השולחן או"ח סי' תריח סע' ה ו־ו. וכותב שם על המג"א ס"ק ג שהדבר תמוה והרבה פעמים אנו רואים שהחולה מבקש דבר ומזיק לו ואין נותנים לו ע"פ ציווי הרופא, וכי מפני שעתה יוהכ"פ מיגרע גרע ?

(9) או"ח תריח סע' א מ"ב ס"ק ב וביה"ל ד"ה חולה.

(10) או"ח סי' תריח סע' ז ומ"ב ס"ק יז. שו"ת חתם סופר סי' קכז ד"ה תו צל"ע.

(11) שו"ת אבקת רוכל סוסי' נג. וכן דעת הרשב"ץ ח"ב סי' רצא. פרי חדש יו"ד סי' צט סע' ו. שו"ת יד הלוי יו"ד סי' ר. זבחי צדק סי' צח סע' ד. וראה גם אנציקלופדיה תלמודית, כרך ג ערך ביצה

(ב) עמ' קמד ד"ה בקביעת השיעורים.

(12) שמירת שבת כהלכתה פל"ט סע' יח.

(13) או"ח סי' תריח מ"ב סע' כא.

(14) שמירת שבת כהלכתה פל"ט סע' כ.

(15) מ"ב סי' תריח ס"ק כא.

b. The minimum time permitted is, if possible, nine minutes for both solids[16] and liquids.[17] If this is not possible, competent halachic authority must be consulted.

After the minimum time allowed for the consumption of a maximum amount of solid and/or liquid has elapsed, there should be a pause of an equivalent period of time before the patient repeats the consumption of food. This means that a maximum of 30 cc. of solid and/or 45 cc. of liquid may be consumed during a continuous period of not less than nine minutes. Following this, at least nine minutes must elapse without further intake before the consumption of solid and/or liquid may be repeated.[18]

These measures of solid and liquid are independent, not additive.[19] Therefore, when both are needed, they may be consumed together or one immediately after the other.[20]

7.   In every case a decision must be made by the physician as to whether the patient needs to eat normally or according to the above measures (see paragraph 4 above), and whether liquid alone will suffice or solid food also is essential. An estimate must also be made of the total amount of solid food and/or liquid that the patient will need to consume during Yom Kippur. It is forbidden for the patient to eat or drink more than is necessary for his health[21] (see also paragraph 13 below).

8.   If a patient feels that taking food in measures is

(16) מייב שם בשם שויית חתייס חייו סיי טז. ואם צריך, אפשר גם להקל שתהיה זמן ההפסקה שתי דקות שמירת שבת כהלכתה פלייט סעי יח.

(17) אוייח סיי תריח סעי ח ומייב סייק כא וסיי תריב סעי י. וראה שם מייב סייק לא. שמירת שבת כהלכתה פלייט סעי כ. וגם כאן ניתן להקל בשעת הצורך לכל 2 דקות שמירת שבת כהלכתה שם.

(18) אוייח סיי תריח מייב סייק כא בשם שוייית החתם סופר חייו סיי טז. וראה אוייח סיי תריב סעי ג. שמירת שבת כהלכתה פלייט הערה סז.

(19) אוייח שם תריב סעי ב ומייב סייק ה. מייב סיי תריח סייק כא.

(20) אוייח שם סעי ח. שמירת שבת כהלכתה פלייט סעי ו.

(21) אוייח סיי תריב סעי ב ומייב סייק ה וסיי תריח מייב סייק כא. שמירת שב כהלכתה שם סעי כב, וראה שם הערה פו.

insufficient, food is placed before him and he is reminded that the day is Yom Kippur; he then decides whether to eat in measures or normally.[22]

9.   A patient who consumes food by measure (see paragraph 6 above) should recite the appropriate benedictions before beginning to eat but should not repeat them before consuming each measure, as long as the patient intends to continue eating.[23] After the last measure is eaten, no benediction should be recited.[24]

10.   A patient who takes liquids by measure (see paragraph 6 above) should recite the appropriate benediction before beginning to drink but should not repeat the benediction before consuming each measure, as long as the patient intends to continue drinking. After the last measure is drunk, no benediction should be recited.[25]

11.   A patient who knows that he will have to eat during Yom Kippur should preferably start to take the small statutory quantities early in the day, thereby avoiding the need to take substantial amounts later on.[26]

12.   A patient who needs to eat on Yom Kippur should preferably take food with a high caloric content so as to minimize, as far as possible, the quantity that he will have to eat and the number of times that food will have to be consumed.[27]

13.   A patient who is being fed by nasogastric tube or via a gastrostomy may continue to take food and drink this way

(22) מ״ב סי׳ תריח ס״ק כד.

(23) ארחות חיים סי׳ תריח סע׳ ז. שמירת שבת כהלכתה פל״ט סע׳ כא.

(24) שמירת שבת כהלכתה שם. ואם אכל בשיעורין תוך זמן של כשלש עד ארבע דקות, יברך ברכה אחרונה שמירת שבת כהלכתה שם סע׳ לא. הגר״ע יוסף, נשמת אברהם עמי שלו אות טז.

(25) אוי״ח סי׳ רי סע׳ א ומ״ב ס״ק א ר־י. שמירת שבת כהלכתה פל״ט הערה פה.

(26) הגרש״ז אויערבאך שליט״א מובא בשמירת שבת כהלכתה פל״ט הערה סט.

(27) ראה יומא פ ע״ב. נשמת אברהם אוי״ח סי׳ תריב ס״ק ו ד״ה והדבר (עמי ש).

in normal quantities on Yom Kippur.[28]

14. A diabetic patient receiving insulin, either by continuous infusion pump or by multiple injections, should, if possible, fast on Yom Kippur, adjusting the doses of insulin (by measuring the blood glucose levels).

15. It is preferable that a person stay in bed in order to be able to fast on Yom Kippur rather than consume food or drink (even if only by measure) so that he will be able to attend synagogue.[29]

16. A person who is required to eat on Yom Kippur does not recite *Kiddush*[30] even if Yom Kippur occurs on the Sabbath.[31] Before eating, the hands should be washed up to the wrists.[32] If the patient has eaten normally (that is, not by measures), *Ya'aleh v'yavo* should be included in the *Birkat Ha-mazon,* and if it is also the Sabbath, *Retzeh* should be recited.[33] Should the patient forget to include these passages, *Birkat Ha-mazon* should not be repeated.[34] Similar rules apply to the *Al ha-michyah* benediction after eating cake, etc.[35]

17. Three adult males who are seriously ill (see Chapter 1, paragraph 1) should not form a quorum on Yom Kippur for the benediction of *zimmun*. It is preferable that they do not sit together while eating.[36]

(28) שו״ת חלקת יעקב חי״ג סי׳ סח. שו״ת מחזה אברהם חי״א סי׳ קכט. שו״ת אחיעזר חי״ג סי׳ סא. וראה נשמת אברהם סי׳ תריב סי״ק ז (עמי שג).

(29) שו״ת חתם סופר חי״ו סי׳ כג. שדי חמד מערכת יום הכפורים סי׳ ג אות א.

(30) או״ח סי׳ תריח מ״ב סי״ק כט.

(31) שו״ע הרב סי׳ תריח סעי׳ יח. חיי אדם כלל קמה סעי׳ לב. שו״ת הר צבי או״ח חי״א סי׳ קנה.

(32) שמירת שבת כהלכתה פלי״ט סעי׳ לא.

(33) או״ח סי׳ תריח סעי׳ י ומ״ב סי״ק כט.

(34) מ״ב שם.

(35) שמירת שבת כהלכתה שם.

(36) כף החיים סי׳ קצו סי״ק ט. שמירת שבת כהלכתה פלי״ט סעי׳ לא והערה קה בשם הגרש״ז אויערבאך שליט״א.

18. Although eating heartily the day before Yom Kippur is in itself a specific *mitzvah*, it does not apply to a patient who is seriously ill (see Chapter 1, paragraph 1) and who will, of necessity, eat on Yom Kippur.[37]

19. If a patient, even one who is non-seriously ill (see Chapter 1, paragraph 2), needs to take medicines on Yom Kippur, he or she may do so, but without water.[38] If pleasant to the taste, the medicaments should preferably be taken in capsule form.[39]

20. A patient who has eaten on Yom Kippur may be called up to the reading of the Torah during *Shacharit*.[40] If Yom Kippur occurs on the Sabbath, he may also be called up to the reading of the Torah during *Minchah*.[41] However, only if he has partaken of food in no more than statutory quantities (see paragraph 6 above) may he be called up to the reading of the Torah during *Minchah* of Yom Kippur, even when it occurs on a weekday.[42]

PREGNANT WOMEN, CHILDBIRTH AND NURSING MOTHERS

The following rules apply to a woman after childbirth, or who has had a miscarriage more than forty days after her last ritual immersion in a *mikveh*.[43]

21. Pregnant and nursing women should fast if possible on Yom Kippur.[44] See paragraph 26 below regarding nursing mothers.

(37) שערים מצויינים בהלכה סי׳ קלא ס״ק ג.

(38) שו״ת כתב סופר או״ח סי׳ קיא. שו״ת אגרות משה או״ח ח״ג סוסי׳ צא. שמירת שבת כהלכתה פל״ט סע׳ ח.

(34) שמעתי מהגרש״ז אויערבאך שליט״א.

(39) שו״ת חתם סופר או״ח סי׳ קנז. שו״ת רעק״א סי׳ סט (פסקים כד).

(40) שמירת שבת כהלכתה פל״ט סע׳ לו.

(41) שמירת שבת כהלכתה פל״ט הערה קטו בשם הגרש״ז אויערבאך שליט״א.

(42) או״ח סי׳ תריז ביה״ל ד״ה יולדת. כף החיים סי׳ של ס״ק ב. שדי חמד מערכת יום הכפורים סי׳ ג אות א.

(43) או״ח סי׳ תריז סע׳ א.

(44) מ״ב שם ס״ק ב.

22. A pregnant woman who says that she requires food,[45] or whose facial expression indicates such a need,[46] should be given food, first in statutory measures (see paragraph 6 above) and then, if that does not satisfy her,[47] in the quantity she needs to restore her well-being.[48]

23. From the time a woman is in labor[49] (see Chapter 10, paragraph 125) until seventy-two hours[50] after giving birth,[51] she is required to eat on Yom Kippur as she does normally at any other time. If neither she nor the physician thinks that it is necessary for her to eat, she should still take food, but in statutory measures[52] (see paragraph 6 above).

24. After seventy-two hours following childbirth and until the end of the next ninety-six hours (i.e., a total of seven days), the following rules apply:[53]

a. The woman should eat normally if she feels the need to do so, even if the physician does not consider it necessary,[54] or if the physician considers it necessary, even if she does not feel a need to eat.[55]

b. If the woman says she feels no need to eat and no competent opinion disagrees, she may fast, as long as there is no possibility of affecting the state of a nursing baby[56] (see paragraph 26 below).

(45) או״ח שם סע׳ ב בהגה.

(46) מ״ב שם ס״ק ד.

(47) או״ח שם.

(48) או״ח שם סע׳ ד ומ״ב ס״ק ט.

(49) מ״ב שם ס״ק יג.

(50) או״ח סי׳ של מ״ב ס״ק יא. וראה ביה״ל שם ד״ה כל.

(51) מ״ב שם ס״ק י.

(52) או״ח שם סע׳ ד.

(53) מ״ב שם ס״ק יא.

(54) או״ח סי׳ תריח סע׳ א.

(55) או״ח סי׳ תריז מ״ב ס״ק יא. שדי חמד מערכת יום הכפורים סי׳ ג אות א.

(56) או״ח סי׳ תריז סע׳ ד.

25.   After the seven days following childbirth, the mother is in the same category as any non-seriously ill patient (see Chapter 1, paragraph 2). She should fast[57] unless she feels the need to eat because of weakness as a result of having given birth, in which case she should take food like any seriously ill patient[58] (see Chapter 1, paragraph 1).

26.   A nursing mother who, as a result of her fasting, produces insufficient milk to sustain her baby must take such food, preferably fluids, as is needed and, when feasible, in statutory measures[59] (see paragraph 6 above).

(57) מ״ב שם ס״ק יב.

(58) ביה״ל או״ח שם סע׳ ב ד״ה עוברות.

(59) כף החיים שם ס״ק ב.

14 / SUKKOT (FEAST OF TABERNACLES)

EATING IN THE *SUKKAH*

1. A patient who is suffering from even the mildest of ailments need not eat in the *sukkah* if eating elsewhere is more comfortable for him.[1] This exemption applies also to his attendants.[2] However, on the first night he should make an effort to recite *Kiddush* and eat at least an olive's bulk (30 cc.) of bread in the *sukkah*,[3] without pronouncing the benediction for the *sukkah*.[4]

2. Even a man who just feels out of sorts is not required to eat in the *sukkah* if doing so causes him discomfort; but in such a case his attendants are not exempt.[5] On the first night he should recite *Kiddush* and eat at least an olive's bulk (30 cc.) of bread in the *sukkah*,[6] without pronouncing the benediction for the *sukkah*.[7]

3. A male physician or attendant, even when on duty, should eat in a *sukkah* if possible, when he leaves his patients.[8]

ARBA'AH MINIM (THE FOUR SPECIES)

4. A man may not partake of food prior to performing the *mitzvah* of *lulav*.[9] After *Shacharit* he may recite *Kiddush* and take light refreshment, if necessary[10] (see Chapter 10, paragraph 154).

(1) אוי״ח סי׳ תרלט מ״ב ס״ק ט.

(2) אוי״ח סי׳ תרמ סע׳ ג ומ״ב ס״ק ט. אליה רבה שם ס״ק ח.

(3) בן איש חי שנה א פ׳ האזינו סע׳ יב.

(4) אוי״ח סי׳ תרלט מ״ב ס״ק לה.

(5) אוי״ח שם סע׳ ד.

(6) שם בהגה וסי׳ תרמ סע׳ ד בהגה.

(7) מ״ב סי׳ תרלט ס״ק טו ו־לה.

(8) ראה מ״ב שם ס״ק י.

(19) אוי״ח סי׳ תרנב סע׳ ב ומ״ב ס״ק ז.

(10) אוי״ח סי׳ פט סע׳ ג מ״ב ס״ק כב.

107

5. A man who has lost one of his hands should first take the *lulav* in the remaining hand and afterwards the *etrog*.[11]

6. The above ruling applies also to a person who has a completely paralyzed arm.[12] However, if he is able to move the fingers of his paralyzed arm sufficiently to hold the *lulav* or *etrog*, he should do so while someone lifts his arm for him.[13]

7. If an ill person is unable to stand or sit up, he may perform the *mitzvah* of *arba'ah minim* while sitting or lying down, as the case may be.[14]

8. A man with a band-aid on the hand or a finger should remove it before performing the *mitzvah* of *arba'ah minim*.[15] If removal is inadvisable, he should nevertheless perform the *mitzvah* and pronounce the benediction.[16]

9. A patient who has his hand bandaged or encased in plaster, so that he can hold the *lulav* or *etrog* only with his fingers, may perform the *mitzvah* and should pronounce the benediction.[17]

(11) מ״ב סי׳ תרנא ס״ק כג. וראה שערי תשובה שם ס״ק יא וכף החיים שם ס״ק מג.

(12) שע״ת שם.

(13) ספר ארבע מינים ח״ב עמ׳ קו. וראה נשמת אברהם או״ח שם ס״ק ד (עמ׳ שכה) ומה שכתב הגרא״י וולדינברג שם עמי שמו אות יד.

(14) ראה מ״ב שם ס״ק כז.

(15) או״ח סי׳ תרנא סעי׳ ז ומי״ב ס״ק לו. בן איש חי שנה א פי האזינו סעי׳ יג.

(16) שמעתי מפי הגרש״ז אויערבאך שליט״א.

(17) הגרי״ע יוסף שליט״א בנשמת אברהם עמי שלז אות יח. אך עיין שם סי׳ תרנא ס״ק ה (עמ׳ שכה) בשם הגרש״ז אויערבאך שליט״א.

15 / PESACH (PASSOVER)

Leavened food may not be eaten during the Festival of Pesach. The observance of this prohibition by the sick is discussed in this chapter, as is the performance of various *mitzvot* of the *Seder* night.

CHAMETZ

1. A patient who is not seriously ill (see Chapter 1, paragraph 1) may eat no *chametz* on Pesach, however small the quantity and even if it is only Rabbinically prohibited.[1]

2. Ashkenazim do not eat rice, grains or any leguminous vegetables on Pesach.[2] A non-seriously ill patient (see Chapter 1, paragraph 2) suffering from diarrhea, who needs to eat rice, may do so.[3] The rice must first be thoroughly checked in order to exclude kernels of the five species of grain that are capable of becoming *chametz*.[4] The rice should then be scalded by adding it to boiling water; it should not be placed in cold water and then brought to a boil.[5] Separate utensils should be used for cooking and eating such foods on Pesach.[6]

3. A sick child who needs to eat *chametz* should be fed in an area apart from the rooms prepared for Pesach. The necessary quantity of *chametz* should be kept there, and a parent or other person responsible for the child's welfare should re-

(1) או״ח סי׳ תסו סע׳ א שעה״צ ס״ק ו. שערי תשובה סי״ א.

(2) או״ח סי׳ תנג סע׳ א בהגה ומי״ב ס״ק ו.

(3) חיי אדם כלל קכז סע׳ ו. שו״ת מהרם שיק או״ח סי׳ רמא. שו״ת מלמד להועיל או״ח סי׳ צח.

(4) מי״ב שם ס״ק ז.

(5) שו״ת חתם סופר או״ח סי׳ קכב. מי״ב שם.

(6) כף החיים סי׳ תנז ס״ק כז. שו״ת מהרי״ם שיק סוסי׳ רמא.

nounce ownership of the *chametz* before Pesach. The child should preferably be fed by a non-Jew or a minor. The *chametz* needed during Pesach should be stored with that which was sold before Pesach.[7]

4. If any of the above restrictions may result in a delay with possibly serious consequences, it is not to be applied.[8]

PERSONS FORBIDDEN TO CONSUME
MATZAH, *MAROR* OR WINE

5. A person with celiac disease, who is on a *strict* gluten-free diet and may eat nothing containing wheat flour, is exempt from eating matzah made from wheat flour and, indeed, is forbidden to eat it against the physician's instructions. The physician should be consulted as to whether matzah may be prepared for the patient from oats. Gluten-free flour is *chametz*.

6. No credit is due to a patient who, contrary to medical advice, consumes matzah, *maror* or wine on Pesach. In fact, this is a classic example of a *"mitzvah* performed by transgression,"[9] or, in the opinion of some authorities, no *mitzvah* at all, just a transgression.[10] It should be borne in mind by the physician and the patient that lettuce may be used for *maror*, and grape juice may take the place of wine.

7. No matzah may be eaten on the day preceding Pesach.[11] After the middle of the morning preceding Pesach, one may not even consume matzah prepared without water;[12] nor may a full meal of any kind be taken.[13]

(7) אוו״ח סי׳ תנ מ״ב ס״ק יח.

(8) שם.

(9) שו״ת מהר״י אסאד סי׳ קס. וראה שו״ת ציץ אליעזר חי״ב סי׳ מג.

(10) שו״ת מהרי״ם שיק אוו״ח סי׳ רס. שו״ת מנחת יצחק חי״ד סי׳ קב אות ב.

(11) אוו״ח סי׳ תעא סעי׳ ב בהגה. חק יעקב שם ס״ק א. מג״א שם. כף החיים שם ס״ק ג.

(12) אוו״ח סי׳ תעא סעי׳ ב. וראה סי׳ תסב.

(13) אוו״ח סי׳ תעא סעי׳ א.

MEDICINES

8. No pleasant-tasting medicine, such as lozenges or syrup, containing *chametz* may be consumed on Pesach, no matter how small the quantity of *chametz*, except by a seriously ill patient (see Chapter 1, paragraph 1).[14]

9. If the medicament is unpalatable, even a patient who is non-seriously ill (see Chapter 1, paragraph 2) may take it.[15]

THE *SEDER* NIGHT: ILL PERSONS

10. A patient or an elderly person who finds it difficult to eat the required amount of matzah in its solid form on the *Seder* night may crush it.[16] If the patient is unable to eat it dry, it may be taken with a gulp of water.[17] If this is too difficult, the matzah may be softened beforehand in cold water[18] or, when absolutely necessary, in wine or some other liquid.[19]

11. One should make every effort to drink the four cups of wine on the *Seder* night, even if doing so may result in a headache or a hangover.[20] Wine that has been boiled, wine made of raisins, and grape juice are all acceptable for the four cups.[21]

12. A person is exempt from drinking the four cups of wine or grape juice if doing so might lead to illness severe

---

(14) שמירת שבת כהלכתה פ״מ סע׳ עד.

(15) רמב״ם הל׳ יסודי התורה פ״ה ה״ח. דרכי תשובה יו״ד סי׳ קנה ס״ק כח. חזו״א או״ח סי׳ קטז ס״ק ח. שו״ת אג״מ או״ח ח״ב סי׳ צב וח״ג סי׳ סב. חזון עובדיה עמ׳ סז. שו״ת ציץ אליעזר ח״י סי׳ כה פ״ק. שמירת שבת כהלכתה פ״מ סע׳ עד.

(16) ברכי יוסף סי׳ תסא ס״ק א. ביה״ל שם ד״ה יוצא.

(17) שו״ת בנין ציון סי׳ כט.

(18) מ״ב סי׳ תסא ס״ק יח. ולא ישרה אותם מעת לעת מ״ב שם ס״ק יז.

(19) מג״א שם ס״ק ז. מ״ב שם ס״ק יח.

(20) או״ח סי׳ תעב סע׳ י.

(21) חזון עובדיה עמ׳ קכה.

enough to require bed rest.[22] This rule applies also to eating *maror*[23] (see paragraph 6 above). If a patient thinks that the matzah might be harmful to him and the physician considers it to be safe, the physician's opinion prevails.[24]

13.   A person who cannot eat an olive's bulk (30 cc.) of matzah or *maror* within four minutes[25] should not pronounce the benediction *Al achilat matzah* or *Al achilat maror*, respectively;[26] nor should *Birkat Ha-mazon* be recited after eating the matzah.[27]

14.   A person who consumed matzah, *maror* or wine on the *Seder* night in order to comply with the respective *mitzvah* and then vomited fulfilled the *mitzvah* once the substance was swallowed and need not repeat the *mitzvah*.[28] If this happens after the meal, *Birkat Ha-mazon* should not be recited.[29]

15.   One should preferably consume the matzah and the wine while reclining on one's left side.[30] A person who does not have a right hand or is unable to use it for eating need not recline.[31]

(22) מ״ב סי׳ תעב ס״ק לה. חזון עובדיה שם.

(23) חזון עובדיה עמ׳ קעג.

(24) כי הכלל של ״לב יודע מרת נפשו״ שייך רק לגבי מצב של רעבון ולא לגבי מצבים אחרים שו״ת שרידי אש ח״ב סי׳ קנח. וראה מה שכתב הגרא״י וולדינברג שליט״א בנשמת אברהם או״ח עמי שמב אות ח.

(25) שיעורין דאורייתא בשיעורי המצוות סעי׳ כט. שיעורי תורה סי׳ ג סעי׳ טז. וההבדל בין פסח ליוהכ״פ הוא שביוהכ״פ מדובר על איסור אכילה ובפסח על חיוב אכילה, ומכיון שבשניהם הספק הוא בדיני דאורייתא, נקטינן לחומרא לכאן ולכאן. וראה כף החיים סי׳ רי ס״ק ח ושו״ת חת״ס חי״ו סי׳ טז וסי׳ כג.

(26) או״ח סי׳ תעה סעי׳ א ומ״ב ס״ק ט ו־יב. ביה״ל סי׳ תסא סעי׳ ד ד״ה יוצא.

(27) שמירת שבת כהלכתה פי״מ סעי׳ צג.

(28) שו״ת תורה לשמה או״ח סי׳ קכה.

(29) שם. בן איש חי שנה א פ׳ חקת סעי׳ יג. ברכ״יי סי׳ רח ס״ק א.

(30) או״ח סי׳ תעב סעי׳ ג.

(31) שמעתי ממו״ר הגרי״י נויבירט שליט״א. וראה ביה״ל שם ד״ה ואין. נשמת אברהם שם ס״ק א (עמ׳ רסט).

THE *SEDER* NIGHT: MEDICAL PERSONNEL

16. A physician or an attendant who is likely to be occupied with patients and therefore not able to carry out the complete *Seder* before midnight (the midpoint between sunset and sunrise, which is not necessarily the same as 12 o'clock) should act as follows, depending on the amount of time available:[32]

a. Even if extremely busy, one should try at least to recite *Kiddush,* wash one's hands and pronounce the benediction *Al netilat yadayim,* recite the benedictions *Ha-motzi* and *Al achilat matzah* and eat two olives' bulk (60 cc.) of matzah,[33] one for the *mitzvah* of matzah and the other as the *afikoman,*[34] eating them separately and each within a period of four minutes.[35] If this is not possible, a total of one olive's bulk will suffice for both purposes.[36] However, in this case, the benediction *Al netilat yadayim* should not be pronounced when the hands are washed.[37] The passage *"Rabban Gamliel hayah omer..."* and the *Birkat Ha-mazon* should then be recited.

Before commencing to eat the *afikoman,* one should bear in mind that a full meal might possibly be eaten later (since ordinarily nothing but water, tea, or the like may be consumed after the *afikoman*).[38]

b. If more time is available, one should, in addition, eat an olive's bulk (30 cc.) of *maror,* after reciting the appropriate benediction, and then eat the second olive's bulk of matzah for

---

(32) מהא דדגול מרבבה סי׳ תעז. שערי תשובה שם. מ״ב שם ס״ק ו. כף החיים שם ס״ק י. חזון עובדיה עמ׳ קסז. מעדני שמואל סי׳ קיט ס״ק מד. וראה שו״ת אבני נזר או״ח סי׳ שפא ס״ק ה.

(33) מ״ב סי׳ תעה ס״ק ט וביה״ל ד״ה כזית.

(34) מהא דמ״ב סי׳ תפב סוס״ק ו.

(35) מ״ב סי׳ תעה ס״ק ט. שיעורין דאורייתא בשיעורי המצוות סע׳ כט. שיעורי תורה סי׳ ג סע׳ טז.

(36) מ״ב שם ס״ק יא וביה״ל ד״ה כזית.

(37) או״ח סי׳ קנח סע׳ ב.

(38) שמעתי ממו״ר הגרי״י נויבירט שליט״א.

the *afikoman*.[39] If possible, one should first eat a small quantity of *karpas*, in order to pronounce the *Borei peri ha-adamah* benediction. This benediction is not pronounced on the *maror*.[40] If and when one is able to complete the *Seder* and eat a meal, it is not necessary to eat *maror* again.

    c. With more time available, the first two passages of *Hallel* should be recited, and the second cup of wine should be drunk after the benediction *Asher ge'alanu* has been recited. Matzah and *maror* are eaten as stated above. Following *Birkat Ha-mazon*, the third cup of wine is drunk. The remaining part of *Hallel* is then recited, and the fourth cup of wine is drunk after the appropriate benediction has been recited.

    At the termination of one's duties, the following rules apply:

    a. If duty terminates *before* midnight (see the beginning of paragraph 16), the rest of the *Seder* (depending at which of the above stages it had to be discontinued) should be carried out. *Ha-motzi* is recited over two whole *matzot* at the beginning of the meal and *maror* is eaten after the appropriate benediction (if it has not already been eaten).[41]

    b. If duty terminates only *after* midnight (see the beginning of paragraph 16), an olive's bulk (30 cc.) of *maror* is eaten (if it has not already been eaten) without reciting the appropriate benediction,[42] and the rest of the *Seder* is carried out (depending at which of the above stages it had to be discontinued).[43]

---

(39) כי עדיף לאכול כזית מרור, שבאכילתו יש מצוה דרבנן ומברכים עליה מלאכול אפיקומן שאינו אלא לזכר שמעתי ממו"ר הגרי"י נויבירט שליט"א.

(40) כף החיים סי' תעג ס"ק קט. נשמת אברהם או"ח סי' תעז ס"ק א (עמי רעב) ד"ה ולגבי.

(41) מ"ב סי' רעד ס"ק א. ערוה"ש סעי' ה. ולגבי ברכת אשר גאלנו וחתימת הלל בברכה, ראה נשמת אברהם שם עמ' רעג ד"ה ואם הוא.

(42) ביה"ל סי' תעז ד"ה ויהא.

(43) מ"ב שם ס"ק ז ושעה"צ ס"ק ו.

17. If there is no time before midnight (see the beginning of paragraph 16) to carry out any of the above *mitzvot*, the *Seder* should be conducted any time prior to daybreak,[44] but without reciting *Al achilat matzah* and *Al achilat maror*.[45] The benediction *Borei peri ha-gafen* should be recited on the first and third cups of wine only, even if the person is an Ashkenazi.[46]

18. It should be emphasized that, if a physician is called urgently to treat a patient, he must go immediately, even if, as a result, he may not be able to carry out any of the duties of the *Seder*.

19. All the above rules apply also to the second *Seder* night observed in the Diaspora.[47]

(44) מג״א סי׳ תפה ס״ק א. שערי תשובה בהקדמה לסי׳ תפב.

(45) מ״ב סי׳ תעז ס״ק ו וביה״ל ד״ה ויהא.

(46) שמעתי מהגרש״ז אויערבאך שליט״א. נשמת אברהם שם ד״ה ואם לא.

(47) או״ח סי׳ תפא סע׳ ב בהגה.

16 / CHANUKAH

1. A patient who is confined to bed and cannot get up to kindle the Chanukah lights by the door or a window should not light them next to the bed and have someone else move them. Rather, another person should kindle them in the correct place on behalf of the patient.[1] If this is not possible, they should be kindled by the bedside and left there.[2]

2. The wife of a blind man should perform the *mitzvah* of the Chanukah lights on his behalf. An unmarried blind man who is home with others should take part in the *mitzvah* by making a token payment toward the cost of the oil or candles. If he lives alone, he should kindle the lights with the help of another, but he should not recite the benedictions.[3]

3. The wife of a hospitalized patient should kindle the Chanukah lights at home and bear in mind to include her husband in the *mitzvah*.[4]

4. The *mitzvah* of Chanukah lights ordinarily should not be performed with electric lights.[5] But a hospitalized patient who has no alternative should perform the *mitzvah* with electric lights and not recite the benedictions.[6]

---

(1) שערים מצויינים בהלכה סי׳ קלט ס״ק טז. וראה מ״ב סי׳ תרעא ס״ק ל וסי׳ תרעה ס״ק ו.

(2) שמעתי ממו״ר הגרי״י נויבירט שליט״א.

(3) בן איש חי שנה א פ׳ וישב סע׳ טו (טו). מ״ב סי׳ תרעה ס״ק ט. כף החיים שם ס״ק כג.

(4) מהא דמ״ב סי׳ תרעז ס״ק ב. וראה שם ס״ק טז.

(5) שו״ת בית יצחק יו״ד ח״א סי׳ קכ. שו״ת הר צבי או״ח ח״ב סי׳ קיד אות ב. כף החיים סי׳ תרעג ס״ק יט. שו״ת ציץ אליעזר ח״א סי׳ כ פי״ד. הגרש״ז אויערבאך שליט״א בספר מאורי אש עמי צה.

(6) שו״ת יביע אומר ח״ג סי׳ לה.

17 / PURIM

1. One should not eat a meal before hearing the reading of the *Megillah* on Purim eve, even if the fast (of Esther) has been difficult.[1] If necessary, light refreshment may be taken.[2]

2. One who is unable to go to the synagogue should wait until after the evening service to have the *Megillah* read to him. If such a prolongation of fasting is difficult, he may take light refreshment. Should this not suffice, he may have the *Megillah* read for him any time after *pelag ha-minchah* (one and a quarter hours before sunset, an hour, in this case, being one-twelfth of the period from dawn to dusk).[3]

3. Should it be necessary to eat before the reading of the *Megillah*, and light refreshment is not sufficient, the patient should ask to be reminded to hear the reading of the *Megillah* after the meal.[4]

4. In the morning one may not eat before the reading of the *Megillah* even if *Shacharit* has been recited.[5]

5. A hospitalized patient should try to arrange for the *mitzvot* of *mishlo'ach manot* and *mattanot la-evyonim* to be performed on his behalf by another person.

(1) או״ח סי׳ תרצב סע׳ ד בהגה.

(2)מ״ב שם ס״ק יד.

(3) או״ח שם וביה״ל ד״ה מפלג. מ״ב שם ס״ק יד.

(4) מ״ב שם ס״ק טז.

(5) מ״ב שם ס״ק טו ושעה״יצ ס״ק כז.

18 / TISHA B'AV (THE FAST OF THE NINTH OF AV)

Tisha B'Av is the most important of all fasts other than Yom Kippur.

1. One may not eat meat or drink wine during the week in which Tisha B'Av occurs,[1] and some abstain from the first of the month of Av.[2] Any patient suffering from even a minor illness (see Chapter 1, paragraph 3), is permitted meat and wine.[3]

2. A person who must eat animal protein should consume poultry rather than meat. However, if for reasons of health meat is advisable, the person should not refrain from it.[4]

3. A patient, even a non-seriously ill one (see Chapter 1, paragraph 2), who needs to eat on Tisha B'Av should not hesitate to do so, since the fast was not instituted for those who are ill.[5] However, it is customary to fast as long as doing so does not cause distress or possibly lead to serious consequences. A patient who wishes to eat may do so;[6] but if possible, he should eat later than usual so as to fast at least for a short while. If one has to eat, only the amount needed for physical well-being should be consumed.[7]

(1) או"ח סי' תקנא סעי' ט.

(2) שם ומ"ב ס"" נח.

(3) וה"ה יין, הגה שם ומ"ב ס"ק סא.

(4) מ"ב שם ס"ק סד.

(5) או"ח סי' תקנד ומ"ב ס"ק יא.

(6) הגה שם.

(7) חיי אדם כלל קלה סעי' ב. וי"א שאם די לו בשתיה לא יאכל שו"ת חתם סופר או"ח סי' קנז. שו"ת מהר"ם שיק או"ח סי' רפט. שדי חמד מערכת בהמ"צ סי' ב אות ג. וראה שו"ת משנת יעב"ץ או"ח סי' מט.

4. A person who has not completely recovered from an illness should not fast if fasting might lead to a relapse. Although one does not need to eat in limited measures (as required in some cases on Yom Kippur), one should nevertheless eat only what is needed to sustain health.[8]

5. A person suffering only minor discomfort (see Chapter 1, paragraphs 3 and 4) is required to fast.[9]

6. A patient who needs to eat on Tisha B'Av should, if it occurs on a Sunday, first recite *Havdalah*.[10] He should preferably make *Havdalah* on a halachically acceptable beverage other than wine[11] since in any case he needs to take liquids for his health, while wine is not essential to his health.[12] However, if he does make *Havdalah* on wine, it should be given to a child to drink.[13]

7. A woman who needs to eat on Tisha B'Av should, if it occurs on a Sunday, first ask her husband or another male to make *Havdalah* for her. The rulings stated in the previous paragraph apply in this case as well.[14]

8. A patient who needs to eat on Tisha B'Av may be called up to the reading of the Torah during *Shacharit*. He should not be called up to the reading during *Minchah*[15] unless

(8) כף החיים סי׳ תקנד ס״ק לא.

(9) ערוך השולחן סי׳ תקנד סע׳ ז.

(10) כף החיים סי׳ תקנו ס״ק ט.

(11) או״ח סי׳ תקנו.

(12) שמירת שבת כהלכתה פס״ב סע׳ מו. אך עיין שו״ת יחוה דעת ח״ג סי׳ מ. ומה נקרא חמר מדינה, ראה שמירת שבת כהלכתה פ״ס סע׳ ג-ח.

(13) ברכי יוסף סי׳ תקנו ס״ק ב ו-ג. שערי תשובה שם ס״ק א. שדי חמד מערכת בהמ״צ סי׳ ב אות ה. ארחות חיים סי׳ תקנו ס״ק ב.

(14) שמירת שבת כהלכתה שם סע׳ מח.

(15) ראה שו״ת חתם סופר או״ח סי׳ קנז שמתיר גם במנחה. וראה שו״ת רעק״א (פסקים) סי׳ כד ומ״ב סי׳ תקסו ס״ק כא.

he has eaten only in statutory measures[16] (see paragraph 4 above).

9.   It is preferable, though not mandatory, not to eat a new fruit during the three weeks preceding Tisha B'Av, so as to avoid pronouncing the *Shehecheyanu* benediction.[17] However, a pregnant woman or any patient who so desires may eat a new fruit, preferably choosing the Sabbath or *Rosh Chodesh* on which to do so.[18]

10.   A pregnant woman or anyone who is ill may take a hot bath during the week of Tisha B'Av if it gives relief or comfort.[19] However, on Tisha B'Av itself this is forbidden.[20]

11.   A patient who has been instructed by a physician to swim daily may do so even on the day before Tisha B'Av.[21]

PREGNANT WOMEN, CHILDBIRTH AND NURSING MOTHERS

12.   It is customary for a woman after childbirth to refrain from partaking of meat and wine from the seventh day of Av if it falls within the same week as Tisha B'Av,[22] but only if she is completely well.[23]

13.   The rules concerning fasting on Tisha B'Av by a pregnant woman or a nursing mother are similar to, but not quite the same as, those for Yom Kippur.[24]

14.   A woman may not fast during the seven days

(16) הגרש"ז אויערבאך שליט"א.

(17) או"ח סי' תקנא סע' יז. וראה מ"ב שם ס"ק צט. כף החיים שם ס"ק ריד.

(18) הגרש"ז אויערבאך שליט"א.

(19) מ"ב סי' תקנא ס"ק פח.

(20) שעה"צ שם ס"ק צד.

(21) שמעתי ממו"ר הגרי"י נויבירט שליט"א.

(22) מג"א סי' תקנד ס"ק ט.

(23) מ"ב סי' תקנא ס"ק סא.

(24) או"ח סי' תקנד סע' ה.

following childbirth even if she feels capable of so doing.[25]

15. From the eighth to the end of the thirtieth day following childbirth, a woman may eat as soon as she feels the need to eat.[26] However, if she is certain that she will be able to fast, she should do so.[27]

16. Even after childbirth a woman should try to postpone her regular mealtime for a few hours, unless doing so causes some measure of discomfort.[28]

17. A mother who is breast-feeding a baby who cannot, for one reason or another, be fed artificial milk, should consume all the food and drink that she requires on Tisha B'Av.[29]

18. If Tisha B'Av coincides with the Sabbath, the fast is postponed to Sunday. In such a case a woman within thirty days of childbirth need not fast.[30]

(25) מ״ב שם ס״ק יג.

(26) שם סעי׳ ו.

(27) מ״ב שם ס״ק יב.

(28) שערי תשובה סי׳ תקנד ס״ק ז.

(29) ברכי יוסף סי׳ תקנד ס״ק ה. שערי תשובה שם ס״ק ו. וראה לעיל הערה 7.

(30) מג״א סי׳ תקנד ס״ק ט. סי׳ תקנ״ט סעי׳ ט ביה״ל ד״ה ואינו. שו״ת יביע אומר ח״ה סי׳ מ אות ה.

19 / FAST DAYS OTHER THAN YOM KIPPUR AND TISHA B'AV

This chapter discusses public fast days: the Third of Tishrei (the Fast of Gedalyah), the Tenth of Tevet, the Thirteenth of Adar (the Fast of Esther) and the Seventeenth of Tammuz.

1.   Patients, including those who are non-seriously ill (see Chapter 1, paragraph 2), should not fast on these days, even if they wish to do so[1] (see paragraph 2 below).

2.   Pregnant women and nursing mothers need not fast on these days,[2] particularly if the fast distresses them.[3] However, it is not appropriate for them to eat a hearty meal on a fast day; just enough should be eaten to ensure the well-being of the pregnant woman or the nursing mother and her child.[4]

3.   For the purposes of these rules, the state of pregnancy starts when it is noticeable by others. However, should the woman not feel well, she should not fast any time during her pregnancy.[5]

4.   A person who is fasting and suffers a headache may, in order to obtain relief, take pills without water if the medicament is not agreeably flavored. If it is pleasant to the taste, it should be taken in capsule form.[6]

(1) מ״ב סי׳ תקנ ס״ק ד.

(2) או״ח סי׳ תקנד סע׳ ה.

(3) או״ח סי׳ תקנד סע׳ א בהגה. מ״ב ס״ק ה. שעה״צ ס״ק ג.

(4) או״ח סי׳ תקנד סע׳ ה. מ״ב סי׳ תקנ ס״ק ה.

(5) מ״ב סי׳ תקנ ס״ק ג ושעה״צ ס״ק ב.

(6) הגרש״ז אויערבאך שליט״א.

20 / MEDICAL ATTENDANCE ON PARENTS

The Torah commands us to honor our parents, to revere them and, of course, not to cause them any harm or injury. Problems may thus arise when parents require medical attention.

1. A person may treat a parent by injection or by other traumatic methods for medical purposes, only if no one else is available to do so.[1] The parent's express permission should be obtained if possible.[2]

2. A parent who has become mentally confused should be taken care of by a son or daughter as long as possible. If the parent has become so deranged that he or she can no longer be taken care of by them, others who are competent may be delegated to do so.[3]

3. If a mentally confused and restless parent is causing severe problems at home, and in the physician's opinion needs to be tied down to a bed or a chair, the son or daughter may not do so. The patient should be placed in the care of others who can carry out the physician's instructions.[4] If the parent is likely to harm himself, his son or daughter may tie him down until institutional care is available.[5]

4. If an ill parent requires private nursing care but

‫(1) יו״ד סי׳ רמא סע׳ ג בהגה. בן איש חי שנה ב פ׳ שופטים סע׳ כד. גשר החיים ח״ב פ״א‬
‫סי״ק ג. שו״ת חלקת יעקב ח״ב סי׳ לט. הגרש״ז אויערבאך שליט״א בגשר החיים שם עמ׳‬
‫טז. וראה שו״ת הר צבי יו״ד סי׳ קצז.‬

‫(2) מנחת חינוך מצוה מח סי״ק ב. ערוך השולחן יו״ד סי׳ רמא סע׳ ו. שו״ת מנחת יצחק ח״א‬
‫סי׳ כז.‬

‫(3) יו״ד סי׳ רמ סע׳ י. וראה שם ט״ז סי״ק יד.‬

‫(4) שו״ת ציץ אליעזר ח״ב סי׳ נט.‬

‫(5) שמעתי ממו״ר הגרי״י נויבירט שליט״א.‬

cannot afford it, it is incumbent upon the children to care for their parent as well as they can. This applies to a son, an unmarried daughter,[6] and a married daughter whose husband does not object.[7]

5. If a parent is suffering from a serious illness (see Chapter 1, paragraph 1), and insists on being informed by his children of the nature of the ailment, this should not be done if it is likely to cause the parent to lose hope and thus result in further deterioration of the parent's condition.[8]

6. If a physician orders that a patient not be given a particular food and the patient asks one of his or her children for it, the child should not comply.[9]

7. A blind person should stand up to honor his or her parent on becoming aware that the parent has entered the room. Similarly, one should stand up to honor a blind parent who enters the room.[10]

8. A proselyte who is requested by his or her ailing parent to visit, must comply with the parent's wish.[11]

9. When praying for an ill parent, one should mention the parent by name, adding only the title "my father" or "my mother" before the name.[12]

10. An ill person, one of whose relatives has died, should not be informed if such knowledge is likely to affect the patient mentally and thereby result in a serious deterioration of

(6) יו״ד סי׳ רמ סע׳ יז.

(7) ש״ך שם ס״ק יט.

(8) שערים מצויינים בהלכה סי׳ קצג ס״ק ב. וראה ש״ך סי׳ שלח ס״ק א.

(9) ערוך השולחן סי׳ רמ סע׳ מא. וראה שם ברכי יוסף ס״ק י.

(10) פ״ת שם ס״ק ו. וראה נחלת צבי שם. שערים מצויינים בהלכה סי׳ קמג ס״ק ה.

(11) שו״ת אגרות משה יו״ד ח״ב סי׳ קל.

(12) ברכי יוסף יו״ד סי׳ רמ ס״ק ד. הגהות רעק״א על או״ח סי׳ קיט סע׳ א. שו״ת תשובה מאהבה ח״ג סי׳ רמ. שו״ת ציץ אליעזר רמת רחל סי׳ יג.

the patient's condition.[13] Even if the deceased was a parent, for whom the patient would ordinarily have to say *Kaddish*, such a patient should not be informed.[14]

11. One may care for his or her parent even when this involves contact with those parts of the body that are normally covered, if no one else is available to do so.[15]

(13) יו״ד סי׳ שלז סע׳ א.

(14) בית הלל שם.

(15) נשמת אברהם אהע״ז סי׳ כג ס״ק ט (עמ׳ קיט).

21 / DENTAL TREATMENT

1. A tolerable toothache may not be treated on the Sabbath or on a Festival.[1]

2. If the toothache is such as to affect the whole body (see Chapter 1, paragraph 2), medicines may be taken on the Sabbath or on a Festival.[2]

3. If the pain is severe, or if the gums are swollen (even without pain), or if the toothache is accompanied by an elevated temperature, the patient is to be treated by all the necessary means on the Sabbath or on a Festival, even if this involves the setting aside of Torah prohibitions.[3]

4. During *chol ha-moed* (the intermediate days of the Festivals) one may receive treatment for even minor dental problems[4] (see Chapter 11, paragraph 7).

5. On fast days other than Yom Kippur, a person being treated by a dentist may rinse the mouth during treatment.[5] The patient should be careful, however, not to swallow any of the fluid.[6] This also applies to Tisha B'Av if there is a real need for dental treatment.[7]

6. One may suck and swallow blood from a bleeding tooth or gum,[8] but not on the Sabbath or on a Festival.[9]

---

(1) או״ח סי׳ שכח סע׳ א ומ״ב ס״ק י וביה״ל ד״ה ומצטער.

(2) מ״ב שם סוס״ק קב.

(3) או״ח שם סע׳ ג. ועל אף שהמ״ב שם ס״ק י כותב שעקירת השן אינה מותרת ע״י ישראל בשבת, זהו משום שבזמנם עקירת שן היתה בגדר של רפואה שאינה ידועה — שו״ת ציץ אליעזר ח״ח סי׳ טו פי״י. וכן שמעתי ממו״ר הגרי״י נויבירט שליטי״א.

(4) מהא דאו״ח סי׳ תקלב סע׳ ב ומ״ב ס״ק ה.

(5) או״ח סי׳ תקסז סע׳ א.

(6) חיי אדם כלל קלב סע׳ כ. מ״ב סי׳ תקסז ס״ק יא.

(7) חיי אדם ומ״ב שם.

(8) יו״ד סי׳ סו סע׳ י.

(9) מג״א סי׳ שכח סוס״ק נג. שו״ע הרב שם סי׳ נד. מ״ב שם סוס״ק קמז.

22 / DISEASES AFFECTING THE EYE

1. Even a mild eye infection may be treated on the Sabbath or on a Festival with eye drops or oral medication, since the patient is in the category of the non-seriously ill[1] (see Chapter 1, paragraph 2f).

2. A person who has a severe pain in or infection of the eye or who suddenly loses his sight is considered seriously ill (see Chapter 1, paragraph 1), and all the Sabbath laws are set aside for him as necessary.[2]

3. If a *niddah* needs to have eye drops administered and no one but her husband is available to help, he may do so, but if possible without touching her.[3]

See Chapter 23, paragraphs 4-17, regarding the blind.

(1) שמירת שבת כהלכתה פל"ג סע' א ס"ק ו. פל"ד סע' ח

(2) או"ח סי' שכח סע' ט.

(3) דרכי תשובה יו"ד סי' קצה ס"ק נו. ואם אי אפשר בלי שיגע בה מותר — שמעתי מהגרש"ז אויערבאך שליט"א.

23 / THE HANDICAPPED

THE PARALYZED AND THE AMPUTEE

1. One who is unable to walk without a cane or a crutch may walk with either of them in the street on the Sabbath.[1] If it is used only as an added precaution, it should not be taken into the street on the Sabbath[2] unless there is an *eruv*.[3]

2. A person who is confined to a wheelchair may leave the house in it on the Sabbath (as long as no form of motor or electricity is used, of course) if there is an *eruv*.[4]

If there is no *eruv* the cripple may go out only for the purpose of fulfilling a *mitzvah* such as attending synagogue or learning Torah, and then a distinction is made between an indefinite and a definite public domain[5] (competent halachic opinion must be sought): (a) If the public domain is *not definite*, the cripple may go out either propelling the chair himself by hand or having a non-Jew propel it. (b) If the public domain is a *definite* one, the cripple may go out only if both he and a non-Jew together propel the chair.[6]

All articles that are not necessary for the cripple's immediate transport must be removed from the chair and pockets. A cushion for support or sitting on may be left in the chair,[7] but

(1) או"ח סי' שא סע' יז ומ"ב ס"ק סג. ערוך השולחן שם סע' ע. והוא הדין לגבי יום טוב ארחות חיים סי' תקכב ס"ק א. פמ"ג מ"ז ס"ז ס"ק א.

(2) סי' שא סע' יז. תקכב סע' א בהגה.

(3) שערי תשובה סי' שא ס"ק ב. שו"ת נודע ביהודה מהדו"ת סי' כח. שו"ת שואל ומשיב מהדו"ת סי' עד. ערוך השולחן סי' שא סע' עא. שמירת שבת כהלכתה פי"ח סע' יג.

(4) שערי תשובה סי' שא ס"ק ג. שו"ת נודע ביהודה מהדו"ק סי' יא. ערוה"ש סי' תקכב סע' ב.

(5) שמירת שבת כהלכתה פי"ז סע' ג. ועיין שם פל"ד סע' כז במושג של רשות הרבים "גמורה".

(6) שו"ת מנחת יצחק ח"ב סי' קיד. וכן כתב לי הגר"ע יוסף שליט"א. וכן שמעתי מהגרש"ז אויערבאך שליט"א. וראה שו"ת הר צבי או"ח ח"א סי' קע. שמירת שבת כהלכתה פל"ד סע' כז.

(7) שמירת שבת כהלכתה שם.

not crutches needed for later use.[8]

3. One may go out on the Sabbath wearing an artificial limb.[9]

THE BLIND

4. A blind person is obligated to carry out all the *mitzvot*,[10] including those that relate to sight, such as *tzitzit*.[11] He recites the benedictions *Poke'ach ivrim*[12] and *Yotzer ha-meorot*,[13] and, if a *kohen*, he pronounces the priestly benediction.[14]

5. A blind person may lead prayer services.[15]

6. A blind person may be called up to the Torah,[16] and he is obligated to hear the reading of the Torah and of the *Megillah*.[17]

7. A blind person should preferably hear *Havdalah* from someone else. If no one else is available, the benediction *Borei meorei ha-esh* should not be pronounced.[18]

8. The wife of a blind person should light Chanukah

(8) שמעתי ממו״ר הגריי״י נויבירט שליט״א.

(9) מהא דאו״ח סי׳ שא סע׳ טו ומ״ב ס״ק נו. שמירת שבת כהלכתה פי״ח סע׳ טו.

(10) פמ״ג או״ח סי׳ שא בא״א ופתיחה כוללת סוף ח״ב. מ״ב שם ס״ק מא.

(11) או״ח סי׳ יז סע׳ א ומ״ב ס״ק א. שו״ת רב פעלים ח״ב או״ח סי׳ ז. שו״ת שבות יעקב ח״ב סי׳ לח.

(12) מ״ב סי׳ מו ס״ק כה.

(13) או״ח סי׳ סט סע׳ ב.

(14) ראה פרטי דינים או״ח סי׳ קכח סע׳ ל וביה״ל שם ד״ה וכן. וראה שו״ת רדב״ז סי׳ לט וסי׳ ב׳ אלפים קיז. שו״ת יעב״ץ ח״א סי׳ עה.

(15) או״ח סי׳ נג סע׳ יד. וראה מ״ב ס״ק מא.

(16) כף החיים סי׳ קלט ס״ק טו. וכן שמעתי מהגרש״ז אויערבאך שליט״א. וראה או״ח סי׳ נג סע׳ יד. סי׳ קלט סע׳ ג ומגי״א ס״ק ד. ט״ז סי׳ קמא ס״ק ג. קיצור שו״ע סי׳ כג סע׳ יז. מ״ב סי׳ קלט ס״ק יב.

(17) שו״ת רדב״ז סי׳ תתסז (תכה). פמ״ג פתיחה כוללת סוף ח״ב.

(18) או״ח סי׳ רצח סע׳ יג ומ״ב ס״ק לד. ולפי הגר״ע יוסף שליט״א גם שאר ההבדלה אינו אומר. וראה כף החיים סי׳ רצח ס״ק סח. נשמת אברהם סי׳ רצח ס״ק א (עמ׳ קכג).

candles on his behalf. If the blind person is unmarried and lives with others who light Chanukah candles, he should take part in the *mitzvah* by making a token payment toward the cost of the oil or candles. If he lives alone, he should kindle the lights himself with the help of others, but he should not recite the benedictions.[19]

9. When *Kiddush Levanah* is being recited, a blind person should ask a sighted person to include him in the latter's *Birkat Ha-levanah*, and he may then recite the rest of the prayer himself.[20]

10. A blind woman should light Sabbath candles with the help of another person and recite the benediction over them even if she lives alone. If she is married and her husband is not blind, it is preferable that he light the candles and recite the benediction. If she was married and now lives with others who light Sabbath candles, she too should light candles after them, but not pronounce the benediction.[21]

11. A blind person may not go out with a cane on the Sabbath if there is no *eruv*.[22]

12. A blind person may go out with his guide dog on the Sabbath.[23]

(19) מור וקציעה סי׳ תרעה. בן איש חי שנה א פ׳ וישב סע׳ טו (טו). מ״ב סי׳ תרעה ס״ק ט. כף החיים שם ס״ק כג.

(20) ברכי יוסף או״ח סי׳ רכד ס״ק א ומחזיק ברכה סי׳ רכט ס״ק ו. בן איש חי שנה ב פ׳ ויקרא סע׳ כד. כף החיים סי׳ תכו ס״ק ב. שו״ת יחוה דעת ח״ד סי׳ יח הערה יב.

(21) או״ח סי׳ רסג מ״ב ס״ק יד. קיצור שו״ע סי׳ עה סע׳ יג. מג״א סי׳ רסג ס״ק ט. פמ״ג א״א שם. וראה מחצית השקל ס״ק ט ומ״ב ס״ק יד. שמירת שבת כהלכתה פמ״ג סע׳ י.

(22) או״ח סי׳ שא סע׳ יח. שמירת שבת כהלכתה פי״ח סע׳ יג. וראה ערוה״ש סע׳ עב דאם אינו יכול ללכת כלל בלי מקל, דינו כחיגר שמותר לו לצאת במקלו. וכן הוא בעטרת זקנים על שו״ע סי׳ תקכב. וע״יש פמ״ג מ״ז ס״ק א. ולהלכה יש לשאול שאילת חכם — שמירת שבת כהלכתה שם הערה סב.

(23) שו״ת אגרות משה או״ח ח״א סי׳ מה ד״ה ולכן כיון. שו״ת לב אריה ח״ב סי׳ ז. וראה אג״מ שם, שו״ת חלקת יעקב ח״ג סי׳ פז ושערים מצויינים בהלכה סי׳ יג ס״ק ב בנוגע לכניסתו לבית הכנסת עם הכלב.

13. A blind person whose wife is a *niddah* may go out with her on the Sabbath even though she may have to help him avoid colliding with objects or other people by pulling on his sleeve or, if unavoidable, his hand. However, this is permitted only for the purpose of attending synagogue or performing some *mitzvah*, not just going for a walk.[24] The same ruling applies if the wife is blind and a *niddah*.[25]

14. One may turn on a light on the Sabbath for a seriously ill patient (see Chapter 1, paragraph 1) even if the person is blind, because the patient is reassured by the knowledge that thereby he or she can be cared for properly[26] (see also Chapter 10, paragraph 35).

15. One should not have a blind child committed to a non-Jewish institution, unless the child can there receive treatment not otherwise available.[27]

16. A blind person should stand up on becoming aware that a parent or a *talmid chacham* has entered the room.[28] Similarly, a person should rise when a blind parent or *talmid chacham* enters the room.[29]

17. A blind person may not pray or study Torah in the presence of excreta[30] (for details, see Chapter 9, paragraphs 1-3).

(24) שמעתי מהגרש״ז אויערבאך שליט״א. וראה דרכי תשובה יו״ד סי׳ קצה ס״ק ז ושו״ת ציץ אליעזר חי״ב סי׳ נח.

(25) הגרש״ז אויערבאך שליט״א.

(26) או״ח סי׳ של סע׳ א ומ״ב ס״ק ג ו־ד.

(27) שו״ת מהרי״ם שיק או״ח סי׳ קסג. וראה חכמת שלמה או״ח סוסי׳ שכח. הגרש״ז אויערבאך שליט״א בנשמת אברהם יו״ד סי׳ פא ס״ק ב (עמי״ט).

(28) יו״ד סי׳ רמ פ״ת ס״ק ו. וראה נחלת צבי שם.

(29) שערים מצויינים בהלכה סי׳ קמג ס״ק ב.

(30) או״ח סי׳ עט סע׳ א. חיי אדם כלל ג סע׳ יב ו־יג.

THE DEAF

18. A deaf person is obligated to carry out all the *mitzvot*[31] except that of *shofar*.[32]

19. A deaf person should recite the benediction ...*la-sechvi vinah*,[33] but should wait until daylight to do so.[34]

20. A deaf person may form part of a *minyan*[35] if he is able to make the appropriate responses by observing those made by the congregation.[36] If there is no *minyan* without him, the *Amidah* is not repeated.[37]

21. A deaf person may use a hearing aid on the Sabbath provided that it was turned on before the Sabbath.[38] One may adjust the volume on the Sabbath if doing so does not cause a wire to reach red heat when the current is increased[39] or cool from red heat when the current is reduced.[40] Expert technical advice should be obtained before the Sabbath.

22. A hearing aid may not be worn in the public domain on the Sabbath unless there is an *eruv*.[41]

THE MUTE

23. A mute person (who can hear) is obligated to carry out all the *mitzvot*, including those dependent upon speech,

(31) או״ח סי׳ נה סע׳ ח. פמ״ג פתיחה כוללת חי״ב סי״ק ד.

(32) סי׳ תקפ״ט סע׳ ב.

(33) מ״ב סי׳ מו סי״ק כה.

(34) חיי אדם כלל ח סע׳ א.

(35) או״ח סי׳ נה סע׳ ח. כף החיים סי״ק נב. וכי״כ שו״ת רשב״ץ חי״ג סי׳ קיג.

(36) מ״ב שם סי״ק לח וראה בן איש חי שנה א פ׳ ויחי סע׳ ו וכף החיים שם סי״ק נג.

(37) אלא מתפללים בקול רם עד הא-ל הקדוש. שמעתי ממו״ר הגרי״י נויבירט שליטי״א.

(38) שו״ת יביע אומר חי״א סוסי׳ יט.

(39) שמירת שבת כהלכתה פל״ד סע׳ כח.

(40) הגרש״ז אויערבאך שליט״א שם הערה קז.

(41) שו״ת הר צבי או״ח חי״א סי׳ קעג. שמירת שבת כהלכתה פל״ד סע׳ כח. וראה שו״ת מנחת יצחק חי״א סי׳ לז וח״ב סי׳ יז וסי׳ קיב שכתב להתיר, אולם חזר בו בח״ב סי׳ קיג (אחרי שראה את ההר צבי).

such as recital of the *Shema*, the *Amidah*, *Birkat Ha-mazon* after meals and the benedictions before the performance of *mitzvot*. He should, therefore, either utter them silently or listen to another person who recites them with the intention of including him in the pronouncements.[42]

THE DEAF-MUTE

24. A deaf-mute is not obligated to perform *mitzvot*.[43] However, if he has been taught to speak, he is treated as a deaf person with regard to *mitzvot*,[44] and he may be counted to form a *minyan* if without him there would not be one; in that case the *Amidah* is not repeated.[45]

(42) או״ח סי׳ נה סע׳ ח. שו״ת שאגת אריה סי׳ ו. פמ״ג פתיחה כוללת ח״ב ס״ק ד.

(43) או״ח סי׳ נה סע׳ ח.

(44) שמעתי מהגרי״ע יוסף שליטא״א. וראה שו״ת יחוה דעת ח״ב סי׳ ו. נחלת צבי ח״א עמ׳ סא. שו״ת מהרש״ם ח״ב סי׳ קמ. ויש חולקים שו״ת מהר״ם שיק אהע״ז סי׳ עט. שו״ת דברי חיים אהע״ז סי׳ עב. שו״ת זכר שמחה סי׳ ט. וראה שו״ת דברי מלכיאל ח״ו או״ח סי׳ לה. שו״ת צמח צדק סי׳ עג. שו״ת משפטי עוזיאל אהע״ז סי׳ פט. וראה גם מה שכתבו הגרח״פ שיינברג והגרש״ז אויערבאך שליטא״א, מוריה אלול תשמ״ב עמי נא ו־סה.

(45) ויתפלל שמונה עשרה בקול רם עד סוף הא־ל הקדוש. הגרי״ע יוסף שליטא״א, לב אברהם ח״ב עמי יג. שו״ת יחוה דעת ח״ב סי׳ ו.

24 / MENTAL ILLNESS

1. *Halachah* does not differentiate between physical and mental illness, and the psychiatric patient also is categorized as enumerated in Chapter 1. Thus, where necessary, the laws of the Sabbath, Yom Kippur, *kashrut*, etc., are set aside for him as explained previously for the patient with a physical illness. In all cases, competent halachic authority must be consulted.[1]

2. A Jewish patient should not be committed to a non-Jewish hospital for psychiatric care if he will be given forbidden foods, unless there is a question of danger to life.[2]

3. One may commit a mentally retarded child to a non-Jewish institution for treatment or training, but the child should be taken out upon reaching age thirteen, if a boy, or twelve, if a girl, unless it is possible to arrange for kosher food to be provided.[3] However, a child who is so severely retarded that there is no possibility of corrective treatment or training may be committed indefinitely to a non-Jewish instititon.[4]

4. A person in need of psychiatric help should, if possible, consult a psychiatrist or psychologist who is an observant Jew. If such a person is not available, one may consult any expert, after having been assured by him that he will not discuss matters of faith or Torah with the patient.[5]

5. A patient who is at times normal and at other times mentally disturbed is obligated to perform *mitzvot* like any other person during the times when he is normal.[6]

(1) שו"ת ציץ אליעזר ח"ד סי' יז אות ג, ח"ח סי' טו פי"ב אות ה.

(2) שו"ת אגרות משה יו"ד ח"ב סי' נט. וראה גם שו"ת מלמד להועיל ח"ב סי' לא.

(3) שו"ת חתם סופר או"ח סי' פג.

(4) הגרש"ז אויערבאך שליט"א, נשמת אברהם יו"ד סי' פא ס"ק ב (עמ' יט). שו"ת אג"מ יו"ד ח"ב סי' פח.

(5) שו"ת אג"מ שם סי' נז.

(6) או"ח סי' נה סע' ח. וראה יו"ד סי' א סע' ה.

6. A severely mentally retarded person is not obligated to perform *mitzvot*.[7]

7. A seriously mentally ill person (see Chapter 36, paragraph 2) should recite the *Ha-gomel* benediction upon recovery.[8] However, on recovery from attempted suicide the benediction should not be pronounced.[9]

8. The Sabbath laws are set aside, if necessary, in order to prevent serious mental illness which could endanger life.[10]

(7) חו״מ סי׳ לה סע׳ ט. ביה״ל או״ח שם סוד״ה הוא.

(8) שו״ת ציץ אליעזר חי״ב סי׳ יח אות ח.

(9) שו״ת יחוה דעת ח״ד סי׳ יד. שו״ת ציץ אליעזר חי״י סי׳ כה פכ״ג.

(10) הגרש״ז אויערבאך שליט״א, נשמת אברהם אהע״ז סי׳ קמה ס״ק ג (עמ׳ קסא).

25 / THE STUDY OF MEDICINE

The study and practice of medicine are essential for the welfare of mankind.[1]

1.   A physician may study medical texts on the Sabbath.[2]

2.   Rather than ask a non-Jewish student to make a carbon copy of notes of lectures given on the Sabbath, one should copy them after the Sabbath.[3] However, one may ask a non-Jew to make a carbon copy for himself, promising to buy it from him after the Sabbath.[4]

3.   The use of animals in medical research and investigation is not prohibited on account of cruelty to animals[5] (see Chapter 29, paragraph 1). However, all possible care must be taken to avoid causing animals unnecessary suffering.

4.   One must be careful during bedside teaching and rounds to say or do nothing that might embarrass the patient or cause him or her to worry. It is proper that the patient's permission first be obtained for bedside teaching.[6]

(1) שו״ת רשב״א ח״א סי׳ תטו. שאילת יעב״ץ ח״א סי׳ מא. שו״ת חלקת יעקב ח״א סי׳ פד. וראה ספר חסידים סי׳ תתרתרסט ופירוש הר״ע מברטנורה נדרים פ״ד מ״ד ד״ה רפואת.

(2) באר היטב או״ח סי׳ שז ס״ק כ. ושמעתי מהגרש״ז אויערבאך שליט״א דרופא ודאי מותר וקעביד נמי מצוה.

(3) שו״ת מנחת יצחק ח״ה סי׳ לו.

(4) או״ח סי׳ שז סע׳ ג ומ״ב ס״ק יג. סי׳ תמח סע׳ ד ומ״ב ס״ק כג. ארחות חיים סי׳ שז ס״ק ה. שמירת שבת כהלכתה פל״א סע׳ טו.

(5) אהע״ז סי׳ ה סע׳ יד בהגה. קיצור שו״ע סי׳ קצא סע׳ א. חידושי חת״ס על שבת קנד ע״ב וב״מ לב ע״ב. שו״ת שבות יעקב ח״ג סי׳ עא. שו״ת בנין ציון סי׳ קח. שו״ת שרידי אש ח״ג סי׳ ז. שו״ת חלקת יעקב ח״א סי׳ ל ו-לא.

(6) שו״ת ציץ אליעזר חי״ג סי׳ פא.

26 / THE PHYSICIAN

1. The fact that the Torah permits medical treatment of the sick renders it a *mitzvah* for the physician to provide it, and to avoid doing so is equivalent to "shedding blood."[1] If the patient is seriously ill and requests to be treated by a particular physician, that physician should treat him even if others are available.[2]

2. Physicians are encouraged to practice preventive medicine.[3]

3. A person may not practice medicine without qualification from a recognized school of medicine.[4]

4. A patient, even when in need of medical help, should realize that ultimately cure is not due to a particular physician or treatment[5] but depends on Divine Providence, for whose mercy we pray, for, as Scripture says (*Deuteronomy* 32:39): "I strike and I heal." But the Almighty has so willed it that the physician is, in the natural order of things, the agent for healing.[6]

5. One may not treat patients with the medicaments

(1) יו״ד סי׳ שלו סע׳ א. שו״ת ציץ אליעזר ח״ד סי׳ יג. וראה גם פירוש המשניות להרמב״ם פסחים פ״ד מ״י ונדרים פ״ד מ״ד וברמב״ם הלכות נדרים פ״ו ה״ח. וראה מהר״ץ חיות על ב״ק פא ע״ב ופי׳ ר״ע מברטנורה נדרים פ״ד ד״ה רפואת. מדרש שמואל פ״ד על הפסוק אנוש כחציר ימיו, מובא בדברי שאול יו״ד סי׳ שלו. רש״י ב״ק פה ע״א ד״ה ניתנה. תוס׳ שם ד״ה שניתנה. החיד״א פתח עינים ב״ק שם. נשמת אברהם יו״ד בהקדמה לסימן שלו (עמ׳ רכ).

(2) ערוך השולחן יו״ד סי׳ שלו סע׳ א.

(3) קל וחומר מהא דהרמב״ם הל׳ גזילה ואבידה פי״א ה״כ. וראה גם שם הל׳ רוצח פי״א ה״ד. חו״מ סי׳ רנט סע׳ ט. נשמת אברהם יו״ד סי׳ שלו ס״ק ד (עמ׳ רכח).

(4) שיורי ברכה או״ח סי׳ שכח ס״ק ט ויו״ד סי׳ שלו ס״ק א. ערוך השולחן יו״ד סי׳ שלו סע׳ ב.

(5) יד אברהם יו״ד סי׳ שלו. שו״ת הרשב״א ח״א סי׳ תיג.

(6) יו״ד סי׳ שלו בט״ז ס״ק א. שו״ת הרשב״א שם.

that are suggested in the Talmud. These cannot be identified with certainty, the dosages and exact instructions for administration are not known,[7] and times and conditions have changed.[8]

6. If a patient dies as a result of a genuine error on the part of a physician, the physician is not held guilty.[9]

7. A physician who while praying or having been called up to the reading of the Torah is urgently needed to treat a patient should leave immediately,[10] even if the time for that particular prayer will have passed by the time he finishes tending the patient.[11]

8. A person ordinarily may not leave his home during the seven days of mourning, but a physician in mourning may go to treat any patient who feels that this particular physician would be able to help.[12] It is preferable that the physician not accept payment for services rendered, but he may receive reimbursement for expenses incurred.[13]

9. A physician may drive a car or be driven by another Jew on the Sabbath and the Festivals if necessary in order to treat a patient who is seriously ill (see Chapter 1, paragraph 1; Chapter 10, paragraphs 113-119); but the physician may not

(7) חידושי רעק״א יו״ד שם ס״ק א. כף החיים להגר״ח פאלאג׳י סי׳ כד סע׳ נ. שו״ת חות יאיר סי׳ רלד.

(8) תוס׳, מו״ק יא ע״א ד״ה כוורא, ע״ז כד ע״ב ד״ה פרה וחולין מז ע״א ד״ה כל. ים של שלמה חולין פ״ח סי׳ יב. הרב חיד״א בברית עולם על ספר חסידים סי׳ תעז. וראה תפארת ישראל בועז שבת פי״ט ס״ק א. או״ח סי׳ שלא סע׳ ט. אהע״ז סי׳ קנו סע׳ ד בהגה. מג״א סי׳ קעג ס״ק א וסי׳ קעט ס״ק ח. חזו״א נשים סי׳ כז ס״ק ג ויו״ד סי׳ ה ס״ק ג.

(9) שו״ת ציץ אליעזר ח״ד סי׳ יג וח״ה רמת רחל סי׳ כג. הגרש״ז אויערבאך שליט״א, לב אברהם ח״ב פי״ד סע׳ ה הערה 17 ועמי׳ יט. נשמת אברהם יו״ד סי׳ שלו ס״ק ז (עמי׳ רל).

(10) שו״ת ציץ אליעזר ח״ט סי׳ יז פי״ז.

(11) שו״ת לב חיים סי׳ קמח. שו״ת ציץ אליעזר שם וח״י סי׳ יג.

(12) שו״ת שבות יעקב ח״א סי׳ פו. פי״ת יו״ד סי׳ שפ ס״ק א. הגרש״ז אויערבאך שליט״א, נשמת אברהם יו״ד סי׳ שפ ס״ק א (עמי׳ רפג).

(13) הגרש״ז אויערבאך שליט״א שם.

return by car unless it will probably be needed again during the Sabbath for a seriously ill patient.[14]

10.   A physician may travel by car within the city boundaries on the Sabbath and the Festivals in order to visit a non-seriously ill patient (see Chapter 1, paragraph 2) if he is driven by a non-Jew and is not able to reach the patient on foot. He also may return home that way.[15] (Similarly, essential personnel may be brought to and from duty in a hospital by a non-Jew.) If the physician uses public transportation and has to pay for it, a non-Jew should, if possible, be asked to make the payment. Where there is an *eruv*, a token, pre-paid ticket or pass may be used. Otherwise, the required fee may be paid, but the money should be carried in an unusual manner,[16] and no change may be accepted.[17]

11.   Where there is no *eruv*, a physician may not carry a medical bag, etc., except to visit a patient who is seriously ill[18] (see Chapter 1, paragraph 1). Similarly, a physician may not carry a beeper outside a private domain unless there is an *eruv*.[19]

12.   Physicians and nurses in hospitals outside Israel should make every effort to avoid working on the Sabbath and the Festivals. They should either exchange their day of duty for a Sunday or any other weekday, even if thereby they have to work more than their share of days, or they should pay a non-Jewish colleague to take their tour of duty.[20]

14) שמירת שבת כהלכתה פ"מ סע' סט. שו"ת ציץ אליעזר חי"א סי' לט.

15) שמירת שבת כהלכתה שם.

16) הגרש"ז אויערבאך שליט"א, שמירת שבת כהלכתה פל"ח הערה נא.

17) שמירת שבת כהלכתה פל"ח סע' יג. או"ח סי' שכט סע' ט ומ:ב ס"ק כ.

18) שמירת שבת כהלכתה פ"מ סע' י.

19) שמעתי מהגרש"ז אויערבאך שליט"א. ואמנם מתיר השו"ת אג"מ או"ח ח"ד סי' פא אך צ"ע אם טעמו עוד נכון היום.

20) שו"ת אג"מ או"ח ח"ד סי' עט. הגרש"ז אויערבאך שליט"א, שמירת שבת כהלכתה פל"ב הערה קכה. נשמת אברהם או"ח סי' רמה ס"ק א (עמ' קד).

13.   A computer may not be used on the Sabbath, either to type in information or to obtain a print-out. Even though typing in the information on the screen and storing it in the diskette does not involve a Torah prohibition of writing, it does involve a Torah prohibition of "construction" since the diskette has now been converted into something of greater worth.[21]

14.   Although one is not obligated to endanger one's own life in order to save the life of another, a physician and paramedical staff should treat patients with infectious diseases (including AIDS), even at risk to themselves. Indeed, this is considered a great *mitzvah*.[22]

15.   Medical personnel may not strike if doing so could possibly cause harm to patients.[23]

16.   On the battlefield, everyone, whether he is a physician or a soldier, is duty bound to risk his life for the sake of his fellow.[24]

With regard to the treatment of parents, see Chapter 20.

TRIAGE (THE MEDICAL SCREENING OF PATIENTS
TO DETERMINE THEIR PRIORITY FOR TREATMENT)

17.   One may not sacrifice a life for a life. It is forbidden to save oneself or another, even a person of outstanding learning and piety who serves the world at large, by means which hasten the death of another person, even one who is very aged, mentally incapacitated and a burden to others.[25] Thus, if a physician has already *started* treating a patient, such treatment may not be interrupted for the benefit of another patient. This

21) שמעתי מהגרש"ז אויערבאך שליט"א. וראה בשמירת שבת כהלכתה פס"ו הערה ריא ופס"ח הערה קכד.

22) שו"ת ציץ אליעזר ח"ט סי' יז פ"ה.

23) ראה נשמת אברהם חו"מ סי' שלג ס"ק א.

24) שו"ת ציץ אליעזר חי"ב סי' נז.

25) הגרש"ז אויערבאך שליט"א, נשמת אברהם יו"ד סי' רנב ס"ק ב (עמ' קנו).

applies to treatment by the physician personally, to the use of equipment such as a respirator, when there is only one available, or to the mandatory use of an intensive-care bed. No matter what the medical or other status of the two patients may be, nothing is permitted that could result in the sacrifice of the patient who is already under treatment for the benefit of the other.

18.   If two patients come into the emergency room or the physician's office at the same time, or are already present when the physician arrives, and they are in the same category of illness (see Chapter 1), and are equally ill, the physician should treat them according to the priorities laid down in the Mishnah.[26] If they did not arrive at the same time and have the same medical status, the physician may treat them on a "first come, first served" basis, unless there is some valid reason for giving the later arrival priority over the earlier.

However, if one patient would certainly die if not treated immediately whereas it is not certain that the other would, the physician should first treat the patient who would certainly die. Similarly, if one patient has no chance (or only a very small chance) of survival even if treated and the other stands a good chance of survival if treated, the latter should be given priority.[27]

(26) הוריות יג ע״ב. יו״ד סי׳ רנא סע׳ ט. וראה גם הגרי׳עב״ץ מגדל עוז אבן בוחן פנה א ס״ק צא, צב.

(27) פרי מגדים או״ח סי׳ שכח מ״ז ס״ק א. שו״ת ציץ אליעזר ח״ט סי׳ יז ס״ק ה וסי׳ כח ס״ק ג. שו״ת אגרות משה חו״מ ח״ב סי׳ עג אות ב.

27 / THE PHYSICIAN'S FEE

1. Although a physician may not charge for specialized knowledge,[1] a fee may be requested for the time and effort spent.[2] A patient is legally bound to pay an agreed-upon fee, even if he considers it exorbitant.[3]

2. A physician may charge for services confirming death and for issuing the appropriate certificate.[4]

3. A physician who refuses to treat a patient who is unable to pay for his services may be compelled to render them if no other physician is available.[5]

4. A patient must pay for legitimate medical expenses incurred by others on his behalf.[6]

SABBATH FEES

5. A physician may accept a fee after the Sabbath for services rendered on the Sabbath.[7]

6. A Jewish physician who is in partnership with a non-Jew should make it a condition of the partnership that the

(1) יו"ד סי' שלו סע' א ש"ך וט"ז שם.

(2) שם סע' ב. נשמת אברהם יו"ד סי' שלו ס"ק ט (עמ' רלב).

(3) יו"ד שם סע' ג ש"ך ס"ק ז. ואסיא דמגן במגן מגן שוה ב"ק פה ע"א. וראה גם סמ"ג מ"ע עד.

(4) שו"ת מהר"ם שיק יו"ד סי' שמג.

(5) שו"ת תשובה מאהבה ח"ג יו"ד סי' תח (שלו). הגרא"י וולדינברג שליט"א, לב אברהם ח"ב עמ' כד. נשמת אברהם יו"ד סי' שלו סוס"ק יט (עמ' רלד).

(6) חו"מ סי' קח סע' א. ערוך השולחן שם סע' ג. סמ"ע שם ס"ק ט. וראה נשמת אברהם חו"מ סי' קח ס"ק א (עמ' קפה), סי' רסד ס"ק א (עמ' קצח) וסי' תכו ס"ק א (עמ' רמא).

(7) שו"ת ציץ אליעזר ח"ח סי' טו פי"ג. מהרש"ם על ארחות חיים סי' שו ס"ק ה. מ"ב או"ח סי' שו ס"ק כד. מנחת שבת סי' צ ס"ק יט. יסודי ישורון ח"ד עמ' רעב. שו"ת הר צבי או"ח ח"א סי' רד. שערים מצויינים בהלכה סי' צ ס"ק ז. שמירת שבת כהלכתה פל"ב סע' יב. שו"ת יביע אומר ח"ה סי' כה.

non-Jew receive the fees of the Sabbath while he takes the fees of another day of the week; the fees for the remaining five days may then be divided between them.[8] The non-Jewish physician should be on duty on the Sabbath and the Jew on another day of the week (see also Chapter 26, paragraph 12).

7.   In a partnership between an observant and a non-observant Jewish physician, only the fees of the six weekdays may be divided between them, so that the observant physician takes nothing of the Sabbath earnings.[9]

(8) או״ח סי׳ רמה סע׳ א ומ״ב בהקדמה לסימן.

(9) שו״ת לבוש מרדכי סי׳ ג, מובא ביסודי ישורון ח״ג עמ׳ קיז. שו״ת מלמד להועיל או״ח סי׳ לד. נשמת אברהם או״ח סי׳ רמה ס״ק א (עמ׳ קד).

28 / CONFIDENTIAL MEDICAL INFORMATION

1. One may not divulge medical information concerning a patient to anyone other than those members of the family who need such information.[1]

2. However, if the non-disclosure of such information might cause harm to others, it is the duty of the physician to reveal the appropriate information to the party concerned. Thus the family of a patient and those who have come into contact with the patient should be informed if he is suffering from an infectious disease. The spouse of a patient who is a carrier of the AIDS virus should be informed, so that appropriate steps can be taken to avoid infection of the spouse.[2] The appropriate authorities should be notified if an uncontrolled epileptic patient insists on driving.[3]

3. A person *may* be told if his or her spouse-to-be has an illness that may affect married life or future children.[4] If the prospective spouse's illness is fatal, the person *should* be told.[5] Similarly, when a condition is present which might severely affect the married life of the prospective partner (such as certain inability to beget children), that person *should* be informed.[6]

4. A person who knows that he or she is a carrier of the gene for Tay-Sach's disease should inform the prospective spouse so that the appropriate test can be performed in order to determine whether or not they are both carriers.[7]

(1) שו״ת ציץ אליעזר חי״ג סי׳ פא.

(2) שמעתי מהגרש״ז אויערבאך שליט״א.

(3) שו״ת ציץ אליעזר שם סי׳ קד. שו״ת יחוה דעת ח״ד סי׳ ס.

(4) הגרש״ז אויערבאך שליט״א, נשמת אברהם אהע״ז סי׳ ב ס״ק א
(עמ׳ כז) מהא דחפץ חיים הל׳ איסורי רכילות כלל ט ציור שלישי סע׳ ד.

(5) שו״ת חלקת יעקב ח״ג סי׳ קלו.

(6) שו״ת ציץ אליעזר חט״ז סי׳ ד.

(7) שו״ת אגרות משה אהע״ז ח״ד סי׳ י.

5. Evidence must be given in court, when required, in order that justice be done.[8]

6. A battered child must be removed from its culpable parent in order to save it from further injury and danger.[9]

(8) שו״ת ציץ אליעזר חי״ג סי׳ פא.

(9) הגרש״ז אויערבאך שליט״א, נשמת אברהם חו״מ סי׳ תכד ס״ק ב (עמי ריט).

ANIMAL

1.   Scientific research using animals is permitted if its purpose is to help mankind.[1] All possible care must be taken to avoid causing the animals unnecessary suffering.

2.   It is forbidden to feed the animals food prepared by cooking meat or its derivatives together with dairy products, even if the cooking was done by a non-Jew.[2]

3.   During Pesach one may not feed the animals anything containing *chametz*. If this is unavoidable, the animals, together with their food, should be sold to a non-Jew before Pesach and he should take care of them.[3] Such animals may not be used for research purposes during Pesach.[4]

4.   It is forbidden to castrate a male or spay a female animal.[5]

5.   During *chol ha-moed* only research that had already been started before the Festival may be carried out, and then only if its postponement would result in financial loss. A manuscript may not be prepared during these days, even if only as a draft.[6]

HUMAN

6.   One may not risk the life of one person in order to

(1) אהע"ז סי' ה סע' יד בהגה. שו"ת שבות יעקב ח"ג סי' עא. שו"ת בנין ציון סי' קח. שו"ת שרידי אש ח"ג סי' ז. שו"ת חלקת יעקב ח"א סי' ל ו-לא.

(2) יו"ד סי' פז סע' א. פמ"ג מ"ז שם סי"ק ב. פ"ת שם סי"ק ו. דרכי תשובה שם סי"ק לא.

(3) מהא דשו"ת אג"מ או"ח ח"א סי' קמז. נשמת אדם כלל קכד שאלה ח. תשובת מהרי"ם מרוטנברג, מובא בכף החיים סי' תמח סי"ק קט. ארחות חיים סי' תמח סי"ק כא. נודע ביהודה, בשו"ת תשובה מאהבה ח"א סי' מב. שו"ת חתם סופר או"ח סי' סב. וראה שדי חמד מערכת חמץ ומצה סי' ט סי"ק ג, מעדני שמואל על קיצור שו"ע סי' קיד סי"ק לה.

(4) שמעתי ממו"ר הגרי"י נויבירט שליט"א.

(5) הגרש"ז אויערבאך שליט"א, נשמת אברהם אהע"ז סי' ה סי"ק ט (עמ' נד).

(6) שמעתי ממו"ר הגרי"י נויבירט שליט"א.

save the life of another. Therefore, a physician may not endanger the life of one person in order to help another.[7] If no risk is involved and only minimal discomfort is caused, a person may agree to take part in a research project for the sake of others or for the advancement of medicine.[8] However, for the sake of a patient who is seriously ill (see Chapter 1, paragraph 1) not only is it permissible to volunteer to undergo a procedure that carries a relatively small risk (such as the donation of a kidney for transplantation into a patient with terminal kidney failure) but it is, indeed, meritorious to do so.[9]

7. A patient who is seriously ill (see Chapter 1, paragraph 1) and will in all probability die within a short period of time may, on expert advice, and with his consent, be given an experimental drug or other treatment that offers a chance of cure, even if there is also a risk that his life may thereby be further curtailed.[10]

8. As in all cases involving seriously ill patients (see Chapter 1, paragraph 1), such experimental treatment may be carried out on the Sabbath, even if this requires the setting aside of Torah prohibitions.[11]

(7) שו"ת רדב"ז סי' אלף נב (תרכז). מנחת חינוך מצוה רלז. פתחי תשובה חו"מ סי' תכו. שו"ת ציץ אליעזר ח"ח סי' טו פ"י.

(8) הגרש"ז אויערבאך שליט"א, נשמת אברהם יו"ד סי' קנז ס"ק ד(2) (עמ' סו).

(9) הגרש"ז אויערבאך שליט"א שם.

(10) שו"ת אחיעזר ח"ב סי' טז אות ו. שו"ת בנין ציון ח"א סי' קיא. מהרש"ם דעת תורה סי' שכח סע' י. שו"ת שבות יעקב ח"ג סי' עה. שו"ת ציץ אליעזר ח"ד סי' יג וח"י סי' כה פי"ז. וראה גם נשמת אברהם יו"ד סי' שמט ס"ק ג(ג)4 (עמ' רסה).

(11) שמירת שבת כהלכתה פל"ב סע' לו.

30 / AUTOPSIES

1.   There is almost complete consensus among halachic authorities in prohibiting the performance of an autopsy on a Jew for the purpose of studying medicine.[1] The reasons include the prohibition of desecration of the dead,[2] of deriving any benefit from the dead,[3] of delaying burial,[4] and of not burying the corpse or parts of it.[5]

2.   One may not will or sell one's body or part of it for the purpose of autopsy or anatomical dissection.[6] Even if this was done, the prohibition of performing such an autopsy or dissection remains in force.[7]

3.   An autopsy is, however, permitted and even mandatory if it may help to save the life of another *known* patient,[8] or in the case of a fatal familial illness, if other family members or

(1) נודע ביהודה יו״ד סי׳ רי. שאילת יעב״ץ ח״א סי׳ מא. שו״ת חתם סופר יו״ד סי׳ שלו. שו״ת מהר״ם שיק יו״ד סי׳ שדם ר־שמז. שו״ת בנין ציון סי׳ קע ו־קעא. חזון איש אהלות סי׳ כב ס״ק לב. כל בו אבלות ח״א סי׳ ג סע׳ יב. גשר החיים ח״א פ״ה סע׳ ו. שו״ת שרידי אש ח״ב סי׳ קיט. שו״ת יביע אומר ח״ג סי׳ כג אות כו. שו״ת אגרות משה יו״ד ח״ב סי׳ קנא וח״ג סי׳ קמ. שו״ת ציץ אליעזר ח״ד סי׳ יד. שו״ת מנחת יצחק ח״ה סי׳ ט. וראה רשימה ארוכה בהמעין שנת תשכ״ז טבת עמ׳ 43 וניסן עמ׳ 71 וספר אסיא ח״ד עמ׳ 32.

(2) דברים כא:כג. חולין יא ע״ב. נודע ביהודה שם. חת״ס שם. שו״ת שאגת אריה החדשות סי׳ ו. שו״ת כתב סופר יו״ד סי׳ קעד.

(3) שו״ת חת״ס שם. ש״ך יו״ד סי׳ עט ס״ק ג וסי׳ שמט ס״ק א. שאילת יעב״ץ שם.

(4) אנציקלופדיה תלמודית ערך הלנת המת, כרך ט עמ׳ תלח. כל בו אבלות ח״א סי׳ ג סע׳ יא.

(5) תוס׳ יו״ט שבת פ״י מ״ה. מנחת חינוך מצוה תקלז. שו״ת נודע ביהודה מה״ק יו״ד סי׳ כ. שו״ת ציץ אליעזר ח״ד סי׳ יד. וראה נשמת אברהם יו״ד סי׳ שמט ס״ק ב (עמ׳ רנה).

(6) הגרש״ז אויערבאך שליט״א, נשמת אברהם יו״ד סי׳ שמט ס״ק ב 3 (עמ׳ רנז).

(7) שו״ת אגרות משה יו״ד ח״ג סי׳ קמ.

(8) הגרי״י אריאלי ז״ל, תורה שבעל פה כרך ו, תשכ״ד עמ׳ מ, עפ״י הפוסקים המובאים לעיל הערה 1.

contacts may be helped.[9] The autopsy must be carried out with due reverence for the deceased and with only the minimum dissection required in order to confirm or negate the diagnosis. After the autopsy, care must be taken to bury all the separated parts together with the rest of the body.[10]

4. Autopsy of a fetus is prohibited.[11] However, if the mother has had repeated miscarriages and an autopsy of a fetus or of a child who died within thirty days of birth might help to prevent another miscarriage or perinatal death, an autopsy is permitted. The remains must be buried as usual.[12]

(9) הגר״י אריאלי שם. כל בו אבלות ח״א סי׳ יג סע׳ יב ס״ק 10.

(10) שו״ת משפטי עוזיאל יו״ד סי׳ כח ו־כט.

(11) הגר״י אריאלי ז״ל שם. וראה גם שו״ת בנין ציון סי׳ קיט ומהר״ם שיק יו״ד סי׳ שדמ.

(12) נשמת אברהם יו״ד סי׳ שמט ס״ק ב 4 בשם מו״ר הגר״י נויבירט שליט״א והגרש״ז אויערבאך שליט״א.

31 / BIOPSY

1. An urgent diagnostic biopsy may be performed on the Sabbath on a patient who is seriously ill (see Chapter 1, paragraph 1).

2. A diagnostic testicular biopsy may be performed on a man who has been persistently sterile.[1] It should preferably be done on the left testis.[2]

FROM A CORPSE

3. A needle biopsy specimen, blood or other fluids may be taken from a corpse for diagnostic purposes.[3]

(1) שו״ת אגרות משה אהע״ז ח,ב סי׳ ג. שו״ת מנחת יצחק ח״ג סי׳ קח. שו״ת ציץ אליעזר ח״ט סי׳ נא שער א פי״ב.

(2) שו״ת מנחת יצחק שם. שו״ת ציץ אליעזר שם.

(3) שו״ת אגרות משה יו״ד ח״ב סוסי׳ קנא. וכן שמעתי מהגרש״ז אויערבאך שליט״א.

32 / THE HOSPITAL

Much of the hospital routine should be altered or modified on the Sabbath and the Festivals. The details are discussed in this chapter.

1. Everything that is urgently and directly necessary for the health of a patient who is seriously ill (see Chapter 1, paragraph 1) must be performed on the Sabbath and on the Festivals as on a weekday.[1] If time is not of the essence, whatever needs to be done that involves the setting aside of Sabbath laws should be carried out in an unusual manner.[2]

WRITING

2. When a patient who is or may be seriously ill (see Chapter 1, paragraph 1) is first seen in the emergency room or the ward on the Sabbath or a Festival, one may write whatever information is essential for identification, so as to avoid any possibility of confusion. This includes the patient's full name, age, identity number and father's name. If possible, the writing should be done with the left hand[3] or, preferably, by a non-Jew.

3. The patient's complaints, the essential physical findings, and orders for investigations to be carried out or treatment to be given during the Sabbath should be documented, if possible, with the left hand or, preferably, by a non-Jew.

4. It is customary in many hospitals to attach a name tag to a newborn infant in order to avoid the possibility of interchange. The tag should be prepared, if possible, before the Sabbath. If this was not done or if the mother was admitted only on the Sabbath,

(1) או״ח סי׳ שכח סע׳ יב בהגה ומ״ב ס״ק לה.

(2) שמעתי מהגרש״ז אויערבאך שליט״א.

(3) מ״ב סי׳ שמ ס״ק כב אות ז.

the name may not be written on the Sabbath by a Jew. If a non-Jew is available, he may be requested to write the name on the tag. Otherwise, previously prepared numbered tags, with identical numbers for the mother and the infant, should be used. A non-Jew should be asked to tie on the tag. If a non-Jew is not available the tag should be secured with a safety pinw4 or a bandage clip. If this is not possible, one may tie a double knot while specifically having in mind to undo the knot immediately after the termination of the Sabbath.[5]

Regarding letters of discharge from a hospital, see paragraph 30 below.

Regarding death certificates, see paragraph 31 below.

PHYSICAL EXAMINATION OF THE PATIENT

5. A physical examination including pulse, temperature and blood pressure may be carried out in the usual way.[6] The results should be recorded by attaching previously prepared figures to the patient's chart with paper clips,[7] or the results may be written in by a non-Jew.

6. A folding screen may be opened on the Sabbath to screen the patient before examination or treatment, or so that the patient can rest. The screen should then be left in place to allow the patient to study Torah or recite prayers.[8]

THE USE OF INSTRUMENTS

7. Examination of the throat, fundus and ears, which

(4) שו"ת אג"מ או"ח ח"ב סי' פד, שו"ת מנחת יצחק ח"ב סי' יט, הגרש"ז אויערבאך שליט"א שמירת שבת כהלכתה פט"ו הערה רכד. וראה שם סע' ע שאם אפשר, אל יתחב את הסיכה פעמיים אלא פעם אחת בלבד.

(5) שמירת שבת כהלכתה פל"ו סע' יב.

(6) מהא דאו"ח סי' שו סע' ז מ"ב ס"ק לו. וראה גם בספר מאורי אש להגרש"ז אויערבאך שליט"א, דף לג ע"ב.

(7) ראה שו"ת חלקת יעקב ח"ג סי' קנא.

(8) שמירת שבת כהלכתה פ"מ סע' מב.

involves the use of lighted instruments, may be carried out, when necessary, only on patients who are or may be seriously ill (see Chapter 1, paragraph 1). The lights may not be switched off at the end of the examination, since it is a simple matter to put in new batteries when necessary. If the instrument is plugged into a wall socket at the patient's bedside, it must be left there at the end of the examination without the light being switched off, to be moved to the next seriously ill patient when necessary.

Electronic devices are now available whereby the light is automatically activated, for example, for two to three seconds every two minutes. If, when the light is off, a switch is moved, the light will stay on for ninety seconds (or any other pre-set period), allowing sufficient time for the instrument to be used to examine the patient. When the light goes out automatically, the switch is returned to its original position.[9]

8. Electrocardiography involves a number of Torah prohibitions, such as switching on lights, writing and tearing (of the strip from the roll), and may therefore be performed on the Sabbath only for a patient who is or may be seriously ill (see Chapter 1, paragraph 1). It is preferable, before the Sabbath, to remove the lamp that is activated when the machine is switched on. Information regarding the identity of the patient or treatment may be written on the strip; if possible, it should be written with the left hand or, preferably, by a non-Jew.

In the newer, computerized models, the relevant information is typed onto a screen and appears on the strip at the time that the cardiogram is produced. This type of model poses less of a problem in terms of Torah prohibitions and is to be preferred when available.[10] Writing must still be limited to the essential.

(9) מורשה, חורף תשל"יו עמ' 58.

(10) שמעתי ממו"ר הגרי"י נויבירט שליט"א. וראה מ"ב סי' שיח ס"ק יג מחלוקת אם האיסור במרבה בשיעורין בבת אחת הוא דאורייתא או דרבנן.

The electrocardiograph should be left switched on and plugged into the wall socket until needed elsewhere.

Electrocardiographic jelly may be used in order to obtain good electrical contact between the patient's skin and the leads of the electrocardiograph.[11]

9. Battery-operated instruments such as ophthalmoscopes and auroscopes should not be switched off after use, since the time lost in replacing the batteries, when necessary, is of no consequence. However, battery-operated instruments such as laryngoscopes, which must be ready for *immediate* use in an emergency, must be switched off after use.[12]

10. Radiography involves many Torah prohibitions, such as switching on lights and developing film.[13] Hence it may be performed on the Sabbath only for a patient who is or may be seriously ill (see Chapter 1, paragraph 1) for whom it is essential that he be X-rayed immediately.[14] For example, one should not X-ray a simple, uncomplicated broken finger on the Sabbath if no danger is involved in waiting till the termination of the Sabbath. "Routine" X-rays are prohibited on the Sabbath.

11. Radiography should not be performed on the Sabbath in order to confirm an obvious diagnosis.[15]

12. The X-ray viewing screen should remain lit throughout the Sabbath. If the screen is not lit and a film has to be viewed for a seriously ill patient (see Chapter 1, paragraph 1), one may switch on the light but, if possible, in an unusual manner (such as with the elbow or the back of the hand). Of

11) שמעתי ממו"ר הגריי"י נויבירט שליט"א ולא כפי שכתוב בשמירת שבת כהלכתה פ"מ סעי' לא.

12) שמעתי ממו"ר הגריי"י נויבירט שליט"א.

13) שו"ת שבט הלוי או"ח ח"א סי' קכא אות ג. שו"ת הר צבי יו"ד סי' רל. שו"ת יביע אומר ח"ד סי' כ. שו"ת אבני נזר או"ח סי' רג. מנחת שבת בדף האחרון.

14) שמירת שבת כהלכתה פ"מ סעי' לב.

15) מהא דאו"ח סי' שכח סעי' ד מ"ב ס"ק יד, ביה"ל ד"ה כל ושעהי"צ ס"ק יא.

course, the screen light may not be turned off on the Sabbath.

13.   Urgent endoscopic, bronchoscopic, etc., examinations of seriously ill patients (see Chapter 1, paragraph 1) may be carried out on the Sabbath, and biopsy specimens may be taken as necessary. The findings may be photographed[16] if this is required for follow-up of the patient, but not if purely for teaching purposes. The development of the film must be left till after the Sabbath.

14.   It is permitted to "beep" a physician, nurse or technician on the Sabbath for the sake of a patient. If, as a result, a light appears on the beeper or at the central call station, the beeper may be used only for the sake of a patient who is or may be seriously ill (see Chapter 1, paragraph 1).

15.   An internal telephone may be used on the Sabbath for the benefit of a patient, even if he is non-seriously ill (see Chapter 1, paragraph 2). If a light appears at the exchange when the receiver is lifted off the hook, it must be inactivated before the Sabbath; otherwise, use of the telephone must be restricted to cases involving seriously ill patients (see Chapter 1, paragraph 1). If a non-Jew is available to lift up and replace the receiver, an external line also may also be used even for a non-seriously ill patient[17] (see also Chapter 10, paragraphs 47-55).

16.   A physician may not carry a stethoscope, beeper, etc., from one hospital wing to another if in doing so he has to go out into the public domain, unless there is an *eruv* or he does so for the sake of a seriously ill patient (see Chapter 1, paragraph 1). In the latter instance, the instruments should, if possible, be carried in an unusual manner. Regarding the use of a computer, see Chapter 11, paragraph 12 and Chapter 26, paragraph 13.

(16) שו״ת הר צבי צבי יו״ד סי׳ רל. שו״ת שבט הלוי הלוי או״ח ח״א סי׳ קכא סע׳ ג.

(17) שו״ת יביע אומר ח״א סי׳ כ. וביום טוב מותר לטלפן אפילו עבור חולה שאין בו סכנה, כיון שרוב הפוסקים סוברים דהמצאת אש ביום טוב אסורה רק מדרבנן, וגם יתכן דחשיב כפסיק רישא דלא ניחא ליה כיון שהמחייג אינו צריך את הדלקת הנורה במרכזיה שמירת שבת כהלכתה פל״ג הערה כג׳ בשם הגרש״ז אוירבאך שליטי״א.

INVESTIGATIONS

17. The drawing of blood for purposes of examination, whether by pricking a finger or an earlobe, or drawing blood from a vein or an artery, is permitted on the Sabbath only for seriously ill patients[18] (see Chapter 1, paragraph 1). This procedure may be performed on such a patient even if the results will not become available till after the Sabbath, provided that it is necessary in order to obtain a diagnosis or provide treatment as speedily as possible. An autoanalyzer may be used on the Sabbath even if it automatically includes tests, on the same sample of blood, that are not necessary for the patient.[19]

18. Dipsticks may be used on the Sabbath for the examination of urine and feces, even for non-seriously ill patients[20] (see Chapter 1, paragraph 2).

19. Identification should be attached to specimen tubes with rubber bands to obviate writing on the labels. Previously prepared labels should not be stuck onto forms, glassware, etc., if this can be avoided.[21]

20. The results received from the laboratory on various patients should not be sorted on the Sabbath (neither into groups, one group for each patient, nor according to the order of the charts) before they are filed into the patients' charts. Instead, the physician or nurse should take a result at random, examine it, and then file it into the appropriate chart.[22]

(18) או"ח סי' שטז סע' ח מ"ב ס"ק ל.

(19) שמירת שבת כהלכתה פי"מ סע' כט. ולגבי הגדרה של מרבה בשיעורין, ראה שם פל"ב הערה צ. וראה נשמת אברהם או"ח סי' שכח ס"ק מא (עמ' קצב).

(20) שמירת שבת כהלכתה פל"ג סע' כ. וראה שם הערה פג בשם הגרש"ז אויערבאך שליט"א שמפקפק בזה.

(21) או"ח סי' שם סע' יד ביה"ל ד"ה ה"ז. שמירת שבת כהלכתה פי"מ סע' לד.

(22) שמירת שבת כהלכתה פי"מ סע' לה.

TREATMENT

21. A patient should not sign, or be asked to sign, a consent form on the Sabbath in order to permit the physician to carry out an urgent procedure. Verbal consent in the presence of two witnesses should suffice. If the physician insists that the patient sign a consent form before an urgently necessary procedure is carried out, the patient should initial the form with the left hand without adding punctuation or flourishes.[23]

22. The specific instructions of a physician for a seriously ill patient (see Chapter 1, paragraph 1) on the Sabbath must be carried out by the paramedical staff, even if they involve the setting aside of Torah prohibitions.[24]

23. All patients being treated in the post-surgical recovery rooms or in intensive-care units are considered to be seriously ill (see Chapter 1, paragraph 1), and the Sabbath rules are set aside for them as necessary.

24. A patient who is under continuous monitoring may move around freely in bed, even if doing so causes changes in the signals and tracings on the screen.[25]

25. A person who is seriously ill (see Chapter 1, paragraph 1) may, of course, undergo an operation on the Sabbath,[26] unless postponement of the operation till after the Sabbath would in no way threaten life or prejudice recovery.[27]

26. If it can be arranged, an elective operation should be performed during the first half of the week, so as to avoid the need later to set aside Sabbath laws during post-operative care. However, if it is unavoidable, such an operation may be per-

(23) שם סעי כא.

(24) או״ח סי׳ שכח סעי׳ י מ״ב ס״ק כה. יסודי ישורון ח״ד עמי רלט. שו״ת ציץ אליעזר ח״ח סי׳ טו פ״ז. שמירת שבת כהלכתה פל״ב סעי׳ כא.

(25) שמעתי ממו״ר הגרי״י נויבירט שליט״א.

(26) מהא דאו״ח סי׳ שכח סעי׳ ג.

(27) שם סעי׳ ד מ״ב ס״ק טו וביה״ל ד״ה שממתין.

formed as late as Friday, even though this might lead to the setting aside of Sabbath laws later.[28]

27. No preparations may be made on the Sabbath for an operation to be performed after the Sabbath, unless time is of the essence. Thus a patient may not be shaved or given an enema, nor may he undergo any blood tests, X-rays, etc., unless the postponement of such procedures until after the Sabbath would cause the delay of an urgent operation which has to be carried out immediately after the Sabbath.[29] A patient may not be prepared (e.g., by an enema) on the Sabbath for an *elective* examination, such as an X-ray, which is to be performed on the following day.

28. Most fractures and dislocations may be treated on the Sabbath, if necessary.[30]

29. The edges of a superficial cut may be brought together using previously prepared butterfly plasters. Regarding deeper cuts, bleeding should be stopped, if possible, by pressure. When only a short time remains before the termination of the Sabbath, such wounds should be sutured after the Sabbath. If the bleeding continues, or if the risk of infection does not allow delay, the cut should be sutured on the Sabbath.[31]

DISCHARGE

30. A patient who is taken to an emergency room on or before the Sabbath and is discharged on the Sabbath or who is discharged from a ward on the Sabbath should not ask for a letter of discharge.[32] It is preferable to stay in the hospital till

(28) שמעתי ממו״ר הגרי״י נויבירט שליט״א ומהגרש״ז אויערבאך שליט״א. שו״ת ציץ אליעזר חי״ב סי׳ מג. וראה שם סי׳ מו.

(29) שמירת שבת כהלכתה פי״מ סע׳ לח. וראה מ״ב סי׳ תרסז ס״ק ה ואו״ח סי׳ תקג.

(30) או״ח סי׳ שכח סע׳ מז ו־ל ומ״ב ס״ק קמה. ערוך השולחן שם סע׳ יח ו־לט. שו״ת ציץ אליעזר חי״ח סי׳ טו פ״י. שמירת שבת כהלכתה פל״ב סע׳ יא ופל״ג סע׳ יז.

(31) וראה שמירת שבת כהלכתה פל״ה סע׳ ד ו־כד.

(32) שם פי״מ סע׳ מד.

after the Sabbath. If he is in the category of a non-seriously ill patient (see Chapter 1, paragraph 2) and there is a possibility that he may require further treatment at home on the Sabbath, for which the details of his hospital stay may be important, a non-Jew may be asked to write the letter.[33]

DEATHS

31. A death certificate may not be written on the Sabbath, nor may one ask a non-Jew to write one. However, if the physician is going off duty on the Sabbath morning and will be unable to return to write the certificate after the Sabbath, before going off duty he may dictate it to a non-Jew, in order to avoid a delay of burial.[34]

THE DIASPORA

32. Physicians and nurses in hospitals outside Israel should make every effort to avoid working on the Sabbath and the Festivals. They should either exchange their day of duty for a Sunday or any other weekday, even if thereby they have to work more than their share of days, or they should pay a non-Jewish colleague to take their tour of duty.[35]

(33) שם.

(34) שמעתי ממו"ר הגרי"י נויבירט שליט"א והגרש"א אויערבאך שליט"א.

(35) שו"ת אגרות משה או"ח ח"ד סי' עט. הגרש"ז אויערבאך שליט"א שמירת שבת כהלכתה פל"ב הערה קכה. נשמת אברהם או"ח סי' רמה ס"ק א (עמי' קד).

33 / THE NURSE

1. A nurse should help patients to fulfill *mitzvot*, such as washing the hands on awakening in the morning[1] and before meals,[2] cleaning the surrounding area of excreta, etc. (see Chapter 9), and assisting patients to lay *tefillin*.[3]

2. Medical personnel may not take part in a strike if doing so might cause harm to patients.[4]

THE SABBATH AND FESTIVALS

3. If a physician has given instructions that involve setting aside Sabbath laws for a seriously ill patient (see Chapter 1, paragraph 1), the nurse must carry them out, even if she thinks differently.[5]

4. All needs or situations that can be anticipated before-hand should be prepared for before the Sabbath or the Festival, to the extent that this is possible, in order to avoid the setting aside of Sabbath or Festival laws.[6]

5. The Sabbath and Festival laws may not be set aside in order to prepare a patient for an elective examination or treatment scheduled to take place after the Sabbath or Festival. Thus a patient may not have blood taken, be shaved or be given an enema on these days in order to be prepared for an elective

---

(1) או"ח סי' ד סע' א.

(2) או"ח סי' קנח סע' א.

(3) שו"ת מהרם שיק או"ח סי' טו. שו"ת מהרי"י אסאד או"ח סי' יט. שו"ת יד הלוי או"ח ח"ב סי' א. שו"ת ציץ אליעזר חי"ג סי' ז. ולגבי טיפול אחות בגבר ראה אהע"ז סי' כא סע' ה בהגה. יו"ד סי' שלה סע' י בט"ז ס"ק ה.

(4) ראה נשמת אברהם חו"מ סי' שלג ס"ק א.

(5) שמירת שבת כהלכתה פל"ב סע' כא מהא דאו"ח סי' שכח סע' י ומ"ב ס"ק כה ו־כו. שו"ת ציץ אליעזר ח"ח סי' טו פי"ז. יסודי ישורון ח"ד עמ' רלט. שו"ת אגרות משה חו"מ ח"ב סי' עג אות ט.

(6) מ"ב סי' של ס"ק א.

operation or X-ray examination later.[7] However, if the examination or operation is urgent and requires preparation of the patient, this should be carried out on the Sabbath, even if the patient will not be ready for the examination or treatment until after the Sabbath.

6. All measurements, such as temperature (see Chapter 10, paragraphs 90-93), pulse rate, blood pressure and routine fluid balance, may be taken on the Sabbath.[8] The results should be recorded by attaching previously prepared figures to the patient's chart with paper clips[9] or should be written in by a non-Jew. In the case of a seriously ill patient (see Chapter 1, paragraph 1), vital information that may be lost or misplaced, such as blood group, types and amounts of fluids or medications given, results of pressures recorded by monitors or by hand, etc., should be written into the chart by a non-Jew. If a non-Jew is not available, the physician or the nurse should write them in, if possible with the left hand.[10]

7. A flashlight may be handled for patient care (within the hospital precincts), but it may not be switched on or off unless there is a question of serious illness[11] (see Chapter 1, paragraph 1).

8. The patient should preferably be washed with liquid soap.[12] If this is not available, then ordinary soap may be used.[13]

---

(7) מ"ב סי' תרסז ס"ק ה וסי' תקג.

(8) מהא דאו"ח סי' שו סע' ז ומ"ב ס"ק לו. וראה שו"ת חלקת יעקב ח"ג סי' כד. שו"ת אגרות משה או"ח ח"א סי' קכח. שו"ת ציץ אליעזר ח"ג סי' י וח"יא סי' לח. שו"ת מנחת יצחק ח"ג סי' קמב. מאורי אש דף 66. שמירת שבת כהלכתה פ"מ סע' ב.

(9) ראה שו"ת חלקת יואב ח"ג סי' קנא.

(10) ראה שמירת שבת כהלכתה פל"ב סע' מט.

(11) שמירת שבת כהלכתה פל"ג סע' ו. וראה שם שישתדל לטלטל את המוקצה דוקא על ידי שינוי.

(12) ערוך השולחן או"ח סי' שכו סוסע' יא. קצות השולחן סי' קמו בבדה"ש סוס"ק לב.

(13) שו"ת ציץ אליעזר ח"ח סי' טו פי"ד. שו"ת יביע אומר ח"ד סי' כז ו-כח.

The nurse should wash the patient with her bare hands or wearing plastic or rubber gloves, but should not use a sponge or a cloth.[14]

9. Patients who may develop pressure sores if not treated prophylactically may have the necessary treatment applied to the appropriate areas of the body, as described in paragraph 8 above.[15]

10. The nurse should also wash her hands, when possible, with liquid soap, before any treatment is carried out. If it is not available, ordinary soap may be used.[16]

11. One may tear the paper wrapping off a medication or a syringe[17] but should avoid tearing through print.[18]

12. One should not swab with alcohol- or iodine-soaked cotton wool or gauze, even if it is held with forceps or was soaked before the Sabbath.[19] Instead, one should do either of the following:

a. If nylon (non-absorbent) swabs are available, one should use them rather than absorbent cotton wool or gauze.[20]

b. If they are not available, one should pour alcohol or iodine onto the part of the body concerned and then wipe it dry

(14) שמירת שבת כהלכתה פי"ד סעי' יג.

(15) שמירת שבת כהלכתה פי"מ סעי' ה.

(16) ראה או"ח סי' שכו סעי' יב בהגה, באר היטב ס"ק ח ומ"ב ס"ק ל. שמירת שבת כהלכתה פי"מ סעי' יא.

(17) מ"ב סי' שיד ס"ק כה. חזו"א או"ח סי' סא ס"ק ב. כף החיים סי' שם ס"ק פה.

(18) או"ח סי' שמ סעי' יג ומ"ב ס"ק מא. וראה מ"ב ס"ק יז. כף החיים סי' שז ס"ק קד. נשמת אדם כלל כט סעי' ב.

(19) הגרש"ז אויערבאך שליט"א מובא בשו"ת ציץ אליעזר ח"ט סי' יז. שמירת שבת כהלכתה פל"ב סעי' יא.

(20) שמעתי ממו"ר הגרי"י נויבירט שליט"א. וראה שו"ת ציץ אליעזר ח"ח סי' טו פי"ד אות יא. ואין משום צובע בחיטוי מקום הזריקה ביוד וכדומה, לא לגבי הצמר גפן (מהא דשו"ע הרב סי' שב בקונטרס אחרון) ולא לגבי העור (או"ח סי' שג מ"ב ס"ק עט) — מובא בשמירת שבת כהלכתה פל"ב סעי' נט.

with cotton wool, gauze[21] or tissue.[22]

13. A nurse may be driven by a non-Jew to and from duty in a hospital in Israel (see Chapter 26, paragraph 12) if it is difficult for her to reach it on foot[23] (see also Chapter 26, paragraph 10).

Regarding the lighting of Sabbath and Festival candles, see Chapter 10, paragraphs 142-146.

Regarding the *mitzvah* of *Kiddush*, see Chapter 10, paragraphs 148-157.

Regarding the *mitzvah* of *Havdalah*, see Chapter 10, paragraphs 161 and 162.

Regarding working in a hospital in the Diaspora, see Chapter 32, paragraph 32.

(21) שמירת שבת כהלכתה שם.

(22) שו״ת הר צבי או״ח ח״א סי׳ קצ. שו״ת אגרות משה או״ח ח״ב סי׳ ע.

(23) שמירת שבת כהלכתה פ״מ סע׳ סט.

34 / OPERATIONS

1. If in the physician's opinion a patient is likely to die within a few months and there are no prospects of recovery unless an operation is performed, the patient may undergo the operation even if the procedure carries a definite mortality risk.[1] However, all the facts must be seriously taken into account, with the advice of the most expert physicians available[2] and in consultation with competent halachic authority.

2. A patient who is non-seriously ill (see Chapter 1, paragraph 2) may undergo an operation for the purpose of relieving or reducing suffering, and thereby being restored to good health.[3]

3. A person who has a prostatic obstruction may undergo a prostatectomy and is not thereby considered as having mutilated genitals.[4] However, the vasa connecting the testes to the urethra may not be tied or severed at any site outside the abdominal cavity.[5]

4. The recommended therapy today for advanced prostatic cancer includes the removal of both testes. This operation is permissible in such a case.[6]

---

(1) שו״ת אחיעזר יו״ד סי׳ ט״ז אות ו. פ״ת יו״ד סי׳ שלט ס״ק א. גליון מהרש״א על יו״ד סי׳ קנה סע׳ א. שו״ת בנין ציון סי׳ קיא. שו״ת שבות יעקב ח״ג סי׳ עה. שו״ת ציץ אליעזר ח״ד סי׳ יג וח״י סי׳ כה פ״ז. שו״ת יד הלוי ח״א יו״ד סי׳ רז. דעת תורה סי׳ שכח סע׳ י. הגראי״י אונטרמן נועם כרך יג עמי ה.

(2) שו״ת אחיעזר שם.

(3) שערים מצויינים בהלכה סי׳ קצ ס״ק ד.

(4) חזון איש נשים סי׳ יב אות ז. שו״ת חלקת יעקב ח״ב סי׳ כב. שו״ת ציץ אליעזר ח״י סי׳ כה פכ״ד. שו״ת מנחת יצחק ח״ב סי׳ קכג אות ו.

(5) ראה נשמת אברהם אהע״ז סי׳ ה ס״ק ו (עמי מז).

(6) הגרש״ז אויערבאך שליט״א, נשמת אברהם ס״ק ה (עמי מה).

5. A woman may undergo cosmetic surgery which might enable her to get married, or to preserve a marriage, should her appearance be a factor causing marital discord.[7]

6. A baby born with hypospadias should be circumcised in such a way as not to jeopardize the plastic correction to be performed later[8] (see Chapter 45, paragraph 15).

7. A limb or any other part of the body containing flesh and bone which is removed during an operation should be interred.[9]

8. A man who is to undergo an operation scheduled for the early morning and who knows that he will not be able to lay *tefillin* or recite *Shacharit* that day after the operation should try to start praying after dawn, so that he will reach the benediction *Yotzer or* at daybreak,[10] and then put on the *tallit* and *tefillin*, recite the appropriate benedictions[11] and continue with the rest of *Shacharit*.[12] If the operation is scheduled to start so early that even this is not possible, he may put on the *tallit* and *tefillin*

(7) שו"ת חלקת יעקב ח"ג סי' יא. שו"ת אגרות משה חו"מ ח"ב סי' סו. הגרש"ז אויערבאך שליט"א, נשמת אברהם חו"מ סי' תכ ס"ק ד (עמ' ריז). הרב יעקובוביץ שליט"א, נועם כרך ו עמ' רעג. וראה שו"ת ציץ אליעזר חי"א סי' מב ושו"ת מנחת יצחק חי"ו סי' קה שאוסרים.

(8) ראה נשמת אברהם יו"ד סי' רסב ס"ק ט 3 (עמ' קסח). וראה שו"ת חשב האפוד ח"ב סי' ח. וראה נשמת אברהם אהע"ז סי' ה ס"ק ד (עמ' מא).

(9) גשר החיים ח"א פט"ז סע' ב ס"ק ב. שו"ת אגרות משה יו"ד ח"א סי' רלא וח"ג סי' קמא.

(10) וראה ביה"ל סי' פט סע' א ד"ה ואם, על זמן עמוד השחר ועיין מג"א ס"ק ג. וע"ע א"ר והגר"א שם ושו"ת מלמד להועיל סי' ל.

(11) בכדי שיראה את חברו ברחוק ד' אמות. עיין או"ח סי' ל סע' א ופמ"ג סי' נח א"א ס"ק ב. כף החיים ס"ק יח. שו"ת אגרות משה או"ח ח"ד סי' ז.

(12) ועיין רמב"ם הל' תפילין פ"ד הי"א שאף עובר על לאו אם מניחם בלילה. אולם ע"ע או"ח סי' ל סע' ב ומג"א ס"ק א.

immediately after dawn, without reciting the benedictions.[13] If
time does not allow even for this, the *mitzvot* of *tallit* and *tefillin*
may be performed before dawn (in which case the benedictions
are not recited);[14] *Shacharit* may be recited only after dawn.[15]

    9. If it can be arranged, an elective operation should
be performed during the first half of the week, so as to avoid the
need later to set aside Sabbath laws during post-operative care.
However, if it is unavoidable, such an operation may be performed as late as Friday, even though this might lead to the
setting aside of Sabbath laws later.[16]

    10. No preparations may be made on the Sabbath for
an operation to be performed after the Sabbath, unless time is of
the essence. Thus a patient may not be shaved, be given an
enema or undergo any blood tests, X-ray examinations, etc.,
unless the postponement of such procedures until after the
Sabbath would lead to the delay of an urgent operation which
has to be carried out immediately after the Sabbath.[17]

    11. Students may not attend the operating theater on
the Sabbath in order to watch an operation.[18]

    12. A woman who has undergone a total hysterectomy
should immerse herself in a *mikveh* after the operation (without a

---

(13) מהא דמ״ב סי׳ ל ס״ק יג וסימן נח ס״ק יג וביה״ל סע׳ א ד״ה זמן. כף החיים סי׳ נח
ס״ק יז. ועיין תפארת ישראל ברכות סוף פ״א. ברכי יוסף סי׳ נח ס״ק ד. שערי תשובה על סי׳
תרסד. שו״ת אגרות משה או״ח ח״ד סי׳ ו. שו״ת יחוה דעת ח״ב סי׳ ח.

(14) שמעתי ממו״ר הגרי״י נויבירט שליט״א. וראה ערוך השולחן סי׳ ל סע׳ ה.

(15) וראה נשמת אברהם או״ח סי׳ נח ס״ק א (עמי כד).

(16) שמירת שבת כהלכתה פל״ב סע׳ לג. וראה מ״ב סי׳ תסח ס״ק לח, שו״ת ציץ אליעזר
חי״ב סי׳ מו ונשמת אברהם או״ח סי׳ תסח ס״ק ב (עמי רסח) דבערב שבועות ובהושענא
רבה אין להתיר אלא בחולה שיש בו סכנה.

(17) שמירת שבת כהלכתה פ״מ סע׳ לח וראה מ״ב סי׳ תרסז ס״ק ה ובאו״ח סי׳ תקג.

(18) שאילת יעב״ץ סי׳ מא ד״ה לכן. וראה נשמת אברהם או״ח סי׳ שו ס״ק ג (עמי קמא).

benediction) even if she was not a *niddah* before the operation.[19] If only a partial hysterectomy was performed, she must continue to observe all the rules of *niddah* just as she did before the operation.

13.   A limb that has been severed may be rejoined to the body even on the Sabbath, since the patient's life is in danger.[20]

14.   A *kohen* may be the recipient of a transplant[21] (see Chapter 37, paragraph 1).

(19) כתב לי הגרש"ז אויערבאך שליט"א.

(20) הגרש"ז אויערבאך שליט"א, נשמת אברהם יו"ד סי' שסט ס"ק ב
(עמי רע) וראה שם טעמו. ולגבי חיבור אבר אצל כהן, ראה שו"ת ציץ אליעזר חי"ג סי' צ,
דלפי הש"ך יו"ד סי' קנז ס"ק ג, על אף שהכהן עובר על ל"ת דאיסור טומאה כדי לרפאות
ולהשיב עי"ז לתחיה האבר שנקטע ממנו, שרי.

(21) שו"ת ציץ אליעזר. שו"ת אגרות משה יו"ד ח"א סי' רל.

35 / VISITING THE SICK

1. It is a *mitzvah* to visit those who are ill,[1] to take an interest in their condition and, what is most important, to help them with whatever they may require.[2] One who visits a patient and does not pray for the patient's recovery has not properly fulfilled the *mitzvah*.[3]

2. A person who visits a patient should avoid sitting in a position higher than that of the patient.[4]

3. Prayers on behalf of an individual patient should be included in a prayer for all those who are ill:[5]

הַמָּקוֹם יְרַחֵם עָלֶיךָ בְּתוֹךְ שְׁאָר חוֹלֵי יִשְׂרָאֵל.

4. Patients who are too ill to talk should not be visited, but inquiry should be made about their condition to find out what may be done to help, and one should pray for them.[6]

5. The rabbi of the community should be asked to pray for the patient. It is customary to recite the *Mi sheberach* prayer in the synagogue on behalf of a seriously ill patient (see Chapter 1, paragraph 1), and sometimes the patient is given an additional name.[7]

6. Although telephoning to inquire about the health of a patient is not to be equated with fulfilling the *mitzvah* of

(1) ראה נשמת אברהם יו"ד סי' שלה ס"ק א (עמי רו), אם המצוה היא דאורייתא או דרבנן.

(2) טור יו"ד סי' שלה.

(3) יו"ד שם סעי' ד בהגה. וראה שם סעי' ב לגבי ביקור אדם גדול אצל אדם פשוט. ולענין ביקור גבר אצל אשה או להפך ראה ערוך השולחן שם סעי' יא והגרש"ז אויערבאך שליט"א, נשמת אברהם יו"ד סי' שלה ס"ק ד (עמי רט). וע"ע שו"ת ציץ אליעזר ח"ה רמת רחל סי' טז.

(4) יו"ד שם סעי' ג בהגה.

(5) יו"ד שם סעי' ו. וראה שם סעי' ה, ואו"ח סי' קא סעי' ד.

(6) יו"ד שם סעי' ח.

(7) יו"ד שם סעי' י בהגה.

visiting the sick,[8] if the patient cannot be visited, telephoning is commendable.[9]

7. The *mitzvah* of visiting the sick applies even if the patient's disease is contagious, as long as no actual danger is involved.[10] However, physicians, nurses and paramedical staff or other persons who are on duty must treat such a patient in spite of the risk; indeed, doing so is a great *mitzvah*.[11] Thus a patient with AIDS should be treated (with all the appropriate precautions).

8. A patient who is seriously ill (see Chapter 1, paragraph 1), and who would be seriously compromised by an added infection should not be visited except by close relatives and friends who are needed in order to care for the patient and who will take the necessary precautions to avoid infecting the patient.

9. Those who offer a patient unasked for and unwanted suggestions and advice, such as to try a different medication or consult with another physician, only succeed in adding confusion and difficulty.[12] But, if a person gives *constructive* advice, which does not contradict that of the patient's physician, and thereby encourages the patient physically or mentally, a great *mitzvah* is thereby performed.[13]

10. Priority should be given to visiting the poor patient (who is likely to have few or no visitors) over visiting the rich (who is likely to have many visitors), even if the latter is a well-known Torah scholar. However, if both need help,

(8) שערים מצויינים בהלכה סי׳ קצג ס״ק א.

(9) שו״ת אגרות משה יו״ד ח״א סי׳ רכג. שו״ת חלקת יעקב ח״ב סי׳ קכח. שו״ת מנחת יצחק ח״ב סי׳ פד. שו״ת ציץ אליעזר ח״ה רמת רחל סי׳ ח ס״ק ו. שו״ת יחוה דעת ח״ג סי׳ פג.

(10) שו״ת רמ״א סי׳ יט (דפוס וורשא סי׳ כ). וראה נפש כל חי להגר״ח פלאג׳י ח״ב סי׳ מט.

(11) שו״ת ציץ אליעזר ח״ט סי׳ יז פ״ה.

(12) גשר החיים פ״א ס״ק ג.

(13) או״ח סי׳ רפז ביה״ל סוד״ה וכן.

the scholar should be visited first. A poor, pious, though not learned, patient takes precedence over a scholar if the latter is not also a man of piety.[14]

11. It is commendable to visit the sick on the Sabbath and the Festivals,[15] with the appropriate greeting:[16]

שַׁבָּת הִיא (וְיוֹם טוֹב הוּא) מִלִּזְעוֹק וּרְפוּאָה קְרוֹבָה לָבוֹא.

12. One may go beyond the Sabbath boundary (as long as there is no violation of Torah commandments, such as driving there by car) in order to ask a relation to visit a seriously ill patient (see Chapter 1, paragraph 1) who has expressed a wish to be visited.[17]

13. One should not inform a patient of the serious nature of his or her illness if doing so might result in despair and lead thus to further deterioration.[18] However, if the patient is likely to realize the nature of the illness (for example, a patient who is referred to an oncology or radiotherapy service), the physician should disclose the nature of the illness in a gentle, optimistic manner, without necessarily giving all the details of the prognosis.[19]

Regarding a *kohen* who needs to visit a sick relative, see Chapter 42, paragraphs 8 and 9.

---

(14) ספר חסידים סי' שסא.

(15) או"ח סי' רפז. וראה שם מ"ב ס"ק א וביה"ל ד"ה וכן.

(16) יו"ד סי' שלה סע' ו.

(17) ילקוט הגרשוני או"ח סי' שו ס"ק ה. קצות השולחן סי' קלה בבדה"ש ס"ק א. שו"ת ציץ אליעזר ח"ח סי' טו פי"ט. וראה גם שו"ת חלקת יעקב ח"א סוסי' סד ושו"ת שואל ומשיב מהד"ג ח"ב סי' קף.

(18) יו"ד סי' שלח ש"ך ס"ק א.

(19) נשמת אברהם יו"ד סי' שלח ס"ק א ו־ג (עמ' רלח). אסיא חוברת מב, ניסן תשמ"ז עמ'

.24

36 / *BIRKAT HA-GOMEL* (THANKSGIVING)

The *Ha-gomel* benediction is recited after deliverance or recovery from certain categories of danger or illness, to acknowledge the good fortune as a special gift from the Almighty.

1. There are four indications for reciting the *Birkat Ha-gomel*,[1] one of which is recovery from illness. The benediction should be recited in the presence of ten adult males, including the cured patient.[2]

2. The benediction is recited by a Sephardi after any illness for which the person was confined to bed for three or more consecutive days.[3] An Ashkenazi should recite the benediction only after recovery from a serious illness[4] (see Chapter 1, paragraph 1 and 2), and not after a minor illness (see Chapter 1, paragraph 3) that did not affect the whole body.[5]

3. A person who has unsuccessfully attempted to commit suicide should not recite the benediction upon recovery.[6]

(1) או״ח סי׳ ריט סע׳ א.

(2) שם סע׳ ג.

(3) שם סע׳ ח. בן איש חי שנה א פ׳ עקב סע׳ ז.

(4) שם בהגה ומ״ב ס״ק כח וביה״ל ד״ה כגון.

(5) בן איש חי שם. וראה או״ח שם ט״ז ס״ק ה ומ״ב ס״ק כח וביה״ל ד״ה כגון.

(6) שו״ת יחוה דעת ח״ד סי׳ יד. שו״ת ציץ אליעזר חט״ו סי׳ לב אות ה. וראה גם ח״י סי׳ כה פכ״ג. וע״ע כף החיים סי׳ ריט ס״ק מח.

37 / ORGAN TRANSPLANTS

1. One may offer part of one's body for transplantation into a seriously ill patient[1] (see Chapter 1, paragraph 1) provided that according to expert medical opinion the donor will not thereby suffer permanent harm, and this is regarded as a most meritorious act.[2] Thus a kidney transplant from a live, healthy donor is permissible if, according to expert medical opinion, it carries only a small risk for the donor.[3] (Competent halachic authority must first be consulted.)

2. Bone-marrow transplantation carries only a minimal risk for the donor and is, likewise, permitted; indeed, it is praiseworthy.[4] (Competent halachic authority must first be consulted.)

3. Transplantation of skin from a corpse in order to save the life of a badly burned patient is permitted under certain circumstances.[5] (Competent halachic authority must first be consulted.)

4. The cornea removed from a corpse may be transplanted into a blind person.[6] (Competent halachic authority must first be consulted.)

5. The kidneys may be removed from a corpse, under certain circumstances, for transplantation into seriously ill patients[7]

(1) שו"ת ציץ אליעזר ח"י סי' כה פ"ז.

(2) שו"ת יחוה דעת ח"ג סי' פד.

(3) שו"ת ציץ אליעזר ח"ט סי' מה. שו"ת יחוה דעת שם. וכן שמעתי מהגרש"ז אויערבאך שליט"א. וראה שו"ת מנחת יצחק ח"ו סי' קג.

(4) שמעתי מהגרש"ז אויערבאך שליט"א.

(5) שמעתי מהגרש"ז אויערבאך שליט"א.

(6) שו"ת שבט מיהודה עמ' 314. שו"ת הר צבי יו"ד סי' רעז. שו"ת אגרות משה יו"ד ח"א סי' רכט. שו"ת יביע אומר ח"ג סי' כב, כג. שו"ת ציץ אליעזר חי"ד סי' פד. אך ראה שו"ת מנחת יצחק ח"ה סי' ח ושו"ת שבט הלוי יו"ד חי"א סי' ריא.

(7) שמעתי מהגרש"ז אויערבאך שליט"א.

(see Chapter 1, paragraph 1). (Competent halachic authority must first be consulted.)

6. It is not permissible to remove any organ from a *dying* person for transplantation, even if the recipient's life might thereby be saved.[8]

7. A definitive consensus of halachic authorities has not yet been reached regarding the point at which a person is held to be dead in the case of brain-stem death with the heart still beating. Therefore a competent halachic authority should be consulted in every case.[9] One must continue to set aside the Sabbath laws for such a patient, unless and until consensus to the contrary is reached.[10] His status is one of a *terefah*[11] (for definition see Rambam[12]).

8. An anencephalic baby who is still breathing spontaneously and whose heart is still beating is considered to be alive and may not be used as a donor for organ transplantation.[13]

9. A person who during his lifetime sells one of his kidneys for transplantation into a seriously ill patient (see Chapter 1, paragraph 1) because of poverty or debts nevertheless performs the *mitzvah* of saving life.[14]

(8) שו״ת אגרות משה יו״ד ח״ב סי׳ קעד. שו״ת מנחת יצחק ח״ה סי׳ ז ו-ט. שו״ת ציץ אליעזר חי״ג סי׳ צא.

(9) ראה אסיא סיון תשמ״ז כרך יא עמ׳ 70 שועדת רבנים מטעם הרבנות הראשית של ישראל התירו השתלות לב בתנאים מסויימים, לעומתם הגר״ש ואזנר שליט״א (אסיא שם עמ׳ 92), הג״ר וויס ז״ל, ויבדל מחיים לחיים הגרא״י וולדינברג שליט״א (שו״ת ציץ אליעזר חי״ז סי׳ סו), הגרי״ש אלישיב והגר״ע יוסף שליט״א (שמעתי מפיהם) אוסרים כי לדעתם חולה כזה עדיין נקרא חי.

(10) שמעתי מהגרש״ז אויערבאך שליט״א.

(11) שמעתי מהגרי״ש אלישיב שליט״א.

(12) הל׳ רוצח פ״ב ה״ח.

(13) פתחי תשובה יו״ד סי׳ קצד ס״ק ה. שמעתי מהגרש״ז אויערבאך שליט״א.

(14) שמעתי מהגרש״ז אויערבאך שליט״א.

38 / THE DYING PATIENT

1. Nothing may be done to a dying person that might hasten death[1] (see Chapter 39).

2. Since there are rare cases in which critically ill patients, for whom all hope has been abandoned, do nevertheless recover, it is the duty of the physician to continue to treat a dying patient until the very end. One should set aside the Sabbath laws for such a patient[2] (see Chapter 10). This is equally valid if treatment may prolong life for only a short time, but not if the treatment would *add* suffering to a patient who has reached the natural end of the disease[3] (see Chapter 39 for further details).

3. A patient who appears to be close to death should be asked to make a final confession of sins, but at the same time he should be reassured that this does not necessarily mean that death is impending. On the contrary, confession of sins may be rewarded by an extension of life, and anyone who confesses sincerely has a portion in the World-to-Come. Many have confessed and not died, and many have died who had not confessed. If the patient cannot recite the confession aloud, it should be said silently. One should not discuss such matters in the presence of those who may weep and thereby unnerve the patient.[4]

4. A person with a mortal illness should confess as follows:[5]

(1) יו״ד סי׳ שלט סע׳ א וש״ך ס״ק א.

(2) ברכי יוסף או״ח סי׳ שכט ס״ק ד. ביה״ל שם ד״ה אלא. שו״ת שבות יעקב ח״א סי׳ יג. וראה שמירת שבת כהלכתה פל״ב הערה קנ בשם הגרש״ז אויערבאך שליט״א.

(3) שו״ת שבות יעקב ח״א סי׳ יג וח״ג סי׳ עה. גשר החיים ח״א פ״ב סע׳ ב(ב).

(4) יו״ד סי׳ שלח סע׳ א.

(5) שם סע׳ ב.

מוֹדֶה אֲנִי לְפָנֶיךָ ד' אֱלֹקַי וַאלֹקֵי אֲבוֹתַי שֶׁרְפוּאָתִי וּמִיתָתִי
בְּיָדֶךָ, יְהִי רָצוֹן מִלְּפָנֶיךָ שֶׁתִּרְפָּאֵנִי רְפוּאָה שְׁלֵמָה, וְאִם אָמוּת
תְּהֵא מִיתָתִי כַּפָּרָה עַל כָּל חֲטָאִים וַעֲוֹנוֹת וּפְשָׁעִים שֶׁחָטָאתִי
וְשֶׁעָוִיתִי וְשֶׁפָּשַׁעְתִּי לְפָנֶיךָ, וְתֵן חֶלְקִי בְּגַן עֵדֶן וְזַכֵּנִי לָעוֹלָם הַבָּא
הַצָּפוּן לַצַּדִּיקִים.

"I acknowledge unto Thee, O Lord my God and God
of my fathers, that both my cure and my death are in Thy hands.
May it be Thy will to heal me completely. Yet, if I am to die, let
my death be an atonement for the sins, iniquities and transgres-
sions of which I have been guilty before Thee. Give me my
portion in the Garden of Eden and let me merit the World-to-
Come that is reserved for the righteous."

If the patient is capable he may recite the Yom Kippur
confession (*Al chet*) said at the end of the *Shemoneh Esreh* prayer;[6]
if not, his confession may be reduced to the minimum of:

מִיתָתִי תְּהֵא כַּפָּרָה עַל כָּל עֲוֹנוֹתַי.

"Let my death atone for all my sins."[7]

5. In time of need, one may make confession even in
a location where prayers may otherwise not be recited (see
Chapter 9); but the Names of the Almighty should not be uttered.[8]

6. Death is established only when spontaneous respiration, heartbeat and brain function have all ceased.[9] With regard to

(6) שם בהגה.

(7) שם סע' א.

(8) שמעתי ממו"ר הגריי"י נויבירט שליט"א מהא דאו"ח סי' תרו שעה"צ ס"ק כב.

(9) שו"ת חתם סופר חי"ב סי' קמו. שו"ת מהרש"ם חי"ו סי' קכד. דברי שאול יו"ד סי' שצד
סע' ג. וראה גם שו"ת חכם צבי סי' עז. שו"ת אגרות משה יו"ד חי"ב סי' קמו וחי"ג סי' קלב.
שו"ת ציץ אליעזר חי"ט סי' מו וחי"י סי' כה פ"ד.

the problem of "brain death," see Chapter 37, paragraph 7.

7. A dying patient should not be left alone.[10]

8. A patient who is about to die may not be moved, however slightly,[11] unless it is for his benefit. Thus a patient who is beyond all further treatment, for whom nothing more will avail, should not have his pulse, temperature or blood pressure checked. Blood may not be withdrawn for laboratory examinations, since in any case the results would lead to no change in the handling of the patient.[12] If such unnecessary procedures are performed on the Sabbath they are considered to be a desecration of the Sabbath.

However, routine *treatment* such as essential medical and nursing care, should not be discontinued, even on the Sabbath, lest the patient realize the hopelessness of the situation and his death thereby be hastened.[13] For the same reason a patient in an intensive-care unit may not be moved out to make room for another patient with a better prognosis.[14]

(10) יו״ד סי׳ שלט סע׳ ד.

(11) יו״ד סי׳ שלט סע׳ א. וראה שו״ת אגרות משה חו״מ ח״ב סי׳ עג אות ג.

(12) שמעתי מהגרש״ז אויערבאך שליט״א.

(13) ראה שו״ת אגרות משה חו״מ ח״ב סי׳ עה אות ו.

(14) שו״ת אגרות משה שם סי׳ עג.

39 / EUTHANASIA ("MERCY" KILLING)

ACTIVE EUTHANASIA[*]

1. One may not hasten death, even that of a patient who is suffering greatly and for whom there is no hope of a cure,[1] even if the patient asks that this be done.[2] To shorten the life of a person, even a life of agony and suffering, is forbidden. If one does so, albeit for reasons of compassion and even at the request of the patient, it is equivalent to murder and is punishable accordingly.[3]

2. Under no circumstances does Jewish law permit escape from suffering at the price of one's life, for, as the Psalmist says:[4] "God has caused me suffering and not permitted me to die." The value of life is infinite and therefore the value of every part of it, however brief, is similarly infinite. Thus seventy years of life have exactly the same value as thirty years, one year, an hour or even a second.

This conclusion is not merely a mathematical or logical one but is based on deep moral considerations. Once one denies the value of human life because of the nearness of death, one destroys the absolute value of all life and gives it instead a relative value only—in relation to age, health, further use to the community or any other factors one wishes to consider. The moment one is willing to shorten, by however little, the life of a dying patient, on the grounds that it is of no further value, one

*See *Assia, Jewish Medical Ethics*, vol. 1, no. 2 [May 1989], pp. 36-39.

(1)יו״ד סי׳ שלט סע׳ א בהגה וש״ך ס״ק א. חכמת אדם כלל קנא סע׳ יד. ערוך השולחן יו״ד סי׳ שלט סע׳ ג. שו״ת ציץ אליעזר ח״ה רמת רחל סי׳ כט. וראה גם דעת זקנים מבעלי התוספות בראשית ט,ה. רמב״ם הל׳ רוצח פ״ב ה״ז והל׳ סוטה פ״ג ה״כ. תוס׳ יו״ט סוטה פ״א מ״ט.

(2) ספר חסידים סי׳ תשכג. שו״ת ריב״ש סי׳ תפד. מנחת חינוך מצוה לד. שו״ע הרב חו״מ הל׳ נזקי גו״נ סע׳ ד. חזון איש נזיקין סי׳ יט ס״ק ה.

(3) שו״ת אגרות משה יו״ד ח״ב סי׳ קעד.

(4) קיח, יח.

destroys the infinite value of all human life.[5]

Thus, even if death is near and absolutely certain, the life of a patient is still of infinite and inestimable value, and shortening it is in no way different from killing an absolutely healthy individual.[6]

3. A patient in pain should be treated with such pain-relieving medication, including morphine, as is necessary. However, under no circumstances may morphine be injected in order to *shorten* life. A patient with severe pulmonary disease who requires morphine because of intense pain may be so treated, only if the dose is carefully titrated so as not to cause life-threatening respiratory depression, or if the treatment is accompanied by artificial respiration.[7]

4. The prohibition of shortening life applies also to a fetus who is about to die.[8] Regarding abortions, see Chapter 48.

5. An anencephalic baby who is still breathing spontaneously and whose heart is still beating is considered to be alive, and may not be used as a donor for organ transplantation.[9]

PASSIVE EUTHANASIA*

6. It is the duty of the physician to treat the patient even if only to prolong life for a short time. It is therefore forbidden, for instance, to withhold food, fluids, or drugs such as insulin or antibiotics, to discontinue oxygen, or to refrain from giving transfusions, even if such measures result in the

*See *Assia, Jewish Medical Ethics*, vol. 1, no. 2 [May 1989], pp. 36-39.

(5) הרפואה והיהדות עמ' 152.

(6) וראה גם גשר החיים ח״א פ״ב ס״ק א וח״ג פ״ב סע' ב אות ד.

(7) הגרש״ז אויערבאך שליט״א בנשמת אברהם יו״ד סי' שלט ס״ק ד (עמ' רמו). וראה שו״ת ציץ אליעזר חי״ג סי' פז.

(8) שו״ת רדב״ז סי' תרצה. וראה גם נודע ביהודה תניינא חו״מ סי' נט. שו״ת חות יאיר סי' לא. שו״ת מהר״ם שיק יו״ד סי' קנה.

(9) פתחי תשובה יו״ד סי' קצד ס״ק ה. שמעתי מהגרש״ז אויערבאך שליט״א.

prolongation of suffering.[10] All procedures needed to nourish or sustain the patient must be carried out, even if they can be performed only by artificial means. Thus the patient must be given food and fluids by nasogastric tube, feeding gastrostomy or intravenously, as necessary.[11]

7. Although the life of a totally paralyzed person, for example, may seem not to be a valuable life according to our simplistic ideas, and in spite of the very real suffering of the patient and the family, we are nevertheless commanded to do everything in our power to prolong life, even by setting aside the Sabbath laws. We have no yardstick by which to measure the worth and importance of a life, not even in terms of the person's knowledge of Torah and fulfillment of *mitzvot*. One must set aside the Sabbath laws even for a person who is old and sick, who may be socially unacceptable because of a repulsive external disease, who may be mentally retarded and incapable of performing any *mitzvah*.

Everything possible must be done to prolong life even if the patient is a severe burden and a source of suffering to members of the family, who themselves may thereby be prevented from studying Torah and performing *mitzvot*; and even if the patient, in addition to inflicting suffering on others, causes them financial distress. Moreover, if the patient is suffering so much that it is permissible to pray for the person's death,[12] even while praying to the Almighty that the patient should die one must simultaneously do everything in one's power to keep the patient alive, even if in doing so the Sabbath laws are repeatedly set aside.[13] Thus a patient with Alzheimer's Disease, for example, must be treated as any other patient.

(10) שו״ת ציץ אליעזר חי״ג סי׳ פט.

(11) הגרש״ז אויערבאך שליט״א, נשמת אברהם יו״ד סי׳ שלט ס״ק ד (עמ׳ רמה). שו״ת אגרות משה חו״מ ח״ב סי׳ עד אות ג.

(12) ר״ן נדרים מ ע״א.

(13) הגרש״ז אויערבאך שליט״א, מנחת שלמה סי׳ צא אות כד.

8. Every attempt must be made to resuscitate a patient, and the effort must be continued as long as there is any hope of success. However, if the patient is merely being kept in such an artificial state of life that the cessation of treatment would not be followed by spontaneous breathing or heartbeat within a few minutes, and there is no chance of revival, resuscitation should not be continued.[14]

9. One need not resuscitate a patient with a terminal illness whose heartbeat or breathing cease in the natural course of events; indeed, it may be wrong to do so. Also, desperate major interventions to prolong the final, inevitable death process, which only add further agony and suffering, are not called for.[15]

(14) מהא דיו״ד סי׳ שלט סע׳ א בהגה. שו״ת ציץ אליעזר חי״ד סי׳ פט.

(15) שו״ת אגרות משה יו״ד ח״ב סי׳ קעד וחו״מ ח״ב סי׳ עג ו־עה..

40 / THE DECEASED

1.   The body is sacred even after life has departed.[1] Therefore, a corpse must be treated with respect, and no act of levity should take place in its presence.[2]

2.   In Jerusalem it is customary not to move the corpse for twenty minutes following death.[3] The limbs are straightened, the eyes are closed, the lower jaw is bound and the body is covered.[4]

3.   All those present at the moment of death say *"Baruch Dayyan Ha-emet."*[5] But, if any of the persons present is one of the seven close relatives who are required to sit *shivah* for the deceased (see the introduction to Chapter 41), the benediction is recited in full,[6] even on the Sabbath and the Festivals.[7]

4.   No part of a corpse may be moved on the Sabbath.[8] If the lower jaw has dropped, it may be tied with a knot and bow[9] to prevent the mouth from opening further.[10]

5.   Blood or feces on the corpse may be washed off with water on the Sabbath using plastic or rubber gloves.[11] Infusions, other external tubing[12] and a permanent pacemaker may be removed.[13]

(1) שו"ת חתם סופר יו"ד סוסי' שלו. גשר החיים ח"א פי"ה סע' א ס"ק א.

(2) גשר החיים שם ס"ק ג.

(3) גשר החיים שם פי"ג סע' ב ס"ק א.

(4) שם ס"ק ב.

(5) או"ח סי' רכג מג"א ס"ק ד.

(6) מ"ב שם ס"ק ח.

(7) גשר החיים שם סע' א ס"ק ו.

(8) או"ח סי' שיא סע' א וסע' ז.

(9) שם סע' ז.

(10) או"ח סי' שיז סע' ה וראה שם מ"ב וביה"ל.

(11) או"ח סי' שיא מג"א ס"ק כ. גשר החיים פי"ה סע' ה ס"ק ז.

(12) שמירת שבת כהלכתה פס"ד סע' ט.

(13) שו"ת ציץ אליעזר חי"ד סי' פב. הגרש"ז אויערבאך שליט"א, נשמת אברהם יו"ד סי'

6. All these services, whether performed on a weekday or on the Sabbath, must be rendered by Jews.[14]

7. The corpse may be carried from the hospital to another building within the hospital grounds on the Sabbath.[15]

8. If the corpse has to be moved within the hospital via an elevator on the Sabbath, this should be done by a non-Jew, and a Jew may accompany the corpse.[16]

9. A death certificate may not be written on the Sabbath, nor may one ask a non-Jew to write it on the Sabbath. However, if the physician is going off duty on the Sabbath and will be unable to return to write the certificate immediately after the Sabbath, before going off duty he may ask a non-Jewish colleague to write it after the Sabbath, in order to avoid a delay in burial.[17]

10. A physician may charge for services confirming death and for issuing the appropriate certificate.[18]

11. A needle biopsy may be performed, and blood or other fluids may be taken from a corpse for diagnostic purposes.[19]

Regarding autopsies, see Chapter 30.

שמט ס״ק ג (עמ' רס). וע״ע שו״ת מנחת יצחק ח״ז סי' קא שאוסר.

(14) שו״ת הרדב״ז סי' תקז. גשר החיים פי״ב סע' ב ס״ק ה. שמירת שבת כהלכתה פס״ד סע' יב. וראה גם או״ח סי' תקכו סע' א ומ״ב ס״ק יב.

(15) או״ח סי' שיא סע' א ו־סע' ד מג״א ס״ק טז מ״ב ס״ק א ו־טז וביה״ל ד״ה יש. גשר החיים פ״ג סע' ב ס״ק ג ופי״ה סע' ה ס״ק ב. וכן שמעתי מהגרש״ז אויערבאך שליט״א.

(16) ראה שמירת שבת כהלכתה פכ״ג סע' מט הערה קמ בשם הגרש״ז אויערבאך שליט״א, שו״ת ציץ אליעזר חי״ג סוסי' קד. וכן ראיתי מעשה רב אצל מו״ר הגריי״י נויבירט שליט״א.

(17) שמירת שבת כהלכתה פס״ד סע' כט.

(18) שו״ת מהרי״ם שיק יו״ד סי' שמג.

(19) שו״ת אגרות משה יו״ד ח״ב סוסי' קנא. וכן שמעתי מהגרש״ז אויערבאך שליט״א.

41 / THE OBSERVANCE OF MOURNING

One is required to sit *shivah* after the death of any one of the following seven relatives: mother, father, sister and brother (even if there is only one parent in common), son and daughter (if more than thirty days old) and spouse.

1.   An ill person should not be informed of the death of a close relative if that is likely to lead to a serious deterioration of his medical condition.[1] Even if the deceased was a parent, for whom the patient would ordinarily have to say *Kaddish*, the patient should not be informed.[2]

2.   Even if the patient knows that a member of the family has died,[3] one should avoid doing anything that may further upset the patient, such as rending garments, crying or delivering a eulogy in the patient's presence.[4] This applies even if the deceased was not related to the patient.[5]

3.   If the patient was informed of the death of a relative and recovers from his or her illness during the first week after the burial (the *shivah* week), only the remaining days of *shivah* are observed. Similarly, if the patient recovers during the thirty days of mourning, only the remaining days are observed.[6] These rules apply also to a woman following childbirth.[7]

4.   If an ill person was not informed of the death of a

(1) יו"ד סי' שלז סע' א.

(2) בית הלל שם.

(3) שייך שם ס"ק א.

(4) יו"ד שם.

(5) שייך שם ס"ק ב.

(6) קיצור שולחן ערוך סי' ריז סע' ג.

(7) שם.

relative,[8] or was informed but was unable to appreciate or comprehend the significance of the information (because of a clouded consciousness), *shivah* is observed if recovery from the illness takes place within thirty days of the relative's death.[9]

5. During *shivah* a person may not ordinarily leave home; but a physician in mourning may go to treat any patient who feels that this particular physician will be able to help.[10] It is preferable that the physician not accept payment for services rendered; but reimbursement may be charged for expenses incurred.[11]

(8) ערוך השולחן יו״ד סי׳ שלז סע׳ ג. קיצור שולחן ערוך שם.

(9) ערוך השולחן שם וסי׳ שצו סע׳ ג. שו״ת שבות יעקב ח״א יו״ד סי׳ פח. שו״ת ציץ אליעזר חי״ה רמת רחל סי׳ כו.

(10) שו״ת שבות יעקב ח״א יו״ד סי׳ פו. פתחי תשובה יו״ד סי׳ שפ ס״ק א. הגרש״ז אויערבאך שליטא״א בנשמת אברהם יו״ד סי׳ שפ ס״ק א (עמ׳ רפג).

(11) הגרש״ז אויערבאך שליטא״א בנשמת אברהם שם.

42 / THE *KOHEN*
(A MALE OF PRIESTLY DESCENT)

A *kohen* is bound by certain obligations and prohibitions. These may affect him as a patient, a physician, a member of the hospital staff, a medical student or as a visitor in a hospital.

1. A *kohen* may not enter a room containing a corpse or part of one, or a severed limb of a living person.[1] This prohibition applies also when there is a corpse in a neighboring room if there is an open door or window or an opening of 8x8 cm. or more in a wall separating the two rooms. The same applies to all rooms, corridors and staircases through which the corpse will be transported to the outside. Thus a *kohen* who is not seriously ill may not enter a hospital when it is known that a corpse is in the building.[2]

2. The wife of a *kohen* may enter a hospital for obstetric care, even though she may give birth to a male child who would be governed by the same rules as an adult *kohen*.[3] The baby should be kept in the hospital[4] no longer than twenty-four hours, medical opinion allowing.[5]

THE HANDICAPPED

3. A *kohen* who has a marked tremor of the hands or who is unable to raise them even for a short time may not *duchan*

---

(1) יו״ד סי׳ שסט וסי׳ שעא סע׳ א.

(2) שערים מצויינים בהלכה סי׳ רב ס״ק ו בהסתמך על ש״ך יו״ד סי׳ שעב ס״ק ב. שו״ת שואל ומשיב מהד״ג ח״ג סי׳ כו.

(3) יו״ד סי׳ שעא סע׳ א. וראה שו״ת נודע ביהודה תניינא יו״ד סי׳ רז. שאילת יעב״ץ ח״ב סי׳ קעז. שו״ת חתם סופר יו״ד סי׳ שנד.

(4) מהא דאו״ח סי׳ שכח סע׳ יז בהגה. ערוך השולחן שם סע׳ ב. קצות השולחן סי׳ קלד בבדה״ש ס״ק יח. שו״ת חלקת יעקב ח״א סי׳ כח. שו״ת שבט הלוי יו״ד סי׳ רה

(5) שמעתי מהגרש״ז אויערבאך שליט״א.

(pronounce the priestly benedictions).[6] He should leave the synagogue before *Retzeh* and return only after the other *kohanim* have completed the benedictions.[7]

4. A *kohen* who has lost an arm or a hand,[8] or who cannot stand unsupported,[9] or who has lost his voice[10] may not *duchan* and should leave the synagogue before *Retzeh,* and return only after the other *kohanim* have completed the benedictions.[11]

5. A *kohen* may *duchan* if he has a urinary catheter inserted, provided that his outer clothes are clean and there is no unpleasant odor.[12] Similarly, a *kohen* who has a colostomy or ileostomy may *duchan* if there is no unpleasant odor[13] (see Chapter 9, paragraph 14).

A *KOHEN* AS A PHYSICIAN OR MALE NURSE

6. A *kohen* may not come in contact with a corpse or part of one;[14] nor may he stay under the same roof with it.[15] Therefore, he should not take up the study of medicine or nursing, which unavoidably involves such contacts during training.[16]

7. If, in spite of this prohibition, a *kohen* does study

(6) או"ח סי' קכח סעי' יד ומ"ב ס"ק נב ו־ב. שו"ת נודע ביהודה מהדו"ק או"ח סי' ה. כף החיים סי' קכח ס"ק עח. וראה שו"ת כתב סופר או"ח סי' יג.

(7) או"ח שם ומ"ב ס"ק יב.

(8) שו"ת רדב"ז סי' ב אלפים קיז. וראה שו"ת אבני נזר או"ח סי' לא.

(9) או"ח סי' קכח סעי' יד ומ"ב ס"ק נא. שו"ת נודע ביהודה מהדו"ק או"ח סי' ה.

(10) מ"ב שם ס"ק נג.

(11) כף החיים שם ס"ק צ.

(12) שו"ת ציץ אליעזר חי"א סי' ז וח"ח סי' א.

(13) שו"ת מנחת יצחק חי"ו סי' יא ו־יב. שו"ת ציץ אליעזר חי"ט סי' ו. וכן שמעתי מהגרש"ז אויערבאך שליט"א.

(14) יו"ד סי' שסט.

(15) יו"ד סי' שעא סעי' א.

(16) כל בו על אבלות חי"א עמ' 81. גשר החיים חי"א פ"ו סעי' א ס"ק ד. וראה שם סעי' ג, שו"ת חתם סופר יו"ד סי' שלח, נשמת אברהם יו"ד סי' שע ס"ק ב1 (עמ' רעב).

medicine or nursing[17] and qualifies as a physician or a nurse, he may treat dying patients[18] even if other physicians or nurses are available.[19]

VISITING THE SICK IN THE HOSPITAL

8. In the Diaspora a *kohen* may visit a close relative (such as a parent or a child, or his wife's close relatives) in the hospital.[20]

9. In Israel a *kohen* may not enter a hospital even to visit a close relative, unless it is absolutely necessary to do so, without being assured that there is no corpse (or part of one) in the building.[21]

A *KOHEN* AS A PATIENT

10. In the Diaspora a *kohen* may attend any hospital department, even if he is not seriously ill.[22]

11. In Israel a *kohen* may attend a hospital out-patient department, unless he knows that there is a corpse (or part of one) in the building.[23]

---

(17) ואם הוא מטמא למתים, ראה או"ח סי' קכח ומ"ב ס"ק קן ושו"ת חתם סופר יו"ד סי' שלח. אך עיין שו"ת מהרי"י אסאד סי' מז ושו"ת מלמד להועיל ח"א סי' לא. וראה נשמת אברהם יו"ד סי' שע ס"ק 11 (עמי רעג).

(18) שו"ת חתם סופר שם. גשר החיים ח"א פ,ב ס"ק ב(ב). שו"ת מחזה אברהם ח"ב יו"ד סי' יט.

(19) פתחי תשובה יו"ד סי' שע ס"ק א כי לא מכל אדם זוכה להתרפאות (יו"ד סי' רכא סע' ד ט"ז וש"ך ס"ק כ). ואם יש מת בבית החולים, ראה נשמת אברהם יו"ד סי' שע ס"ק 22 בשם שו"ת אגרות משה יו"ד ח"א סי' רמח ובשם מו"ר הגרי"י נויבירט שליטי"א והגרש"ז אויערבאך שליטי"א.

(20) שו"ת אגרות משה יו"ד ח"ב סי' קסו.

(21) הגרש"ז אויערבאך שליטי"א, נשמת אברהם יו"ד סי' שלה ס"ק ד (עמי רי). אך עיין שו"ת שבט הלוי יו"ד סוסי' רה שאוסר.

(22) שו"ת חלקת יעקב ח"א סי' כז. שערים מצויינים בהלכה סי' רב ס"ק ו.

(23) שמעתי ממו"ר הגרי"י נויבירט שליטי"א.

12. If hospitalized in Israel, on hearing that someone has died in the hospital a *kohen* must remain in his room and close the doors and windows until the corpse has been removed.[24]

---

(24) הגרש״ז אויערבאך שליט״א, נשמת אברהם יו״ד סי׳ שעב ס״ק א (עמי רפ).
וראה נשמת אברהם שם לגבי הבאת ילד לבית החולים ע״י אביו כהן.

43 / SECLUSION WITH AND TREATMENT OF THE OPPOSITE SEX

A man should not be secluded in a closed room with a woman, single or married, other than his wife, mother or daughter.[1]

1. A man may study professions such as medicine, nursing and related technologies, such as radiography, etc., even though the practice of such professions necessitates examining or treating women patients.[2]

2. A male physician may examine a married woman if her husband is in the city,[3] or if the examination room door is not locked,[4] even if the husband does not know where she is.[5] Similarly, a man may be examined by a female physician if her husband is in the city or if the examination room door is not locked.[6] In all cases it is preferable that a nurse or a member of the patient's family be present in the room.

3. It is customary to permit a nurse to attend to a male patient.[7]

4. A woman in the *niddah* state who is ill may not be

(1) אהע"ז סי' כב סע' א ו-ב. הגרש"ז אויערבאך שליט"א, נשמת אברהם סי' כב ס"ק ב (עמ' צח) שה"ה אפילו בחולה גוסס ונוטה למות. וראה שם עמ' קד בשם הרשב"א.

(2) הגרש"ז אויערבאך שליט"א, נשמת אברהם יו"ד סי' קצה ס"ק ז (עמ' קטו).

(3) וראה נשמת אברהם סי' כב ס"ק ט (עמ' קד) מה שכתבנו לגבי גודל העיר.

(4) שו"ת ציץ אליעזר ח"ו סי' מ פי"ב מהא דאהע"ז סי' כב סע' ח וברכי יוסף ס"ק ז. שו"ת אגרות משה אהע"ז ח"ד סי' סה אות א.

(5) שו"ת יוסף אומץ סי' צז. דבר הלכה סי' ז ס"ק ב בשם החזו"א. וראה שם או"ק ב ד"ה וכ"פ מרן. נשמת אברהם אהע"ז סי' כב ס"ק א (עמ' צא).

(6) שו"ת ציץ אליעזר ח"ז סי' כז.

(7) אהע"ז שם סע' ה בהגה. יו"ד סי' שלה סע' י. וראה שם בט"ז ס"ק ה וש"ך ס"ק ט וברכי יוסף. שערים מצויינים בהלכה סי' קנב ס"ק ח.

attended to by her husband if this involves bodily contact,[8] unless no one else is available to care for her.[9]

5. A husband may be present in the room while his wife is giving birth if she is very frightened and his presence will reassure her. However, he may not look at those parts of her body that are usually covered, and he may not observe the birth process;[10] nor may he touch her.[11]

6. If the husband of a *niddah* is ill and nobody else is available to care for him, she may attend to him but, if possible, should avoid bodily contact.[12] She should not wash him or make his bed in his presence,[13] unless there is no alternative.[14]

7. An internal examination of a woman which includes the use of an instrument inserted into the vagina *only*, does not render her a *niddah*.[15] Introduction of an instrument into the uterus or the injection of air or contrast material into the uterus or Fallopian tubes does not render her a *niddah* unless blood is found on the instrument, or she finds blood on subsequent self-examination. She should ask the physician to let her see the instrument after the examination.[16]

(8) יו״ד סי׳ קצה סע׳ טז.

(9) הגה שם. וראה גם סע׳ יז ובבית יוסף שם שמסתפק לדעת הרמב״ם אם זה אסור אע״פ שיש פיקוח נפש. ולדעת הערוך השולחן (שם סע׳ כו) גם הב״י מתיר במקום סכנה.

(10) שו״ת אגרות משה יו״ד ח״ב סי׳ נח. הגרש״ז אויערבאך שליט״א, נשמת אברהם יו״ד סי׳ קצה ס״ק ג (עמי קח). ויש אוסרים שו״ת מנחת יצחק ח״ה סי׳ ל אות ב.

(11) הגרש״ז אויערבאך שליט״א, נשמת אברהם שם עמי קט.

(12) הגרש״ז אויערבאך שליט״א, נשמת אברהם יו״ד סי׳ קצה ס״ק ד (עמי קי). בן איש חי בשו״ת רב פעלים ח״ג יו״ד סי׳ יב. וראה ב״י שם וקיצור שולחן ערוך סי׳ קנג סעי יד.

(13) יו״ד סי׳ קצה סעי טו.

(14) דרכי תשובה שם ס״ק נא.

(15) דרכי תשובה סי׳ קצד ס״ק יט. שו״ת מהרש״ם ח״ד סי׳ קמו. שו״ת דברי מלכיאל ח״ב סי׳ נו. טהרת ישראל סי׳ קצד ס״ק ט. שערים מצויינים בהלכה סי׳ קנג ס״ק טז. שו״ת ציץ אליעזר ח״י סי׳ כה פי״א.

(16) שו״ת אגרות משה יו״ד ח״א סי׳ פט. דברי מלכיאל ח״ב סי׳ נו וח״ג סי׳ סא. דרכי

8. A bride who requires incision of the hymen in order to facilitate marital relations does not need immersion after the operation, even if she bleeds as a result.[17] If she bleeds at the first intercourse following the operation, she should wait four days before starting to count seven days free of bleeding prior to immersion (like any other bride). If she did not bleed, she may continue marital relations until just before her next menstrual period is due.[18]

9. A bride-to-be may take oral contraceptives in order to make sure that she will not be a *niddah* on her wedding night. However, since these may lead to "breakthrough" bleeding, she should start taking them the month *before*, stopping fourteen to sixteen days before the wedding. This will result in her menstruating a day or two later, leaving enough time for her to count seven days free of bleeding before immersing herself in a *mikveh* preparatory to her wedding.

תשובה סי׳ קצד ס״ק יט. שו״ת הר צבי יו״ד סי׳ קנב. שו״ת ציץ אליעזר ח״י סי׳ כה פי״א. וראה גם חזון איש יו״ד סי׳ פג ושו״ת אבני נזר סי׳ רכד. ועל אף שלכאורה מחמיר הנודע ביהודה (תניינא יו״ד סוסי׳ קב) ראה בשו״ת תשובה מאהבה ח״א סי׳ קטז.

(17) שו״ת יביע אומר ח״ד סי׳ י. שו״ת אגרות משה יו״ד ח״א סי׳ פז. הגרש״ז אויערבאך שליט״א, נשמת אברהם יו״ד סי׳ קצג ס״ק ב (עמ׳ צז). וראה שו״ת מנחת יצחק ח״ד סי׳ נח, שו״ת ציץ אליעזר ח״י סי׳ כה פי״ב ושו״ת שבט הלוי ח״ה סי׳ קיט שמחמירים. וכן עיין שו״ת מהרש״ם ח״א סי׳ רי ושו״ת חשב האפוד ח״ב סי׳ קיז.

(18) שו״ת אגרות משה שם. שו״ת מנחת יצחק שם.

**Ordinarily, nothing may interpose between the body surface
and the water. If there is any such interposition, competent
halachic opinion must be sought.**

1. A woman who has been advised by a physician to
keep her ear canal dry may immerse herself in a *mikveh*, but she
should insert absorbent cotton wool deep into the ear canal so
that it does not protrude into the external ear. She may attach a
thread in order to be able to withdraw the cotton wool.[1] It is
advisable that during the week preceding her immersion she
keep cotton wool constantly in her ear.[2]

2. A woman may immerse herself in a *mikveh* with her
limb in a plaster cast if it cannot be removed before immersion
without causing pain and possible risk to the limb.[3] However, it
is preferable that immersion be delayed until the plaster is
removed.[4]

3. An intrauterine device (which requires halachic
sanction) does not invalidate immersion.[5] This is true also of the

---

(1) דרכי תשובה סי' קצח ס"ק י. שו"ת מהרש"ם ח"א סי' ז. שו"ת אגרות משה יו"ד ח"א
סי' צח-קג. שו"ת מהרי"י שטייף סי' מו. שו"ת אמרי יושר ח"א סי' קצה וח"ב סי' פב. שו"ת
מלמד להועיל ח"ב סי' ע. וראה בן איש חי שנה ב פ' שמיני סע' י שאוסר. וראה נשמת
אברהם יו"ד סי' קצח ס"ק יב7 (עמ' קלו) בשם הגרש"ז אויערבאך שליט"א.

(2) שו"ת חלקת יואב סי' ל. שו"ת הר צבי יו"ד סי' קע.

(3) שו"ת ציץ אליעזר ח"ד סי' ט.

(4) שו"ת הר צבי יו"ד סי' קסה.

(5) נודע ביהודה מהד"ק יו"ד סי' סד. פתחי תשובה יו"ד סי' קצח ס"ק טז. דרכי תשובה שם
ס"ק פז. ערוך השולחן שם סע' נה. שו"ת חתם סופר יו"ד סי' קצג. שו"ת בנין ציון סי' עא.
שו"ת יד הלוי ח"ב סי' מא. שו"ת זכר שמחה סי' קיט. שו"ת ציץ אליעזר ח"י סי' כה פ"י
או"ק ג.

cord that is attached to it for removal.[6] The woman should ensure that the cord is freely movable in the vagina at the time of immersion.[7]

4. If a pessary has been inserted into the vagina—for example, for uterine prolapse—competent halachic opinion should be sought.[8]

5. Ointment[9] and dried blood[10] must be washed off a wound before immersion. The scab on a healing wound is not considered an interposition once it has dried.[11]

6. Adhesive tape and bandages should be removed before immersion if they can be removed without causing great pain.[12] If there is a likelihood of danger or considerable pain, the area around the adhesive should be washed with warm water before immersion[13] (see paragraph 2 above).

7. Sutures that are visible preclude immersion.[14]

8. If a woman is embarrassed to remove an artificial eye, she may immerse herself in a *mikveh* without removing it.[15]

(6) שו"ת ציץ אליעזר חי"א סי' סג. שו"ת מנחת יצחק ח"ו סי' פז.

(7) שמעתי מהגרש"ז אויערבאך שליט"א.

(8) ראה נודע ביהודה מהד"ת סי' קלה. דרכי תשובה סי' קצח ס"ק פז. ערוך השולחן שם סעי' נה. שו"ת הר צבי יו"ד סי' קנג. וראה נשמת אברהם יו"ד סי' קצח ס"ק יב (עמ' קלד).

(9) ערוך השולחן יו"ד סי' קצח סעי' לב.

(10) יו"ד שם סעי' ט. ערוך השולחן שם.

(11) ערוך השולחן שם סעי' לה.

(12) יו"ד שם סעי' י. חכמת אדם כלל קיט סעי' ז. סדרי טהרה יו"ד שם אות כד. שו"ת הר צבי יו"ד סי' קסט.

(13) שו"ת ציץ אליעזר חי"ד סי' ט בשם דברי חיים יו"ד חי"ב סי' סה. שו"ת יביע אומר ח"ג יו"ד סי' יב. וראה גם מגן אברהם או"ח סי' קסב ס"ק ח.

(14) שו"ת אגרות משה יו"ד חי"ב סי' פז. וראה יו"ד סי' קצח סעי' יא ובש"ך ס"ק טז. סדרי טהרה שם. חכמת אדם כלל קיט סעי' ח.

(15) שו"ת הר צבי יו"ד סי' קסא. שו"ת אגרות משה יו"ד חי"א סי' קד. שו"ת מהרי"י אסאד סי' רכט. שו"ת זכר שמחה סי' קיח. שו"ת מנחת יצחק ח"ג סי' פב.

9. Contact lenses should be removed prior to immersion.[16]

10. A permanent[17] or temporary[18] filling, a dental brace,[19] or a loose tooth which can only be removed professionally,[20] do not invalidate immersion.

Artificial dentures permanently fixed in place do not have to be removed.[21] Removable dentures should be taken out before immersion.[22]

11. A woman with a colostomy may immerse herself after removing the colostomy bag and base and cleaning the surrounding area well.[23]

12. In the case of an ileostomy, because there is often a continuous discharge from the ileostomy opening, a tampon

(16) ואם שכחה להוציאם, אינה צריכה טבילה חוזרת שו"ת אגרות משה שם. וראה שו"ת שואל ומשיב מהד"ג ח"ג סוסי' קח ושו"ת הר צבי יו"ד סי' קסא.

(17) שו"ת שואל ומשיב מהד"ק ח"ג סי' כז ומהד"ג ח"ג סי' קח. דרכי תשובה סי' קצח ס"ק עו. בן איש חי שנה ב פ' שמיני סע' ט. דעת תורה יו"ד סי' קצח סע' כד. טהרת ישראל שם ס"ק צ. מצודת דוד על קיצור שו"ע סי' קסא ס"ק יא. שו"ת אגרות משה יו"ד ח"א סי' צז ענף ו. וע"ע חכמת אדם כלל קיט ובינת אדם ס"ק יב. וראה נשמת אברהם יו"ד סי' קצח ס"ק יא (עמ' קכט).

(18) שו"ת הר צבי יו"ד סי' קסט, שו"ת אגרות משה יו"ד ח"א סי' צז, ודרכי תשובה סי' קצח ס"ק עה מחד גיסא, וטהרת ישראל סי' קצח ס"ק צ, שו"ת אמרי יושר ח"ב סי' קיב ומצודת דוד על קיצור שו"ע סי' קסא ס"ק יא מאידך גיסא. וראה גם שערים מצויינים בהלכה סי' קסא ס"ק יג. נשמת אברהם יו"ד סי' קצח ס"ק יא (עמ' קלא). ושמעתי ממו"ר הגרי"י נויבירט שליט"א שיש להקל.

(19) שו"ת מנחת יצחק ח"ו סי' פו. שערים מצויינים בהלכה סי' קסא ס"ק יב. וראה שו"ת אגרות משה יו"ד ח"א סי' צו.

(20) שו"ת אבני נזר יו"ד סי' רס. שו"ת דובב מישרים ח"א סי' פד. שו"ת שבט הלוי ח"א סי' צו.

(21) שו"ת מהרי"י אסאד סי' רכט. דרכי תשובה סי' קצח ס"ק עה. שו"ת אבני נזר יו"ד סי' רנט.

(22) שו"ת מהרי"י אסאד שם. שו"ת מהרש"ם ח"א סי' עח. שערים מצויינים בהלכה סי' קסא ס"ק יב. וראה נשמת אברהם שם עמ' קלג.

(23) מו"ר הגרי"י נויבירט שליט"א, נשמת אברהם יו"ד שם עמ' קלה.

or gauze should be inserted, with a thread or tape attached to it for removal. The woman must make sure that the tape lies free and is not stuck to the skin.[24]

13. A permanent indwelling catheter does not constitute an interposition.[25]

14. A woman who is paralyzed or otherwise incapacitated may immerse herself with the help of another woman who holds her loosely at the moment of immersion, the latter having first wetted her hands in the *mikveh*.[26]

(24) הגרש"ז אויערבאך שליט"א, נשמת אברהם שם.

(25) הגרש"ז אויערבאך שליט"א שם.

(26) ראה נשמת אברהם שם ס"ק יג (עמי קלו) ושם ס"ק ב (עמי קכה).

45 / *BRIT MILAH* (CIRCUMCISION)

**A male child is ordinarily circumcised on the eighth day
after birth.**

1. A child who is in any way ill may not be circumcised, since the danger to life is of paramount importance. A child can be circumcised at a later date, but a lost life cannot be restored.[1]

2. A sick child whose illness affects the *whole* body may not be circumcised until seven days have passed after his recovery. A rise in temperature (see paragraph 10 below) or any general illness requires that circumcision be delayed for seven days after the child is well, even if recovery takes place rapidly.[2] A person who circumcises such a child on the eighth day after birth when it occurs on the Sabbath is held to have thereby desecrated the Sabbath.[3]

3. A child with a strictly *localized* illness or an injury involving a limited part of the body may not be circumcised until he has recovered. However, he may be circumcised as soon as recovery has taken place, without waiting a further seven days[4] (see paragraph 18 below).

4. A child who is weak, even if he has no obvious illness, should not be circumcised without the physician's clear approval, following which it is still advisable to wait an additional seven days before circumcision[5] (see paragraph 18 below).

(1) יו״ד סי׳ רסג סע׳ א.

(2) יו״ד סי׳ רסב סע׳ ב.

(3) שו״ת בנין ציון סי׳ פז.

(4) יו״ד סי׳ רסב סע׳ ב וש״ך ס״ק ג. וראה שו״ת מנחת יצחק ח״ה סי׳ יא.

(5) שו״ת יד הלוי ח״ב סי׳ מז. שו״ת מהר״יי אסאד יו״ד סי׳ רנד. וראה שו״ת מטה לוי ח״ב

5. If the child is underweight but in no way shows evidence of illness, it is advisable, though not mandatory, to postpone circumcision until normal weight is reached[6] (see paragraph 18 below).

6. An anemic child should not be circumcised. If treatment is not required and recovery is spontaneous, he may be circumcised immediately upon recovery. If the anemia requires treatment, circumcision may take place only after seven days following his recovery[7] (see paragraph 18 below).

7. A "blue baby" should not be circumcised. If according to the physician his condition is stable and will remain so, and no treatment to cure the condition is contemplated, the child may be circumcised if the physician considers him fit to undergo circumcision, but only when he is at least thirty-one days old.[8]

8. A baby who has undergone cardiac catheterization with no complications soon after birth may be circumcised on the eighth day, if he is otherwise healthy.[9]

9. Two types of jaundice may affect the newborn: one is normal and physiological, the other is a manifestation of disease. A child with the first type should not be circumcised while still jaundiced, but should be circumcised as soon as his color becomes normal.[10] If the jaundice is so severe as to necessi-

סי' נב ושו"ת דובב מישרים ח"א סי' סא.

(6) שו"ת אגרות משה יו"ד ח"ב סי' קכא. שו"ת ציץ אליעזר חי"ג סי' פב ס"ק ו. וראה גם מצודת דוד על קיצור שו"ע סי' קסג ס"ק ג.

(7) שו"ת מנחת יצחק ח"ה סי' יא. וכן שמעתי מהגרש"ז אויערבאך שליט"א.

(8) הגרש"ז אויערבאך שליט"א, נשמת אברהם יו,ד סי' רסב ס"ק 21 (עמ' קסו). וראה שו"ת מנחת יצחק שם.

(9) הגרש"ז אויערבאך שם.

(10) שו"ת ציץ אליעזר חי"ג סי' פא ו-פג. שו"ת מנחת יצחק ח"ג סי' קמה, ח"ו סי' צב וחי"ח סי' פח. הגרש"ז אויערבאך שליט"א ומו"ר הגרי"י נויבירט שליט"א, נשמת אברהם סי' רסג ס"ק א(עמי קעא).

tate an exchange transfusion, seven days must pass after his recovery before circumcision may be performed.[11]

If the baby was placed in an incubator in order to help clear the jaundice in time to have the circumcision on the eighth day, and the child is otherwise healthy, he should be circumcised on the eighth day if his color is normal by then.[12]

In the case of a child with the second type of jaundice, circumcision must always be postponed for seven days after recovery[13] (see paragraph 18 below).

10. A baby with a temperature of 38° or more should not be circumcised until seven days have elapsed after the temperature has returned to normal[14] (see paragraph 18 below). If his temperature did not rise to 38°, the baby may be circumcised as soon as the temperature returns to normal.[15] If the slightly raised temperature is, in the physician's opinion, not a manifestation of an illness but a consequence of dehydration or overheating and there is no evidence of disease, the baby may be circumcised on the eighth day if his temperature is normal.[16]

11. A child born with a harelip[17] or a cleft palate,[18] who cannot suck satisfactorily and must therefore be fed artificially, may be circumcised on the eighth day if he is otherwise normal.

---

(11) וראה שו"ת אגרות משה יו"ד ח"ב סי' קכא ומה שכתבתי בנשמת אברהם שם הערה 12.

(12) שו"ת ציץ אליעזר ח"ג סי' פא.

(13) מו"ר הגרי"י נויבירט שליט"א, נשמת אברהם סי' רסב ס"ק 4 ו (עמ' קסו).

(14) שו"ת ציץ אליעזר חי"ג סי' פב ס"ק ה. וכן שמעתי מהגרש"ז אויערבאך שליט"א.

(15) שמעתי מהגרש"ז אויערבאך שליט"א.

(16) שו"ת ציץ אליעזר שם. הגרש"ז אויערבאך שליט"א, נשמת אברהם סי' רסב ס"ק 3 ו (עמ' קסו).

(17) שו"ת מהרש"ם ח"ה סי' ז. זוכר הברית סי' י סע' כא.

(18) שמעתי ממו"ר הגרי"י נויבירט שליט"א.

12. A baby who has to be kept in an incubator for medical reasons (see paragraph 9 above) may not be circumcised until after seven days subsequent to his removal from the incubator, even if the physician approves immediate circumcision[19] (see paragraph 18 below).

13. If two brothers have died as a result of circumcision, a third child may not be circumcised until he has grown older and has proved to be healthy, and until he has been checked medically and has been proved fit to undergo circumcision.[20] A person whose brothers died from circumcision who, having reached adulthood wishes to be circumcised is permitted to take the risk after consulting competent medical opinion.[21]

14. In the disease hemophilia, normal clotting of the blood does not take place. A child may bleed seriously, even fatally, from the slightest wound, and circumcision is therefore dangerous. Such a baby may be circumcised only if he is first appropriately treated.[22] Circumcision of such a baby on the Sabbath is problematic.[23]

15. The circumcision of a baby with hypospadias must be carried out in a special way.[24] It must be done with the agreement of the surgeon, because later a plastic operation will have to be performed to correct the hypospadias. If the surgeon insists that, for surgical reasons, the circumcision be performed only at the time of the operation, the actual circumcision of the foreskin is performed at that time by a *mohel*, who also pronounces the appropriate benedictions. Although the circumcision should be performed by a *mohel*, if that is not possible in this particular case, a

(19) שו"ת אגרות משה יו"ד ח"ב סי' קכא. שו"ת ציץ אליעזר חי"ג סי' פב ס"ק ד.

(20) יו"ד סי' רסג סע' ב. וראה שו"ת נודע ביהודה תניינא יו"ד סי' קסה.

(21) שו"ת חתם סופר יו"ד סי' רמה.

(22) הגרש"ז אויערבאך שליט"א, נשמת אברהם סי' רסג ס"ק ד (עמ' קעב).

(23) ראה שם עמ' קעג.

(24) ראה ספר אסיא ג עמ' 389.

Jewish surgeon must perform the circumcision during the operation and pronounce the appropriate benedictions.[25]

16. If one twin has died within eight days of birth, the other baby should not be circumcised until he is thirty-one days old.[26]

17. A child delivered by Cesarian section may not be circumcised on the Sabbath or a Festival even if it is the eighth day following birth.[27]

18. A child whose circumcision has been postponed may not be circumcised on the Sabbath or a Festival;[28] but he may be circumcised even a day or two prior to a *Festival*.[29] With regard to circumcision on the two days prior to the *Sabbath*, that is, on a Thursday or a Friday, competent halachic opinion should be sought.[30]

19. In the case of an older child or an adult who has to be circumcised, local[31] or general[32] anesthesia may be used.[33]

(25) הגרש"ז אויערבאך שליט"א, נשמת אברהם רסב ס"ק טג (עמי קסח).

(26) תורה לשמה (המיוחס להבן איש חי) סיי שח.

(27) או"ח סיי שלא סעי ה. וראה מ"ב ס"ק ח.

(28) יו"ד סיי רסו סעי ב.

(29) חיד"א, מראית העין ליקוטים, סיי ח אות ב. שו"ת יביע אומר ח"ה יו"ד סיי כג. זוכר הברית סיי ו ס"ק ה.

(30) יש אוסרים רשב"ץ ח"א סיי כא. ט"ז יו"ד סיי רסב ס,ק ג. ברכי יוסף שם ס"ק ב. שו"ת מהרש"ם ח"ה סיי ז. כף החיים או"ח סיי שלא ס"ק לא. שו"ת רב פעלים ח"ד יו"ד סיי כח. שו"ת יביע אומר ח"ה יו"ד סיי כג. זוכר הברית סיי ו ס"ק ג. ויש מתירים שו"ת יו"ד סיי רסו סוס"יק יח. מג"א סיי שלא ס"ק ט. אליה רבה סיי רמח ס"ק ה וסיי שלא ס"ק י. נודע ביהודה תניינא יו"ד סיי קסו. חכם צבי תשובות הנוספות שאלה ט סיי יד. שאילת יעב"ץ ח"ב סיי צה. גליון מהרש"א על יו"ד סיי רסב סעי ב. מ"ב סיי שלא ס"ק לג. הגרש"ז אויערבאך שליט"א, נשמת אברהם סיי רסב ס"ק ג (עמי קסג).

(31) שו"ת שרידי אש ח"ג סיי צו ושו"ת שבט הלוי ח"ה סיי קמז ס"ק ב. וראה שו"ת אמרי יושר ח"ב סיי קם שאוסר אפילו בהרדמה מקומית.

(32) שו"ת מהרש"ם ח"ו סיי קח. שו"ת יביע אומר ח"ה יו"ד סיי כב.

(33) שמעתי מהגרש"ז אויערבאך שליט"א.

As discussed above (in paragraph 2), after a generalized illness he may not be circumcised until seven days have elapsed after recovery.[34]

20. In all instances where there is a danger of cross-infection (such as with the hepatitis or AIDS virus) of either the baby or the *mohel, metzitzah* should be performed by the use of a glass tube.[35]

With regard to a firstborn child whose circumcision has had to be delayed beyond thirty days and the *pidyon ha-ben*, see Chapter 46, paragraphs 1-3.

(34) הגרש״ז אויערבאך שליט״א, נשמת אברהם סי׳ רסב ס״ק ד (עמ׳ קסד).

(35) שו״ת הר צבי יו״ד סי׳ ריד. שו״ת בנין ציון ח״א סי׳ כג. וכך שמעתי מהגרש״ז אויערבאך שליט״א. וראה נשמת אברהם יו״ד סי׳ רסד ס״ק ה (עמ׳ קפג).

46 / PIDYON HA-BEN (REDEMPTION OF THE FIRSTBORN)

This chapter deals with medical questions that bear on the duty of a father to redeem the firstborn child of its mother, if a male, on the thirty-first day after his birth.

1. A mother's firstborn child who is a male and whose circumcision has had to be postponed on account of illness should be redeemed on the thirty-first day even if the child is still sick or in an incubator, as a result of which circumcision will take place only later, after seven days have elapsed following recovery[1] (see Chapter 45, paragraph 12).

2. If the baby was *premature*, redemption must wait until the thirty-first day after he has been taken out of the incubator.[2]

3. If the baby has recovered in time to be circumcised on the thirty-first day, circumcision precedes redemption.[3]

4. If a woman's first pregnancy ended in a miscarriage forty days or more after her last immersion in the *mikveh* and she expelled blood and clots, these should be examined for the presence of fetal parts or membranes. If these were not found and the woman later gives birth to a male child, the father redeems him and recites the benediction *Al pidyon ha-ben*.[4] In this instance the *Shehecheyanu* benediction should be pronounced by

---

(1) שו״ת חיים שאל ח״א סי׳ לא. שו״ת חתם סופר יו״ד סי׳ ש. שו״ת יביע אומר ח״ו יו״ד סי׳ כו. שו״ת חלקת יעקב ח״ג סי׳ קט. שערים מצויינים בהלכה סי׳ קסד ס״ק כ. שו״ת ציץ אליעזר ח״ט סי׳ כח סוף או״ק ח.

(2) שמעתי מהגרש״ז אויערבאך שליט״א.

(3) שייך יו״ד סי׳ שה ס״ק יב. ברכי יוסף סי׳ רסב ס״ק ב. פתחי תשובה יו״ד סי׳ שה ס״ק כג.

(4) יו״ד סי׳ שה בהגה. שו״ת חיים שאל ח״ב סי׳ יז. וראה שו״ת חתם סופר יו״ד סי׳ רצט וזכר שמחה סי׳ קמז.

the *kohen*.[5] If the expelled material was not examined or if it contained fetal parts, the father should redeem the live child without pronouncing the benediction.[6]

5. A child delivered by vaginal forceps or by vacuum suction should be redeemed, and the appropriate benedictions should be recited.[7]

6. A firstborn baby delivered by Cesarian section is exempt from redemption, as is a male child born to the mother subsequently.[8]

(5) שו״ת חתם סופר שם.

(6) שו״ת חתם סופר שם. שו״ת דברי מלכיאל ח״ו סי׳ כ. שו״ת יד הלוי ח״א סי׳ קצב.

(7) שערים מצויינים בהלכה סי׳ קסד ס״ק כ. שו״ת שרידי אש ח״ב סי׳ קיד. שו״ת דובב מישרים ח״ב סי׳ לב. זוכר הברית סי׳ כח ס״ק ה. וראה שו״ת חלקת יואב יו״ד סי׳ כו, שו״ת אבני נזר יו״ד סי׳ שצד ושו״ת חלקת יעקב ח״א סי׳ מא.

(8) יו״ד סי׳ שה סע׳ כד.

47 / CONTRACEPTION

The first commandment in the Torah is that of procreation.

1. For a woman whose life may be at risk if she conceives and for whom contraception is medically necessary the choice of the contraceptive method is a delicate halachic problem and requires expert opinion. A full discussion of the topic is beyond the scope of this book; it may be found in a large number of responsa, which offer a thorough insight into the practical problems resulting from the various methods of contraception.[1]

2. If a woman has been allowed by a competent halachic authority to take an oral contraceptive, she should examine herself every morning and evening during the first month that she takes the pills to ascertain whether there has or has not been any "breakthrough" bleeding (which would make her a *niddah*). If there was no bleeding during the first month, she need not continue to examine herself this way while taking the pill. If she does find blood during the first month, she must continue to examine herself twice daily in the subsequent months until there is no further bleeding for two consecutive months while she continues to take the pill.[2] (This applies also to a woman who is advised to take estrogen tablets at menopause.)

3. The same rules apply to a woman who has been fitted (after halachic approval) with an intrauterine device.

(1) ראה נשמת אברהם אהע"ז סי' ה ס"ק יג (עמ' נט-עב).

(2) שמעתי ממו"ר הגרי"י נויברט שליט"א. שו"ת אגרות משה אהע"ז ח"ג סי' כד.

48 / ABORTION

1. Abortion may be induced in a woman if there is danger to her life from the continuance of pregnancy because of physical or mental illness. Abortion is permitted because under such circumstances the fetus (who is not yet regarded as a separate entity) is viewed as "pursuing (to end) the life of the mother," and her life takes precedence over that of the *unborn* child.[1] However, once the head of the fetus has emerged, the child may not be harmed. It is then a separate, viable entity, whose life is as valuable as that of the mother; and one life may not be sacrificed to save another.[2] In the case of a breech presentation, independent viability is considered established with the emergence of the child's torso,[3] including the navel.[4]

2. An abortion sanctioned by *Halachah* should preferably be performed by a Jewish gynecologist.[5]

3. If an abortion has been sanctioned by *Halachah* because of danger or possible danger to the life of the mother, it is preferable that the abortion be induced within the first forty days after conception.[6]

4. Regarding problems of fetal illness or malformations, such as Tay-Sach's disease, German measles, Down's Syndrome, AIDS, etc., competent halachic authority must be consulted.[7]

(1) ראה נשמת אברהם חו"מ סי' תכה ס"ק א (עמ' רכ-רלה).

(2) חו"מ סי' תכה סע' ב. וראה פתחי תשובה שם ס"ק ב.

(3) טור יו"ד סי' קצד. פתחי תשובה שם.

(4) שמעתי מהגרש"ז אויערבאך שליט"א.

(5) שו"ת מחזה אברהם יו"ד סי' יט. שו"ת ציץ אליעזר ח"ט סי' נא שער ג.

(6) שו"ת ציץ אליעזר שם. שו"ת שרידי אש ח"ג סי' קכז. וראה רמב"ם הל' תרומות פ"ח ה"ג, חו"מ סי' רי ש"ך ס"ק ב, נתיבות המשפט שם ס"ק ה ושו"ת חות יאיר סי' לא.

(7) ראה נשמת אברהם חו"מ סי' תכה ס"ק א (עמ' רל-רלה). וראה שו"ת אגרות משה חו"מ ח"ב סי' עא שכותב: ובכלל יש לידע כי הכל מן השמים ולא שייך להתחכם להמלט מעונשין ח"ו בדברים שמסיתים הרופאים, כי הרבה שלוחים למקום, שלכן צריך לקבל באהבה כל

5. An anencephalic fetus may be aborted.[8]

6. In the case of a multiple pregnancy, it is, under certain circumstances, permitted to abort some of the fetuses in order that the others may develop normally.[9]

מה שעושה השי״ת ואז בזכות זה והבטחון בו ובבקשה ממנו יברך את האשה שתלד ולד קיים בריא ושלם לאורך ימים ושנים, עכ״ל. וראה בגמ׳ ברכות י ע״א, בהדי כבשי דרחמנא למה לך.

(8) הגר״י זילברשטיין שליט״א.

(9) שמעתי מהגרש״ז אויערבאך שליט״א שהתיר במקרה של ששה עוברים.

49 / SEMEN EXAMINATION

1. The wanton and purposeless emission of semen is strictly forbidden; therefore "coitus interruptus" or the use of a condom is prohibited.[1] Under certain circumstances one may be halachically permitted to produce a sample of semen, using a condom, for examination, in order to ascertain the cause of sterility and to indicate possible treatment.[2] Where feasible, the semen should be obtained from the wife after intercourse.[3]

2. Before a husband is permitted to have an examination of his semen the wife must first have been examined to exclude the possibility of her being sterile, and a considerable time[4] must have elapsed without conception having taken place.[5] Competent halachic authority must be consulted.

3. Testicular biopsy for the purposes of examination is permitted under certain circumstances.[6]

---

(1) אהע"ז סי' כג סע' א.

(2) שו"ת יעב"ץ ח"א סי' מג. שו"ת אחיעזר ח"ג סי' כד. שו"ת צפנת פענח סי' ו. שו"ת אבני נזר אהע"ז סי' פג. טהרת ישראל סי' רמ ס"ק לט. חזו"א בספר חיי נפש ח"א עמ' פד מובא בשו"ת ציץ אליעזר ח"ט סי' נא שער א פ"ב. שערים מצויינים בהלכה סי' קנא ס"ק א. אוצר הפוסקים סי' כג סע' א ס"ק י ר-יא. ולפרטי דינים ראה שו"ת ציץ אליעזר שם, שו"ת אגרות משה אהע"ז ח"א סי' ע וח"ב סי' טז, ושו"ת מנחת יצחק ח"ג סי' קח או"ק ו. אולם יש אוסרים שו"ת דברי מלכיאל ח"א סי' ע, ח"ג סי' צא וח"יה סי' קנז. שו"ת מהרי"ש ענגיל ח"ו סי' עה. שדי חמד אסיפת דינים פאת השדה מערכת אישות סי' יג. בעל הארחות חיים מובא בשדי חמד שם. בעל מנחת אלעזר בתשובה בראש ספר דרכי תשובה הלכות נדה.

(3) שו"ת דברי מלכיאל שם. בעל מנחת אלעזר שם. שו"ת מהרי"ש ענגל שם. וראה נשמת אברהם אהע"ז סי' כה ס"ק ב (עמ' קח-קיג).

(4) לפי הרבה פוסקים הזמן הוא לפחות 10 שנים.

(5) ראה שו"ת מנחת יצחק ח"ג סי' קח. שו"ת אגרות משה אהע"ז ח"ב סי' טז. ספר חיי נפש ח"א עמ' פד בשם החזון איש, מובא בשו"ת ציץ אליעזר ח"ט סי' נא שער א פ"ב.

(6) שו"ת אגרות משה אהע"ז ח"ב סי' ג ענף ב. שו"ת ציץ אליעזר ח"ט סי' נא שער א פ"ב. וראה נשמת אברהם אהע"ז סי' כג ס"ק ב (עמ' קיג).

50 / ARTIFICIAL INSEMINATION

1. It is strictly forbidden for a married woman to undergo artificial insemination from a donor (A.I.D.) other than her husband.[1] Mixture of the husband's semen with that of another donor is similarly prohibited.[2]

2. Using the husband's semen for artificial insemination should preferably occur after the wife's ritual immersion at the usual time. However, each case must be evaluated individually and the decision be left to competent halachic authority.[3]

3. Insemination for a test-tube baby is permitted only when other means have failed, and *only* the husband's semen may be used.[4] Competent halachic authority must be consulted.

4. Choosing the sex of a baby by separating the husband's male and female sperm cells and artificially inseminating the wife according to choice is not permitted, even in a situation where artificial insemination with the husband's sperm has been halachically approved.[5]

---

(1) שו״ת אגרות משה אהע״ז ח״א סי׳ עא. שו״ת יביע אומר ח״ב סי׳ א. שו״ת מנחת יצחק ח״ג סי׳ קח. שו״ת ציץ אליעזר ח״ט סי׳ נא שער ד פ״ב. אולם יש אוסרים אפילו מבעל לאשתו שו״ת דברי מלכיאל ח״ד סי׳ קז ו-קח. חזון איש לפי פרושו של שו״ת ציץ אליעזר שם.

(2) יו״ד סי׳ קצה ט״ז ס״ק ז. שו״ת ציץ אליעזר שם. שערים מצויינים בהלכה סי׳ קמה ס״ק ב. וראה שו״ת אגרות משה אהע״ז ח״א סי׳ א וסי׳ עא וח״ב סי׳ יא. אולם ראה שו״ת ציץ אליעזר שם פ״ה שחזר בו האגרות משה למעשה. וראה נשמת אברהם אהע״ז סי׳ א ס״ק ה2 (עמ׳ יא).

(3) ראה שו״ת מהרש״ם ח״ג סי׳ רסח. שו״ת ציץ אליעזר שם. שו״ת מנחת יצחק ח״א סי׳ נ. שו״ת אגרות משה אהע״ז ח״ב סי׳ יח. שו״ת יביע אומר ח״ב סי׳ א. הגרש״ז אויערבאך שליט״א, נועם כרך א תשי״ח עמי קסה.

(4) שמעתי מהגרי״ע יוסף שליט״א. וכן מודפס בשמו בתחומין כרך א עמי 287. וכן כתב הגרי״א נבצל שליט״א, אסיא חוברת לד תשרי תשמ״ג. וע״ע שו״ת ציץ אליעזר חט״ו סי׳ מה שאוסר.

(5) שמעתי מהגרש״ז אויערבאך שליט״א.

The following glossary provides a partial explanation of some of the foreign words and phrases used in this book. The spelling and explanations reflect the way the specific word is used herein. Often, there are alternate spellings and meanings for the words.

Glossary

ADAR: the Hebrew month corresponding to February-March.

AFIKOMAN: MATZAH eaten at the conclusion of the SEDER meal.

AHAVAH: In SHACHARIT, the second of the two prayers which precede the SHEMA.

AL ACHILAT MAROR: the blessing recited before eating the MAROR at the PESACH SEDER.

AL ACHILAT MATZAH: the blessing recited before eating the MATZAH at the PESACH SEDER.

AL HA-MICHYAH: the blessing recited after eating products made of grain, excluding bread.

AL MITZVAT TEFILLIN: the blessing recited before putting the TEFILLIN on one's head.

AL NETILAT YADAYIM: the blessing recited after washing one's hands before eating bread.

AMIDAH: See SHEMONEH ESREH.

ARBA'AH MINIM: the Four Species used on the Festival of SUKKOT.

ASHER GE'ALANU: the prayer of thanks to Hashem for redeeming the Jews from Egyptian bondage, recited at the PESACH SEDER.

ASHER YATZAR: the prayer recited after urinating or defecating.

ASHKENAZI(M): of German or Eastern European origin.

AV: the Hebrew month corresponding to July-August.

BARECHU: the introduction to the prayers which precede the SHEMA in SHACHARIT and MA'ARIV.

BARUCH DAYYAN HA-EMET: "Blessed be the True Judge," a blessing recited upon hearing bad tidings.

BARUCH HA-MAVDIL BEIN KODESH L'CHOL: an abridged form of HAVDALAH said in times of urgency to permit certain light labor before HAVDALAH.

BIRKAT HA-GOMEL: the blessing of thanksgiving recited by one who has been saved from dire circumstances.

BIRKAT HA-MAZON: the grace after meals.

BOREI MEOREI HA-ESH: the blessing recited over the light of the flame of the **HAVDALAH** candle.

BOREI PERI HA-ADAMAH: the blessing recited before eating vegetables and other produce that is newly planted each year.

BOREI PERI HA-GAFEN: the blessing recited before drinking wine or grape juice.

BRIT MILAH: the ritual of circumcision.

CHALLAH: the portion of dough separated as the priest's share.

CHAMETZ: leavened foods that are prohibited during **PESACH.**

CHOL HA-MOED: the intermediate days of **PESACH** and **SUKKOT.**

DUCHANNING: (Y., colloq.) the blessing of the **KOHANIM** during prayer services.

ERUV: halachically constituted boundaries which enable carrying on the Sabbath and Festivals within a city.

ETROG: a citron, one of the four species used on the Festival of **SUKKOT.**

HALACHAH: Jewish law.

HALLEL: Psalms 113-118, recited on Festivals and **ROSH CHODESH.**

HA-MOTZI: the blessing recited before eating bread and bread products.

HAVDALAH: the blessings recited at the termination of the Sabbath and Festivals.

HAVINENU: an abridged version of the **SHEMONEH ESREH**, recited in times of urgency.

KADDISH: a prayer in praise of God, recited only with a **MINYAN**; a mourner's prayer recited for a close relative.

KARPAS: a vegetable dipped in salt water and eaten at the **PESACH SEDER.**

KASHERING: (Y., colloq.) the grilling or the soaking, salting and washing of meat which makes it halachically fit for consumption.

KASHRUT: the Jewish dietary laws.

KIDDUSH: sanctification of the Sabbath and Festivals, usually recited over a cup of wine.

KIDDUSH LEVANAH: the blessing recited on seeing the new moon.

KOHEN (KOHANIM): member(s) of the priestly tribe.

LA-SECHVI VINAH: a morning prayer thanking Hashem for the ability to distinguish between day and night.

LEHANIACH TEFILLIN: the blessing recited before putting the **TEFIL-LIN** on one's hand.

LISHMOA KOL SHOFAR: the blessing recited before blowing the **SHO-FAR** on **ROSH HASHANAH.**

LULAV: a branch of the date palm, one of the Four Species used on the Festival of **SUKKOT;** the term is often used to mean the Four Species.

MA'ARIV: the evening prayer service.

MAROR: bitter herbs eaten at the **PESACH SEDER.**

MATTANOT LA-EVYONIM: the **MITZVAH** of sending gifts to the poor on **PURIM.**

MATZAH (MATZOT): flat, unleavened bread eaten during **PESACH.**

MEGILLAH: lit., a scroll; the scroll of the Book of Esther.

MEKADDESH HA-SHABBAT: the special prayer added to the **SHE-MONEH ESREH** on the Sabbath.

METZITZAH: the requirement of sucking blood from the wound of circumcision.

MI SHEBERACH: a prayer said on behalf of a seriously ill person.

MIKVEH: a ritual bath.

MINCHAH: the afternoon prayer service.

MINYAN: a quorum of ten adult Jewish males, the minimum requirement for congregational prayer.

MISHLO'ACH MANOT: the traditional sending of tasty treats to friends on **PURIM** as prescribed in the Book of Esther.

MISHNAH: the Oral Law, edited by Rabbi Yehudah Ha-Nasi.

MITZVAH (MITZVOT): Torah commandment(s).

MOHEL: a qualified practitioner of circumcision.

MUKTZEH: that which may not be moved on the Sabbath and Festivals.

MUSAF: additional prayers recited on the Sabbath, Festivals and **ROSH CHODESH.**

NIDDAH: the ritually impure state of a woman from the beginning of her menses, or other manifestation of bleeding, until after she has immersed herself in a **MIKVEH** at the proper time.

PESACH: the Festival of Passover.

PIDYON HA-BEN: the ceremony of redemption of the firstborn male child.

POKE'ACH IVRIM: a morning prayer thanking Hashem for the ability to see.

PURIM: the holiday commemorating the victory of the Jews over Haman, as recounted in the Book of Esther.

REFA'ENU: a prayer (the eighth prayer of the **SHEMONEH ESREH**) for the healing of the sick.

RETZEH: a prayer (the seventeenth prayer of the **SHEMONEH ESREH**) for the restoration of the Service to the Temple; a special prayer added to the **BIRKAT HA-MAZON** on the Sabbath.

ROSH CHODESH: the beginning of the Hebrew month.

SEDER: the order of the **PESACH** night ceremony recalling the Exodus from Egypt and the liberation from bondage.

SEPHARDI(M): of Spanish or Middle Eastern origin.

SHACHARIT: the morning prayer service.

SHEHAKOL: the blessing recited before eating food other than fruit, vegetables and grain products.

SHEHECHEYANU: the blessing recited over new fruit, new clothes, or before performing a **MITZVAH** for the first time that season.

SHEMA: "Hear O Israel..." (*Devarim* 6:5), the opening words of the fundamental Jewish prayer which proclaims the unity of God.

SHEMONEH ESREH: the principle daily prayer, also known as the **AMIDAH.**

SHIVAH: the seven days of mourning.

SHOFAR: the ram's horn blown on Rosh Hashanah.

SHOME'A TEFILLAH: a prayer (the sixteenth prayer of the **SHEMONEH ESREH**) for the acceptance of prayer.

SHULCHAN ARUCH: lit., prepared table; the Jewish Code of Law compiled by Rabbi Yosef Caro.

SUKKAH (SUKKOT): booth(s) occupied during the Festival of **SUKKOT.**

SUKKOT: the Festival of Tabernacles.

TALLIT: a prayer shawl.

TALMID CHACHAM: a Torah scholar.

TAMMUZ: the Hebrew month corresponding to June-July.

TEFILLIN: phylacteries; four scriptural sections written on parchment, enclosed in black leather boxes, and worn by men on the left arm and the head during the morning prayers.

TEVET: the Hebrew month corresponding to December- January.

TISHREI: the Hebrew month corresponding to September- October.

TZITZIT: ritual tassels or fringes tied onto the corners of a man's four-cornered garment.

VA-YECHULLU: Scriptural verses (*Bereshit* 2:1-3) which describe Hashem's having "rested" on the seventh day of Creation, recited in the **KIDDUSH.**

YA'ALEH V'YAVO: a special prayer inserted into **RETZEH** (in **SHEMONEH ESREH**) and into **BIRKAT HA-MAZON** on Festivals and **ROSH CHODESH.**

YOM TOV(YAMIM TOVIM): Jewish festival(s).

YOTZER HA-MEOROT: the concluding blessing of the **YOTZER OR** prayer recited in **SHACHARIT** before the **SHEMA.**

YOTZER OR: In **SHACHARIT**, the first of the two prayers which precede the **SHEMA.**

ZIMMUN: three or more adult males who have eaten together, joining to say the **BIRKAT HA-MAZON** as a group.

Index

רשימת ראשי־תיבות במראי המקומות

א״א	אשל אברהם
אב״ג	אבני נזר
אג״מ	אגרות משה
אה״ע	אבן העזר
או״ח	אורח חיים
א״ר	אליה רבה
בדה״ש	בדי השולחן
בהמ״צ	בין המצרים
ב״ח	בית חדש
ב״י	בית יוסף
ביה״ל	ביאור הלכה
ב״מ	בבא מציעא
ב״ק	בבא קמא
ברכ״י	ברכי יוסף
גמ׳	גמרא
ד״ה	דיבור המתחיל
ה׳	הלכה
הגר״א	הגאון ר׳ אליהו מווילנא
הי״ה	הוא הדין
הל׳	הלכה
ח׳	חלק
חו״מ	חושן משפט
חז״א	חזון איש
חיד״א	ר׳ חיים יוסף דוד אזולאי
חכ״א	חכמת אדם
חת״ס	חתם סופר
ט״ז	טורי זהב
י״א	יש אומרים
יו״ד	יורה דעה
יוהכ״פ	יום הכפורים
יו״ט	יום טוב
יעב״ץ	ר׳ יעקב עמדין בן צבי
מ׳	משנה
מ״ב	משנה ברורה
מג״א	מגן אברהם
מהד״ג	מהדורא שלישית
מהד״ק	מהדורה קמא (ראשונה)
מהד״ת	מהדורא תנינא (שניה)
מו״ק	מועד קטן
מ״ז	משבצות זהב
מהרש״ם	ר׳ שלום מרדכי הכהן שוואדרון
נו״ב	נודע ביהודה
סוד״ה	סוף דיבור המתחיל

ראשי־תיבות	פירוש
סוסי׳	סוף סימן
סוס״יק	סוף סעיף קטן
סי׳	סימן
סמ״ג	ספר מצות גדול
סמ״ע	ספר מאירת עינים
סע׳	סעיף
סי״ק	סעיף קטן
ע״א	עמוד א׳
ע״ב	עמוד ב׳
ע״ז	עבודה זרה
ע״י	על ידי
עי״ז	על ידי זה
עכ״ל	עד כאן לשונו
עכ״פ	על כל פנים
עמ׳	עמוד
עפ״י	על פי
עי״ע	עיין עוד
ערוה״ש	ערוך השולחן
עי״ש	עיין שם
פ׳	פרק, פרשה
פמ״ג	פרי מגדים
פ״ת	פתחי תשובה
צ״ע	צריך עיון
קצוה״ש	קצות השולחן
ריב״ש	ר׳ יצחק בר ששת ברפת
רדב״ז	ר׳ דוד אבן זמרא
רמ״א	ר׳ משה איסרליש
רמב״ם	ר׳ משה בן מיימון
רמב״ן	ר׳ משה בן נחמן
ר״ן	ר׳ ניסים בן ראובן גרונדי
רעק״א	ר׳ עקיבא איגר
רשב״א	ר׳ שלמה בן אברהם אדרת
רשב״ץ	ר׳ שמעון בן צמח
שד״ח	שדי חמד
שו״מ	שואל ומשיב
שו״ע	שולחן ערוך
שו״ת	שאלות ותשובות
שי״ך	שפתי כהן
שעה״צ	שער הציון
שע״ת	שערי תשובה
תוס׳	תוספות
תפא״י	תפארת ישראל
תשב״ץ	ר׳ שמעון בן צמח

רשימת הספרים שנזכרו בספר

(פרט לשולחן ערוך ונושאי כליו)

שנת פטירתו	שם המחבר ומקום מגוריו	שם הספר
תר״ע	הג״ר אברהם באראנשטיין, סאכטשאב, פיעטרקוב	אבני נזר שו״ת
שלי״ה	מרן יוסף קארו, בעל השולחן ערוך, צפת	אבקת רוכל שו״ת
	ראה אבני נזר	אגלי טל
תשמ״ז	הג״ר משה פיינשטיין, ניו יורק	אגרות משה שו״ת
ה״א, י	רבינו יצחק ב״ר משה, ווינא	אור זרוע
ת״ש	הג״ר חיים עוזר גראדזענסקי, ווילנא	אחיעזר שו״ת
ת״ע	הג״ר אליה שפירא, פראג	אליה רבה
תרפ״ו	הג״ר מאיר אריק, יאזלוויץ וטרנוב	אמרי יושר שו״ת
	הג״ר מאיר גריינמן שליט״א, בני ברק	אמרי יושר
	ירחון, ירושלים	אסיא
	הג״ר אליהו וייספיש שליט״א, ירושלים	ארבעת המינים
תרס״ד	הג״ר נחמן כהנא, ספינקא	ארחות חיים
תרס״ט	הג״ר יוסף חיים, בגדאד	בן איש חי
תרל״ו	הג״ר יעקב יוקב עטטלינגער, אלטונא	בנין ציון שו״ת
תקס״ו	הג״ר חיים יוסף דוד אזולאי (חיד״א), ליוורנו	ברכי יוסף
	ירחון, קרית צאנז	בשבילי הרפואה
תשט״ו	הג״ר יחיאל מיכל טוקצ'ינסקי, ירושלים	גשר החיים
	שנתון, תל אביב	דיני ישראל
	הג״ר אברהם הלוי הורוביץ שליט״א, בני ברק	דבר הלכה
תשל״ו	הג״ר יהושע מנחם מענדל אהרנברג, תל אביב	דבר יהושע שו״ת
תרל״ו	הג״ר חיים הלברשטאם, צאנז	דברי חיים שו״ת
תר״ע	הג״ר מלכיאל צבי הלוי טננבוים, לאמזא	דברי מלכיאל שו״ת
תשמ״א	הג״ר מנחם מנדל כשר, ירושלים	דברי מנחם שו״ת
	ראה שואל ומשיב	דברי שאול
תשכ״ה	הג״ר דוב בעריש ווידענפעלד, טשעבין וירושלים	דובב משרים שו״ת
תרצ״ה	הג״ר אברהם יצחק הכהן קוק, ירושלים	דעת כהן
תרע״א	הג״ר שלום מרדכי הכהן שוואדרון, ברעזאן	דעת תורה
תרע״ג	הג״ר צבי הירש שפירא, מונקאטש	דרכי תשובה
תשל״ז	הג״ר שלמה יוסף זוין, ירושלים	המועדים בהלכה
	ירחון, ירושלים	המעיין
תרנ״ג	הג״ר נפתלי צבי יהודה ברלין, וואלאזין, ווארשא	העמק שאלה

245

הר צבי שו״ת	הג״ר צבי פסח פראנק, ירושלים	תשכ״א
הרי בשמים שו״ת	הג״ר אריה ליבש הורוויץ, סטריא	תרס״ט
הריב״ש שו״ת	הג״ר יצחק בר ששת ברפת, אלגיר	קס״ח
הרמ״א שו״ת	מו״ר משה איסרליש, קראקא	של״ג
הרפואה והיהדות	הג״ר עמנואל יעקובוביץ שליט״א, לונדון	
הרשב״א שו״ת	רבינו שלמה בן אברהם אדרת, ברצלונה	ה״א, ע
זבחי צדק	הג״ר עבדאללה אברהם יוסף סומך, בגדאד	תרמ״ט
זוכר הברית	הג״ר אנשיל גרינוואלד, אונגוואר	תשי״ד (בערך)
זכר שמחה שו״ת	הג״ר שמחה הלוי באמבערגער	תרס״ז
זכרו תורת משה	ראה חיי אדם	
זכרון שלמה	הג״ר דוד צוקער שליט״א	
חות יאיר שו״ת	הג״ר יאיר חיים בכרך, ווירמיישא	תס״ב
חזון איש	הג״ר אברהם ישעיהו קרליץ, בני ברק	תשי״ד
חזון יחזקאל	הג״ר יחזקאל אברמסקי, ירושלים	תשל״ו
חזון עובדיה	ראה יביע אומר	
חיי אדם	הג״ר אברהם דנציג, וילנא	תק״פ
חיים שאל שו״ת	ראה ברכי יוסף	
חכם צבי שו״ת	הג״ר צבי אשכנזי, אמסטרדם, לבוב	תע״ה
חכמת אדם	ראה חיי אדם	
חלקת יואב שו״ת	הג״ר יואב יהושע וינגרטן, קינצק	תרפ״ב
חלקת יעקב שו״ת	הג״ר מרדכי יעקב ברייש, ציריך	תשל״ז
חשב האפוד	הג״ר חנוך דוב פדוא שליט״א, לונדון	
חתם סופר שו״ת	הג״ר משה סופר, פרשבורג	ת״ר
טבילת כלים	הג״ר צבי הכהן שליט״א, בני ברק	
טהרת ישראל	הג״ר ישראל יצחק ינובסקי, פראג	תרפ״ט (בערך)
יביע אומר שו״ת	הראש״ל הג״ר עובדיה יוסף שליט״א, ירושלים	
יד הלוי שו״ת	הג״ר יצחק דוב הלוי במברגר, וירצבורג	תרל״ט
יוסף אומץ שו״ת	ראה ברכי יוסף	
יחוה דעת שו״ת	ראה יביע אומר	
ילקוט הגרשוני	הג״ר גרשון שטערן, מאראש-לודאש	תר״ץ
ילקוט שמעוני	רבינו שמעון הדרשן, פרנקפורט	ה״א, ק (בערך)
יסודי ישרון שו״ת	הג״ר גדליה פעלדער שליט״א, טורונטו	
כל בו על אבלות	הג״ר יקותיאל יהודה גרינוואלד, קולומבוס	תשט״ו
כף החיים	הג״ר יעקב חיים סופר, ירושלים	תרצ״ט
כרתי ופלתי	הג״ר יהונתן ב״ר נטע אייבשיץ, אלטונה	תקכ״ד

246